the GARDENERS
HANDBOOKS

# Fruits &
# Vegetables

# Fruits &
# Vegetables

CONSULTANT EDITOR
Judy Moore

FOG CITY PRESS

Published by Fog City Press
814 Montgomery Street
San Francisco, CA 94133 USA
Copyright © 2003 Weldon Owen Pty Ltd
Reprinted 2006

FOG CITY PRESS

CHIEF EXECUTIVE OFFICER  John Owen
PRESIDENT  Terry Newell
PUBLISHER  Lynn Humphries
MANAGING EDITOR  Janine Flew
ART DIRECTOR  Kylie Mulquin
COVER DESIGN  John Bull
PICTURE EDITOR  Tracey Gibson
EDITORIAL COORDINATORS  Paul McNally, Kiren Thandi
PRODUCTION MANAGER  Louise Mitchell
PRODUCTION COORDINATOR  Monique Layt
SALES MANAGER  Emily Jahn
VICE PRESIDENT INTERNATIONAL SALES  Stuart Laurence
EUROPEAN SALES DIRECTOR  Vanessa Mori

LIMELIGHT PRESS PTY LTD
PROJECT MANAGEMENT  Helen Bateman/Jayne Denshire
PROJECT EDITOR  Lynn Cole
PROJECT DESIGNER  Katie Ravich
CONSULTANT EDITOR  Judy Moore

ISBN 1 876778 96 2

Color reproduction by Bright Arts Graphics (S) Pte Ltd
Printed by LeeFung-Asco Printers

Printed in China

A Weldon Owen Production

# CONTENTS

# How to Use This Book

This valuable guide will lead you gently through the process of planning and caring for your garden. Whether you are a novice or a more experienced gardener, you'll discover how to get the best results from your soil, whatever the size or design of garden you have chosen.

Colorful photographs give you guidance and inspiration in planning and planting your garden.

There are many helpful illustrations in the book, showing such things as tools, techniques and plant parts.

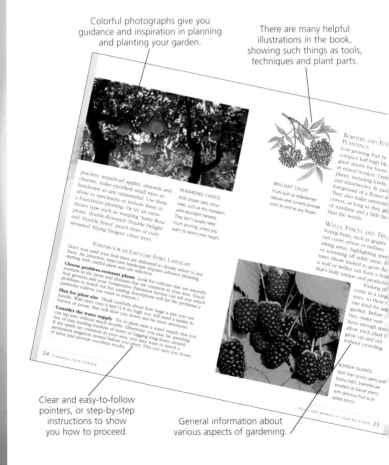

peaches, semidwarf apples, almonds and cherries, make excellent small trees as handsome as any ornamental. Use them alone as specimens or include them in a foundation planting. Or try an extra-showy type such as weeping 'Santa Rosa' plums, double-flowered 'Double Delight' and 'Double Jewel' peach trees or curly stemmed 'Flying Dragon' citrus trees.

**REWARDING CHOICE**
With proper care, citrus trees, such as this mandarin, yield abundant harvests. They don't usually need much pruning, unless you want to restrict their height.

**POINTERS FOR AN EASY-CARE EDIBLE LANDSCAPE**

Don't wait until your fruit trees are delivered to decide where to put them. An attractive, easy-care landscape requires advance planning, starting with careful plant and site selection.

**Choose problem-resistant plants** Look for cultivars that are naturally resistant to the pests and diseases that are common in your area. (Local fruit growers and your Cooperative Extension Service can tell you which problems to watch out for; catalog descriptions will list the problems a particular cultivar can resist or tolerate.)

**Plan for plant size** Think carefully about how large a tree you can handle. With trees over 6 feet (1.8 m) high you will need a ladder to harvest or prune; that will slow you down and be more strenuous.

**Consider the water supply** Try to plant near a water supply that you can tap into without much trouble. Otherwise, you may be spending lots of time hauling buckets of water or dragging long hoses around. If dry spells are common in your area, or you want to install a permanent irrigation system before you plant. This can save you hours of labor and provide excellent results.

**BORDERS AND FOR PLANTINGS**
Low-growing fruit bu compact half-high blu great shrubs for found in mixed borders. Cree plants, including lowbu and strawberries, fit eas foreground of a flower o They also make interestin covers, as long as they ge of sunshine and a little he beat the weeds.

**BRILLIANT COLOR**
Fruits such as elderberries (above) and currants provide color as vivid as any flower

**WALLS, FENCES AND TRE**
Vining fruits, such as grapes can cover arbors or trellises, sitting areas, highlighting spec or screening off utility areas. F trees (those trained to grow fla a wall or trellis) can form a livin that's both unique and productive

Fruiting pl
come in a rang
sizes, so there's
one kind for an
garden. Before
buy, make sure
have enough spa
allow each plant t
grow up and out
without crowding.

**BORDER GUARDS**
With their prickly stems and bushy habit, brambles are excellent as barrier plants, with delicious fruit as an added bonus.

Clear and easy-to-follow pointers, or step-by-step instructions to show you how to proceed.

General information about various aspects of gardening.

*Berberis* spp.

BERBERIDACEAE

HARDINESS
Zones 3–9.

HEIGHT
3–12 feet
(90–360 cm)

SPREAD
3–12 feet
(90–360 cm)

COMMENTS
Common barberry
*Berberis vulgaris*
and other species,
including raisin
barberry
*B. asiatica* and
Nepal barberry
*B. aristata*, are
used for their fruits.

## BARBERRY

BARBERRIES PRODUCE RED, YELLOW OR
BLACK BERRIES; BOTH THE FLESH AND SKIN
OF THE BERRIES ARE EDIBLE. THE FLAVOR IS
USUALLY TART, BUT IN SOME SPECIES THE
FRUITS HAVE ENOUGH SUGAR TO BE DRIED
INTO "RAISINS."

**Position** Barberries prefer full sun
and moist, well-drained soil.
(Evergreen species are generally
less hardy than deciduous species.)

**Cultivation** Set out container-grown
plants anytime the soil isn't frozen,
or plant bareroot shrubs in spring
or autumn, while they are still
dormant. Space plants 3–12 feet
(90–360 cm) apart, depending on
how big the particular species gets.

**Pruning** Cut a few of the oldest
stems to the ground in winter. Also
shorten spindly stems and thin out
suckers if the stems are crowded.

**Propagation** Mix seed with moist
peat moss and refrigerate it for
2–3 months before sowing in a
warm, bright place. Or dig up and
transplant suckers from the base
of a bush.

**Pests and diseases** Generally no
significant problems.

**Harvesting and storage** Harvest the
berries after they are fully colored.
Make the fruit into conserves, jams
or pickles for storage, or dry them
and store in airtight jars.

*Carissa macrocarpa*

APOCYNACEAE

HARDINESS
Zone 10.

HEIGHT
2–18 feet
(60–540 cm), but
cultivars vary in
their eventual
height and spread.

COMMENTS
Natal plum fruit is
usually cooked into
jellies, sauces
and pies.

## NATAL PLUM

THE ROUNDISH FRUIT OF NATAL PLUM IS
THE SIZE OF A PING-PONG BALL, WITH A
CRIMSON SKIN AND STRAWBERRY-RED FLESH.
THE WHOLE FRUIT IS EDIBLE; SOME PEOPLE
PREFER TO REMOVE THE SMALL SEEDS.

**Position** Plant in full sun or partial
shade in well-drained soil. Natal
plum withstands salt spray and is
moderately drought-tolerant.

**Cultivation** Set out container-grown
plants anytime, spacing them
roughly 10 feet (3 m) apart,
depending on the eventual size of
the particular cultivar. Natal plum
generally needs cross-pollination,
so plant at least two seedlings or
cultivars. Hand-pollination often
helps when fruiting is poor. In areas
where Natal plum is not hardy,
grow it indoors in a container.

**Pruning** Prune only as needed to
shape the plant and to remove dead
or crossing branches. You can even
shear this plant as a hedge.

**Propagation** Take cuttings of
semi-woody shoots, or layer a
branch from an established plant.

**Pests and diseases** Generally no
significant problems.

**Harvesting and storage** For fresh
eating, pick fruit when fully ripe
(fully colored); pick fruits slightly
underripe for cooking. Plants
produce fruit almost year-round,
so pick it as you need it.

FRUITS 249

Part One

# Planning
# Your Garden

# CONSIDER YOUR CLIMATE

More than any other single factor, climate influences the selection of plants you can grow. The term describes the interaction of air temperature, moisture, wind and other factors.

Eggplant (aubergine)

Corn

Tomatoes

The climate of your locality also depends on its latitude, altitude and proximity to mountains and bodies of water. The temperate zone, where most of us live, is characterized by alternating periods of moderately wet and dry weather, with predictable winds. Fortunately, most of the vegetables you are familiar with are well suited to this temperate climate.

Often within larger temperate zones there are "mini-regions," which may differ from the average by being drier, wetter, cooler or warmer than the surrounding areas. If you live in one of these extreme locations, seasonal conditions will be affected and you will have to adapt your plans to meet the rigors of the local weather patterns.

Spinach

Summer squash

## OBSERVE SUN AND SHADE PATTERNS
Most crops require ample sunlight to yield a generous supply of produce. Start your sun-and-shade survey as soon as you can—today, if possible. Try to watch the light patterns through one whole growing season before doing any planting. A site that is sunny in early spring or autumn may be in deep shade by midsummer. On one sunny day a

### WARM-WEATHER CROPS
Bell pepper (capsicum), cantaloupe (rockmelon), carrot, corn, cucumber, eggplant (aubergine), lima bean, okra, parsnip, peanut, potato, pumpkin, rutabaga, snap bean, summer squash, sweet potato, Swiss chard (silverbeet), tomato, watermelon.

month, for at least several months before planting, watch your proposed sites through the day. Record when the sun first strikes the ground and when shadows take its place.

Your fruits and vegetables have three basic, climate-dependent requirements: a suitable temperature range, a favorable frost-free period and an adequate supply of moisture. Monitor the weather in your area, and be prepared to take action if your plants aren't getting the conditions they need to grow to their best.

Outside their preferred temperature range, plants may die or become dormant, which means that the chemical

## RAISED BEDS

These are the ultimate in outdoor, custom-built plant containers. They require an initial investment of energy, but you'll save both time and labor later. Raised beds are very productive and working them is easier on your back.

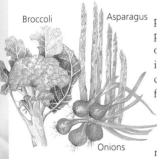

Broccoli
Asparagus
Onions

processes that normally occur inside the plant have slowed to a temporary stage of rest. For example, potato tubers left in the ground in autumn will remain dormant until the soil warms them the following spring. Some gardeners are able to "overwinter" autumn-planted spinach. The young plants remain dormant during the cold season, then resume growing as temperatures rise in the spring. These clever gardeners harvest the earliest crops in their area.

## COOL-WEATHER CROPS

Arugula (rocket), beet, broccoli, brussels sprouts, cabbage, cauliflower, chicory, Chinese cabbage, collard, corn salad (lamb's lettuce, mâche), escarole, kale, kohlrabi, lettuce, mustard, onion, pea, radish, spinach, turnip.

## GROWING SEASON

In temperate climates, the growing season begins after the last frost of the cold season, and ends when frosts begin again in autumn. But gardening activity begins before the technical start of the growing season and continues beyond the end. Frost occurs when the air temperature falls below 32°F (0°C) during the night, after dew has formed. The result is a lacy, white coating of water crystals on leaves the following morning. Frost damage may seem to be limited to the surface, but the plant's interior is also affected. Sensitive plants may die when exposed to frost in the spring or autumn. Hardier vegetables, such as those belonging to the cabbage family, will tolerate some frost damage.

Radish

## SHADE CROPS

There are a few vegetables that can tolerate partial shade. Choose crops that fit your conditions from the following list: arugula (rocket), cabbage, corn salad (lamb's lettuce, mâche), endive, horseradish, lettuce, pea, radish, rhubarb, spinach, Swiss chard (silverbeet).

PRODUCTIVE AND BEAUTIFUL

This mixed cottage garden demonstrates what can be done with a relatively small, but well-sited, space.

# GARDEN PLANNING

When planning your garden, think about how much time you want to spend in it. The amount of work your garden requires will depend on its size and will vary with climate and seasons.

## SITE SELECTION

Consider also how much fresh produce you want. You may need only a small vegetable garden near the kitchen to meet your day-to-day demands for organically grown vegetables. Or you may decide to dedicate a substantial area to growing fruits and vegetables so that you'll have enough produce to freeze or store for later consumption.

**POTS OF GOODNESS**

For a small household, just a few heads of cabbage and some fresh salad greens, planted successively in containers, may be all that you need. This is far better than building a garden that is too big and that will be a chore for you to look after.

## TOPOGRAPHY

Slopes and contours influence the way you arrange your garden. The idea is to minimize the loss of soil through erosion and maximize water retention. If you must plant on a slope, place the rows or beds across the slope. If rows run up and down the slope, water will trickle down the slope instead of penetrating the soil to reach plant roots. It will also carry the precious topsoil away. Also avoid gardening in low-lying areas, where poor air circulation makes your plants more susceptible to disease.

Since most vegetables need at least 1 inch (2.5 cm) of water each week, be prepared to water your vegetable patch during dry periods. Make sure you can reach the site with a garden hose or irrigation pipe, or be prepared to carry water by hand. Avoid gardening in low areas prone to flooding, and on high areas with too much drainage.

## OBSTACLES AND ACCESS

Locate your garden in a place that's easily accessible, both to you and to vehicles that will deliver materials you may need later, such as soil or compost. Avoid areas that have had heavy foot or vehicle traffic, because this activity compacts the soil and damages its structure. Paths should be wide enough for a wheelbarrow or cart. As you choose a site, look for hidden

## HINTS ON CROP ROTATION

Wait 3–5 years before growing the same, or closely related, vegetables in the same spot.

Include soil-improving crops such as rye or clover between early and late crops, or between autumn and spring crops.

Grow legumes, such as clover or peas, the year before grasses, such as corn.

Grow light feeders (such as root crops) before heavy feeders (tomatoes, peppers, cabbages and most leafy vegetables).

Make heavy compost applications to heavy feeders during the growing season.

Make light compost applications to light feeders during the growing season.

### HIGH YIELDS

Before planting a fruit and vegetable garden on this scale, think about how much produce you actually need. Freezing and bottling are time-consuming and must be done when the crops are ready, whether or not that fits in with your schedule.

obstacles such as septic systems, tree roots, shallow boulders and utility lines, and avoid these areas.

## LIGHT

Most plants need 6–12 hours of sunlight each day. Pick a site well away from shade trees and buildings that cast shade for more than half the day. If you have a city garden nestled among tall buildings, you may be limited to shade-tolerant plants. Given a favorable position, the soil in your garden will warm quickly and you may be able to plant early.

## A SIMPLE PLAN

With structured beds, organizing crop rotation is fairly easy. Each year, move your crop over to the next bed in the sequence. Set aside a separate bed for perennials, such as asparagus and rhubarb. Sketch a plan of the bed each year so you're not relying solely on your memory.

Plot A      Plot B      Plot C

**DEMARCATION**

This ornamental red cabbage would make an attractive border to separate sections of your garden.

Plot D

## Turn Lawn into a Vegetable Garden

Use a spade to remove the sod. Slip the blade forward just under the surface to slice through the roots.

Or solarize the area to kill both grass and weeds by covering it with clear plastic for several months during summer.

Or simply mulch the area thickly. It may take a month or two to smother the grass completely. Then dig over the area.

Perhaps the ultimate in space saving, espalier training can also provide your ripening fruit with additional warmth from a sunny wall.

## WIRE CAGES

An alternative to staking for plants such as tomatoes is this cage system. You can also grow vining crops such as cucumbers or gourds this way, with the cage upright, or turn the cage on its side and secure it with several stakes. Plant inside the cage; the vines will loop around and form a horizontal tube. This works well for heavier crops, such as melons.

## MEANS OF SUPPORT

Training plants to grow vertically, instead of horizontally, saves space and makes cultivating and harvesting easier. Because fruits aren't in contact with soil, they're less likely to succumb to soilborne pathogens. Staked plants are also very tidy and leave you more room for special techniques such as interplanting and companion planting. You can purchase stakes made of wood, metal, plastic or bamboo in a variety of heights to fit the needs of the plant.

No matter what method you use, have your support system in place before you plant. Vines such as peas and beans attach themselves by wrapping tendrils or twining stems around the support. Plants such as tomatoes or bell peppers (capsicum) need help. Tie loosely to the stake with scraps of soft cloth or cotton rope.

## Trellising Brambles

Start by setting sturdy 6-foot (1.8-m) posts every 20 feet (6 m) along the planting row. Then construct the trellis in one of these configurations.

A T-trellis makes picking easy for summer-bearing red, black and purple raspberries, as well as blackberries. Add a cross arm to the top of each post and another arm about halfway down the post. Run wires between the ends of opposite arms. After cutting out the fruited canes after harvest, tie the remaining shoots to the bottom wires. When the shoots are tall enough, tie them to the top wires, too.

A hedgerow trellis holds up bramble canes together between the wires. Put one cross arm about three-quarters of the way up each post so it resembles a T. Run wire along the end of each cross arm to support both sides of the plants.

### STOUT STAKES

Staking improves plant health, since better air circulation promotes drying and lessens the chance of disease. Sturdiness is more important than the appearance of the stakes, since your plants will become heavy with fruit as the season progresses.

### TRAINING WIRES

This simple structure provides wires or strings for plants such as beans and cucumbers to climb up. Just remember not to place it where the growing plants will cast shade over their smaller neighbors.

# FRUITS AND BERRIES IN YOUR BACKYARD

## CONTAINERS

Decks, patios and balconies can be fruitful when you grow suitable edibles in containers. Strawberries look superb cascading out of hanging baskets or strawberry pots. Dwarf citrus, apple and peach trees are also good candidates for container culture.

It's surprising that fruiting plants have been neglected so long for landscapes. Most have two irresistible features: attractive flowers and edible fruits.

Many have other features as well, such as showy autumn color or interesting bark. The options for including edibles in your yard are limited only by the space available. Here are some ways to use these beautiful and productive plants.

## SHRUBS AND HEDGES

Fruit- and nut-bearing bushes, such as some hazelnuts, Manchurian bush apricots, elderberries, currants and highbush blueberries, form large shrubs substantial enough to edge the boundary of your property, mass into an informal hedge or naturalize. Prickly shrubs, such as raspberries, blackberries, citrons and gooseberries, make a barrier that the neighborhood children, dogs and other animals won't be quick to push through.

## SHADE TREES

If you're starting a new landscape or renovating an old one, consider growing an edible plant as a shade tree. Walnuts, pecans and other full-sized fruit and nut trees provide height and shade plus a useful crop. Short fruit trees, such as

## APPLE BLOSSOM WALK

A shady path is a striking feature in a large garden.

peaches, semidwarf apples, almonds and cherries, make excellent small trees as handsome as any ornamental. Use them alone as specimens or include them in a foundation planting. Or try an extra-showy type such as weeping 'Santa Rosa' plums, double-flowered 'Double Delight' and 'Double Jewel' peach trees or curly stemmed 'Flying Dragon' citrus trees.

REWARDING CHOICE
With proper care, citrus trees, such as this mandarin, yield abundant harvests. They don't usually need much pruning, unless you want to restrict their height.

## POINTERS FOR AN EASY-CARE EDIBLE LANDSCAPE

Don't wait until your fruit trees are delivered to decide where to put them. An attractive, easy-care landscape requires advance planning, starting with careful plant and site selection.

**Choose problem-resistant plants** Look for cultivars that are naturally resistant to the pests and diseases that are common in your area. (Local fruit growers and your Cooperative Extension Service can tell you which problems to watch out for; catalog descriptions will list the problems a particular cultivar can resist or tolerate.)

**Plan for plant size** Think carefully about how large a tree you can handle. With trees over 6 feet (1.8 m) high you will need a ladder to harvest or prune; that will slow you down and be more strenuous.

**Consider the water supply** Try to plant near a water supply that you can tap into without much trouble. Otherwise, you may be spending lots of time hauling buckets of water or lugging long hoses around. If dry spells are common in your area, you may want to install a permanent irrigation system before you plant. This can save you hours of labor and provide excellent results.

**BRILLIANT COLOR**
Fruits such as elderberries
(above) and currants provide
color as vivid as any flower.

## BORDERS AND FOUNDATION PLANTINGS

Low-growing fruit bushes, such as
compact half-high blueberries, make
great shrubs for foundation plantings or
in mixed borders. Creeping fruit-bearing
plants, including lowbush blueberries
and strawberries, fit easily in the
foreground of a flower or shrub border.
They also make interesting ground-
covers, as long as they get their fair share
of sunshine and a little help from you to
beat the weeds.

## WALLS, FENCES AND TRELLISES

Vining fruits, such as grapes and kiwis
can cover arbors or trellises, shading
sitting areas, highlighting special views
or screening off utility areas. Espaliered
trees (those trained to grow flat against
a wall or trellis) can form a living fence
that's both unique and productive.

Fruiting plants
come in a range of
sizes, so there's at least
one kind for any size
garden. Before you
buy, make sure you
have enough space to
allow each plant to
grow up and out
without crowding.

**BORDER GUARDS**
With their prickly stems and
bushy habit, brambles are
excellent as barrier plants,
with delicious fruit as an
added bonus.

Part Two

# Taking Care of the Soil

# Knowing Your Soil

Good soil is the gardener's key to success. Since it influences your plants' growth, health and yield, it deserves your first consideration. The golden rule is to treat your soil well.

## Soil Composition

Soil is actually a mixture of minerals, water, air and organic matter. Average soil contains about 45 percent mineral matter, 25 percent air, 25 percent water, and 5 percent organic matter.

Soil texture refers to the fineness or coarseness of your soil's mineral matter. Texture is determined by the relative proportions of sand (very coarse), silt and clay (very fine); it influences fertility, water retention and air circulation within the soil. The ideal garden soil is a loam, composed of about 40 percent sand, 40 percent silt and 20 percent clay. The spaces between soil particles, called pore spaces, hold water, air and dissolved nutrients. If the spaces are large, as between sand particles, the soil is unable to retain sufficient water or nutrients.

The way sand, silt and clay particles join together is called soil structure. Both sand and compacted clays have no structure. In between these extremes, various proportions of sand, silt, clay and organic matter are arranged as larger pieces, called aggregates. Soil structure is especially important because it influences pore spaces, which in turn influence

HOME LITMUS TEST

Using a kit like the one above is an easy way to get a rough idea of your soil's acidity or alkalinity. Put some soil in the clean container and stir in distilled water. Let it stand for an hour, then place a strip of litmus paper in the mixture and leave it in for at least 60 seconds. Remove the paper and rinse with distilled water. Match the color of the paper to the chart that came with the kit.

water content and drainage, movement of air in the soil and the release of nutrients. The ideal soil has a crumbly, granular structure that allows water to drain and oxygen and carbon dioxide to move freely from the air into the pore spaces. A light, loose soil structure is known as "friable." Adding organic matter will improve the structure of all soil types.

## AIR AND WATER IN THE SOIL

Plants take in the oxygen they need from the air in the soil, so it is critical for healthy soil and vigorous plant growth. Oxygen is also critical for the well-being of soil organisms, such as earthworms. Air also contains gaseous nitrogen, which specialized bacteria convert into a form that your vegetables can use.

A steady supply of water is vital for the health of almost all plants. Plant roots absorb water and dissolved minerals from pore spaces in the soil. A good garden soil will hold enough water for plant growth while letting excess water drain down to deeper layers. While most vegetables prefer well-drained soil, there

## CHECK YOUR SOIL pH

Soil pH, the relative measure of how acid or alkaline your soil is, can affect nutrient availability for plants. It is measured on a scale from 1.0 (strongly acid) to 14.0 (strongly alkaline). Most plants thrive within a range of 6.0–7.0, from slightly acid to neutral. Nutrients tend to be most accessible to plant roots at this pH range. If you suspect your soil is extremely acid or alkaline, it's wise to have it properly tested. If the results confirm your suspicions, you can make small changes to your soil's pH by incorporating compost or soil amendments, such as powdered sulfur to lower pH or ground limestone to raise it. A soil test report will recommend the types and quantities of amendments to use. But the best solution is to select plants that do well in your natural conditions.

HEALTHY SOIL

Good granular soil is a pleasure to work with. Careful digging and regular additions of organic mulch will keep it healthy.

are a few, such as celery and watercress, that can tolerate more moisture. Raised-bed gardening can help if you need to improve the drainage of your garden beds (see page 13).

## ORGANIC MATTER

Soil organic matter refers to the decomposing remains of plants and animals. Organic matter is important because it attracts and holds important plant nutrients in the soil. It is critical for soil structure because it provides the "glue" that holds individual particles of minerals together as aggregates. When organic matter has decomposed, its stable remains are called humus. The organic matter content of your soil is influenced by many factors, including climate, vegetation, drainage, soil organisms and cultivation. Generally, wetter climates and healthy populations of soil microbes help create soil with a high content of organic matter. Higher annual temperatures, less vegetative growth

## LITTLE HELPERS

Your allies in the battle for good soil structure are the small creatures that crawl through your soil. Earthworms are perhaps the most famous soil builders. Their tunneling loosens and aerates tight soil, and the organic matter they drag down encourages stable soil granules. Rodents churn the soil as they dig and mix organic matter into the subsoil. Plant roots also improve soil structure by adding organic matter below the surface as they break down. Plus, the tiny passages left by the decayed roots allow water and air easier access to lower soil layers, in turn encouraging even better microorganisms and plant growth.

PROTECT YOUR SOIL

Good soil looks dark and has a crumbly texture, with visible organic matter.

and more cultivation lessen the ability of soil to accumulate organic matter.

## Soil Nutrients

The amount and type of soil nutrients that are available to your plants depend on the interaction of many factors, including soil texture, structure, moisture, organic matter and pH. Fine texture, loose structure, ample moisture, high organic matter content and near-neutral pH are all conditions that make the most nutrients available to your plants.

### DO NO HARM
Before you start digging in spring, or after heavy rain, wait until the soil has dried out a bit, or you will damage its structure.

### A Hands-on Test for Soil Texture

To check if your soil is sandy, silty or clayey, take a chunk of soil about the size of your thumb. Moisten it enough so that you can roll it into a ball. Flatten the ball between the pad of your thumb and the side of your bent index finger. Push your thumb forward repeatedly, pressing the soil outward to form a ribbon. The longer the ribbon, the more clay is in the soil. A heavy clay will make a ribbon 1 inch (2.5 cm) long; a sandy soil might not make a ribbon at all. To confirm your findings, put the ribbon in your palm and add enough water to make a runny paste. Rub the index finger of your other hand around in the slop in your palm. If it feels gritty, the soil is sandy. If it's smooth, the soil is silty. If it's on the sticky side, you've got clay.

## SPARE YOUR BACK

Here are some tips that can help save your muscles next time you turn the soil. First, insert the spade into the soil so the blade is straight up and down. Now:

1. Keeping your back straight and your foot on the upper edge of the spade, use your weight to push the spade into the soil.

2. Bend both your waist and knees as you slide the spade under the soil, then straighten up to lift the load.

3. Turn your whole body before depositing the dirt—don't just twist your torso as you fling the soil to the side.

It's easy, in your rush to finish up, to ignore pain. But pain has a purpose: It's telling you to take a break. You'll get more done and feel better if you take regular breaks, before you start to feel pain.

To check the nutrient content of your soil, it may be worthwhile to have a lab test your soil before you plant your crops. It's often a good idea to test the soil in a newly created bed, or in a bed that has been producing for many years. You can get your soil tested by your local Cooperative Extension office or a private soil-testing lab. They will provide you with a statement indicating any nutrient deficiencies or excesses, along with recommendations for fertilizers to add to correct the imbalances. Make sure you ask for recommendations for organic fertilizers. You may want to test the soil again in a few years to monitor the results of your gardening practices and make any necessary adjustments.

## WHEN TO WORK THE SOIL

Each time you work the soil, you have a chance to either destroy or maintain good structure. If you dig when it's too wet, the soil forms clods that are hard to break apart once they dry. And walking around on wet soil while you're digging promotes compaction, another factor that can ruin good soil structure. If you work the soil when it's too dry, the clumps of soil disintegrate, leaving powder that can blow away in the wind or be carried off by the next rainfall.

Even if you don't affect structure, there are other good reasons to avoid working very wet and very dry soils. Wet soils stick to everything—your shoes, your tools and the dog keeping you company. Dry, crusty soils make it hard to push a spade into the ground, so digging is twice as much work as it needs to be.

### SHOULD YOU DIG IN SPRING OR AUTUMN?

In most cases, your odds of finding soil in just the right condition for digging are better in autumn than spring. Rains are usually less frequent then, so the soil gets more time to dry out after soakings. If the soil is too dry, you can just water it and wait a day or two.

Autumn tilling is a bad idea if you garden on a slope because it exposes loose soil to erosion. Because slopes drain faster than level soils, you may be able to work them in spring when other soils are still too moist. If you do till in the autumn, cover the soil with a thick layer of straw or another light mulch that you can rake off in spring. Or protect the soil by growing a cover crop in the winter months.

### SIMPLE READINESS TEST

To check when the soil is at the right stage for digging, pick up a handful of soil and squeeze it. Open your hand. If the soil stays in a firm ball in your palm, it's too wet to work. If it falls apart, it's too dry. If it holds together until you poke it with your finger, it's just right.

# Compost

Composting is an excellent way to manage yard and kitchen wastes and make your own fertilizer. It is a good source of organic matter and nutrients for plants.

Compost improves soil structure and water retention and research shows that it contains beneficial microorganisms that suppress plant pathogens in soil.

## How to Make Fast, Hot Compost

1. Start saving all the organic wastes you normally throw away—leaves, grass clippings, kitchen scraps, rotted straw and other organic wastes. Decomposition is most efficient if materials are shredded. You can use a leaf-shredding machine, but a lawn mower will shred leaves and other light materials to a good size for mulching. Woody prunings, tree bark and newspaper should be shredded to fine pieces. Avoid adding oils, meat scraps and bones

### BREWING COMPOST TEA

To make a good liquid fertilizer, put a shovelful of compost in a cheesecloth or burlap bag. Tie the bag closed and suspend it in a container of water. Keep it covered for a few days. Once it has steeped, use the liquid to drench the soil at the base of plants you want to fertilize. Or dilute the liquid with water until it is the color of weak tea, then spray it on plant leaves. Because the nutrients are dissolved in water, the plants can take them up immediately for a quick burst of energy. (Reuse the "tea bag" several times, then add the soaked compost to the garden.)

### RECYCLING SCRAPS

Keep a small trash bin handy to your kitchen to collect compostable food scraps.

## Fast, Hot Compost

Build up the layers of your compost heap with equal amounts of high-carbon and high-nitrogen materials (see page 37).

Sprinkle water generously over each layer to keep the pile moist and encourage decomposition of the materials.

Aerate the compost pile by turning it over every couple of days with a garden fork. This hastens microbial activity.

## Compost for Busy People

For easy access, put your compost pile on a level, well-drained spot close to the vegetable garden. Some gardeners build elaborate, multi-chambered compost bins, but you can just dump your stuff in a pile. Besides kitchen scraps, toss in pulled weeds (if they don't have seeds) grass clippings, fresh cow or horse manure, sawdust, shredded paper from the office shredder and just about any plant or plant derivative. Don't add diseased plants because the bacteria, fungi or viruses might survive and spread.

Turn the pile every so often with a pitchfork; the more often you turn it, the more air gets in and the faster the soil organisms can break it down. If you're chronically pressed for time, buy a cheap pitchfork and leave it near the compost pile so you can turn the pile when the mood strikes, not at those less-frequent times when you remember to bring the good fork from the shed. When your compost is dark and crumbly (in a few weeks or months), it's ready to use.

because they attract scavenging animals and slow the decomposition process. Do not add human or pet feces, or pesticides, or pesticide-treated grass clippings.

2. Choose a spot near the vegetable garden for composting and store ingredients in piles or bins. Containment is not important, but walls will keep the area neat and

**ULTRA TIDY**

Multiple sturdy bins are great for composting. As the pile ages, fork it into the next bin and start a fresh batch in the first bin. Put a sliding door on each bin if you wish.

## COMPOST TROUBLESHOOTING

If your compost pile doesn't heat up, add more high-nitrogen material (see page 37). If the pile is dry, add water, or try turning the pile.

If the pile smells bad, add more high-carbon material (see page 37). If it is too wet, turning may help to add more air.

If the finished compost is covered with seedlings, your compost has not heated up enough and seeds of weeds and other plants have survived. Either avoid adding materials with seeds or make sure they're in the center of a hot compost pile.

If woody stems, prunings and dry leaves have not broken down, try shredding or chopping them into smaller pieces before adding them to a new pile. Adding more high-nitrogen ingredients can help balance these high-carbon materials.

## TOPDRESSING

Apply compost to a depth of 1–2 inches (2.5–5 cm) over the surface of your garden each year or use it to mulch rows of plants. If soil tests indicate a nutrient imbalance, sprinkle the appropriate fertilizers over the soil before adding the compost, or add fertilizer to the compost itself. You can dig the compost in, or leave it on top as a mulch.

the dog out. Or purchase a ready-made compost bin or tumbler.

3. You'll need enough raw materials to make a pile roughly 3 feet (90 cm) on each side; smaller piles won't heat up as efficiently. Build the pile by stacking the materials layer upon layer, using any kind of garden fork. Alternate materials that are high in carbon (brown, woody materials such as sawdust, straw and newspaper) with layers of material high in nitrogen (green, sloppy materials such as fresh grass clippings, kitchen scraps, weeds and manure).

Use about equal volumes of each. A pile with too much carbon remains cool and breaks down more slowly. Too much nitrogen can create odor problems. As you work, add several shovelfuls of garden soil to inoculate the pile with the right decomposer organisms. Just sprinkle soil on top of alternate layers. You can add dry mineral fertilizers, too, if your soil needs them. If you are adding insect-infested plant material to your pile, make sure you put it in the center, where temperatures will be high enough to kill the pests.

4. Keep the pile moist, but not soggy. As you build the pile, sprinkle the layers with water if the materials are dry. Keep the layered pile covered with a tarpaulin to help maintain the right amount of

**TURN, TURN, TURN**
Forking over the compost pile helps the microbes with their task. A hot compost pile can be ready to use in 2–6 weeks. You'll know it's ready when the temperature has stabilized and the individual materials you added at the beginning are no longer recognizable.

## WORM FARMS

Worm castings are a rich source of organic matter. Buy a commercial worm bin and follow the instructions that come with it to keep your worms healthy and ensure a constant supply of this powerful soil supplement.

moisture. Conditions that are too wet or too dry will change the rate of decomposition, and your compost might not be ready when you want it.

5. To work properly, organisms that hasten decomposition require oxygen. The simplest way to aerate the pile is to turn it every day or two. Invert the pile, one forkful at a time, with your garden fork, next to the original pile. Materials originally on the outside should end up in the middle. Fluff the pile as you go, sprinkling with more water as needed.

Aeration hastens microbial activity, which increases the temperature of the pile. Turning every day or two helps maintain a constant temperature. Use a compost thermometer to monitor the temperature, which should stay below 160°F (71°C), since higher temperatures will kill important decomposer organisms. If the pile gets too cool, turning it will raise the temperature. If the temperature gets too high, let the pile stand for a few days without turning it over, or add a small amount of water.

## TYPES OF WORM FARMS

Basically a worm farm is a simple box with a drainage system to collect liquid waste. Several designs are commercially available, but you could also make your own. Buy worms that are bred for worm farms.

# FERTILIZERS

iron deficiency

phosphorus deficiency

magnesium deficiency

potassium deficiency

nitrogen deficiency

Plants need 16 chemical elements for healthy growth, some in greater amounts (macronutrients) than others (micronutrients or trace elements). Each of these elements performs a particular role.

## FERTILIZERS OR AMENDMENTS?

A fertilizer is a material that contains significant amounts of the chemical elements that plants need to grow, such as nitrogen, phosphorus and potassium. It may also contain material that improves the soil, such as organic matter. But its primary function is to add nutrients. Bloodmeal, bat guano and greensand are examples of organic fertilizers.

An amendment improves the soil physically, usually its structure or drainage, or enhances microbial activity. It may contain some nutrients, but not enough to be called a fertilizer. Compost, grass clippings, lime and peat moss are examples of soil amendments. The material you use depends on what effect you want. Fertilizers provide a general nutrient boost during the growing season and are useful for correcting specific nutrient deficiencies. Amendments are important for long-term soil health, because they add organic matter and humus. Work these in before planting, or use as mulches, but don't count on them to provide enough nutrients to support heavy-feeding plants. Build up soil humus and use a balance of fertilizers and amendments and your plants will have all the nutrients they need.

### DEFICIENCIES

Thankfully, plants rarely show all these nutrient deficiencies at once. If you see any of these symptoms, try a seaweed spray for a quick fix, then amend the soil with compost or a supplement for a long-term solution.

### A BEAUTIFUL CROP

These rutabagas (right) look as if they have everything they need to thrive.

## Nitrogen for Lush Leaves

If you've ever fertilized a lawn, you know what a dramatic effect nitrogen has: It gives plants a deep green color and stimulates leafy growth. It is one of the three primary macronutrients that plants need and is probably the nutrient you'll have to add most often, because it easily washes out of the soil.

Most of the nitrogen in the soil is bound up in organic matter. It is slowly released and converted to a form plants can use, which is dissolved in the water held between soil particles. Unlike many nutrients, the form of nitrogen dissolved in the soil solution leaches readily from the soil. That's why nitrogen is often in short supply, especially in quick-draining sandy soils or in those where it is removed by vigorous plants.

> ### Good Organic Sources of Nitrogen
>
> Alfalfa meal (ground alfalfa hay) contains about 5 percent nitrogen as well as potassium. Bloodmeal contains 13 percent nitrogen. Cottonseed meal contains about 6 percent nitrogen as well as some phosphorus. It is often used on acid-loving crops such as blueberries. Fish emulsion, made of fish by-products dissolved in water, is about 5 percent nitrogen. Spray it on leaves or water it into the soil at the base of the plant. Fish meal consists of dried, ground fish parts; it's a balanced fertilizer that contains 5 percent nitrogen, 3 percent phosphorus and 3 percent potassium. Guano is aged, dry bird or bat droppings mined from roosts and caves. It contains 10–15 percent nitrogen. Because it contains calcium, it raises the soil pH.

GREEN MANURE
Dig a crop of clover into your soil. As it decays, it will release nitrogen in a form accessible to other plants.

## ADDING EXTRA NITROGEN

You can add nitrogen to the soil in several ways. If you have naturally fertile soil, it's enough just to add compost or manure each year to replace the nitrogen that plants remove. These balanced materials will provide a steady supply of nitrogen to growing plants throughout the season.

If your plants need extra nitrogen, you can use a more concentrated source. Depending on the fertilizer you choose, the nitrogen may be available right away, but it may last only a short while or be released gradually over a long period. See "Good Organic Sources of Nitrogen" (opposite) for materials you can add.

Growing a green manure crop of clover, alfalfa, lespedeza or some other legume is a useful way to add extra nutrients to the soil in your vegetable garden. Legumes host beneficial soil bacteria on their roots. These bacteria draw nitrogen gas from air in the soil and convert it to a form that both they and the plants can use. When you work legumes into the soil, the decaying roots release nitrogen other plants can absorb.

### AN EXCEPTION

If you add nitrogen to pea and bean crops, you may actually reduce your harvest.

### HOLD THE NITROGEN

To get the best yield of beautiful tomatoes from your plants, hold off on the nitrogen. It promotes the growth of lush leaves at the expense of the fruit.

## Phosphorus for Roots and Fruits

Plants need large amounts of phosphorus, which, like nitrogen, is one of the primary elements. Crops use it to produce flowers, fruits and to form seeds. It also helps them mature, counteracting the effects of too much nitrogen. Roots, especially the fibrous roots that spread out to absorb water and nutrients, need phosphorus to develop. Phosphorus makes stems strong and improves the quality of your vegetables; it also improves their resistance to disease. A lack of phosphorus limits how well your plants are able to absorb other nutrients, especially nitrogen.

A VITAL ELEMENT
For great crops, remember that phosphorus plays a crucial role in forming healthy roots and strong stems. It also helps in seed formation. Where there is a deficiency, fruits and seeds set and mature late.

## Supplying Phosphorus

Most soils are low in phosphorus, and most of the phosphorus that is there is not available, especially in soils that are very acid or alkaline. In soils with an extreme pH, the phosphorus reacts with chemicals in the soil, such as iron, calcium, aluminum and manganese, to create compounds that plants can't absorb. So, if you add phosphorus to very acid or alkaline soil, much of it binds to these chemicals.

To make more phosphorus available to plants, adjust the pH to near neutral (see page 29). In acid soils, this means adding lime. In alkaline soils, add sulfur. The pH changes slowly, so test your soil once or twice each year for several years, taking samples in the same month each time. Next, add a phosphorus fertilizer, both to increase the supply in the soil and to replace the phosphorus that crops remove (see "Good Organic Sources of Phosphorus" below). Since micro-organisms help make phosphorus more readily available, add phosphorus to your compost rather than directly to the soil.

Because phosphorus doesn't dissolve readily, it doesn't move down through the soil, so dig it in where it's needed, in the root zone. It's best to correct major phosphorus deficiencies before planting, especially for more permanent features such as trees. When it is cold, even soil that has plenty of phosphorus may not supply your plants with what's needed. In permanent plantings, rake off heavy mulches in spring to help soil warm up. Try a temporary black plastic mulch to warm the soil before planting vegetables.

SURE SIGN

Among common signs of phosphorus deficiency is a purplish cast to the leaves, especially on seedlings. Plants may be stunted, including the roots, and the leaves may have yellow streaks. Other signs are skinny, brittle stems.

## GOOD ORGANIC SOURCES OF PHOSPHORUS

Animal manures contain phosphorus, nitrogen and potassium. Poultry manure has the highest content of phosphorus at about 14 percent total. About 2 percent is available at any time. Bonemeal, made from ground animal bones, has 11 percent phosphorus. Steamed bonemeal is a more available source of phosphorus than raw bonemeal, but both release phosphorus more quickly than rock phosphate. Fish emulsion and liquid seaweed give a quick shot of phosphorus when sprayed on plants or watered into the soil. The effect isn't long lasting but can be a big help for young plants forming roots, plants setting fruit and plants showing symptoms of a phosphorus deficiency. Rock phosphate is less expensive than bonemeal, but it takes longer to release its phosphorus. The more finely ground the rock, the more quickly the phosphorus is released. Rock phosphate is about 32 percent total phosphate, but only about 3 percent is available at any one time.

## POTASSIUM FOR HEALTHY GROWTH

Although potassium doesn't get as much attention as the other primary nutrients, plants use as much of it as they do nitrogen and about four times as much as they do phosphorus. Potassium makes plants vigorous by helping them to develop strong root systems and resist disease. It regulates how plants absorb nitrogen, sodium and calcium. Potassium

### TELLTALE SIGNS

If plants don't get enough potassium, they will be stunted and yield poorly, unlike true dwarf cultivars. Potassium deficiency can cause leaves to develop irregular yellow splotches, starting at the bottom of the plant and working upward. In more severe cases, leaves are dry and scorched at the edges. Be aware, however, that other problems can cause similar symptoms.

also balances the tendency of nitrogen to cause leafy growth and of phosphorus to encourage fruiting. Plants use potassium in photosynthesis and it is part of the process that moves newly photosynthesized sugars from the leaves to the roots, then converts them to starches.

## KEEPING A PROPER LEVEL

Most soils, except those composed mostly of sand, are high in total potassium. The problem is that, like phosphorus, much of it is unavailable. Some 90 percent is in rock minerals, such as mica and feldspar, which resist weathering. Fortunately, if you add potassium to the soil, plants can absorb it readily until it is leached away.

The trick to keeping potassium at the right level is to apply it twice a season, half a dose each time, rather than putting it on all at once. This way, your plants get just what they need.

### HEALTHY CROPS

A good balance of soil potassium will promote strong, healthy growth in all your crops. It is especially important in tuber formation, and crops such as potatoes (below) require high amounts of this element to form starches.

## Secondary Macronutrients

Besides nitrogen, phosphorus and potassium, plants need large doses of calcium, magnesium and sulfur. **Calcium** helps plants absorb nitrogen and create proteins. Without it, new leaves and end branches are deformed; the upper leaves curl upward and turn yellow around the edges, then dry and fall off. Stems are hard and roots are brown and stubby. Blossom-end rot, where the bottom of fruits turn brown or black, is a common symptom of calcium deficiency in tomatoes and bell peppers (capsicums). Drought can cause calcium deficiency because plants can't absorb it from the dry soil. Excess potassium can also limit available calcium.

Limestone is the main source of calcium. Limestone also neutralizes soil acidity, making it a useful addition to acid soils but something to avoid on alkaline soils. Add gypsum to alkaline

### ZINC DEFICIENCY

Although not required in large amounts, an absence of trace elements such as zinc can cause problems. Above we see the typical yellowing between dark green veins and the leaves starting to roll along the edges that indicate a lack of zinc.

soil that is calcium-deficient. Calcium is also found in fertilizers that supply other nutrients, such as rock phosphate, bonemeal, kelp meal and wood ashes.

**Magnesium** is part of the chlorophyll molecule, which makes plants green and is essential for photosynthesis. Without it, plants are chlorotic—the leaves are pale with dark green veins. Correct a magnesium deficiency in an acid soil by adding dolomitic limestone, containing magnesium carbonate. In alkaline soils, use Epsom salts, which is magnesium sulfate.

**Sulfur** is part of the proteins that plants build. Plants with a sulfur deficiency are small, pale and spindly. Sulfur also makes soils acid. Deficiencies are rare. Adding ample quantities of organic matter will usually supply all the sulfur your plants need. To lower your soil's acidity, use sulfur dust, also known as flowers of sulfur.

MAGNESIUM DEFICIENCY

Mottling and dead spots on leaves, which may be brittle and curl up, indicate a lack of magnesium. Fruit matures late or not at all. Deficiencies are more common late in the season and in soils with too much potassium or calcium.

SEAWEED

In its fresh form or prepared as an extract, seaweed is an excellent source of calcium and trace elements, or micronutrients, such as iron, zinc, copper and boron.

# MULCHES

Mulching retains soil moisture, controls weed growth, provides a barrier against soilborne diseases, protects soil from erosion and keeps your harvest clean. Its importance cannot be overestimated.

## ORGANIC MULCH

Organic mulches are plant residues, such as compost, bean hulls, grass clippings, shredded leaves, newspapers, pine needles, sawdust, straw and wood chips. Their decomposition enhances soil productivity, enriches the soil with nutrients and supplies organic matter.

Organic mulches encourage and shelter beneficial organisms at the soil surface and just below it. Thick layers of mulch act as a cushion, reducing soil compaction. And at the end of the season, you don't have to remove them, because they decompose naturally. Ideally, organic mulch should be applied before

**SHREDDED LEAVES**
Run autumn leaves through a shredder to make a lightweight insulating mulch that is just the thing for protecting late-season crops.

**GRASS CLIPPINGS**
Use both fresh and dry grass clippings, hay or similar material to mulch around all kinds of plants. Because they contain balanced amounts of carbon and nitrogen, they won't draw nitrogen from your soil as they break down.

annual weeds (such as lamb's-quarters) have a chance to germinate and the perennials (such as quack grass) emerge.

The plants you choose to grow and the location of your garden determine when and how you should apply mulch. Vegetables such as peas and spinach will appreciate early mulching, which can help keep the soil cool. Early mulching is also a good idea in dry climates, since it traps the moisture from spring rains. On the other hand, if you are planting heat-loving crops such as eggplant (aubergine), it's better to wait until the soil has warmed up before you apply the mulch. Mulching later in the season is also useful in wet areas, because the soil will have dried out a bit.

Build a mulch layer 4–12 inches (10–30 cm) thick. Use less material in wet climates, and more in dry climates. Keep the mulch about 4–8 inches (10–20 cm) away from plant stems to promote surface aeration, which helps lessen the chance of disease and problems from slugs and snails.

## BARK MULCHES

Wood chips may contain wood that has been treated with chemicals that could harm plants. If you chip your own bark, let it sit outside for a few months before using it, so that any natural substances harmful to plants are leached out. Turn the pile every few weeks to keep chips from going "sour." Cypress bark can be toxic to young plants.

TWICE AS EFFECTIVE
Compost works best when it is topped with a thin layer of a longer-lasting mulch, such as shredded bark, wood shavings or similar materials.

## LANDSCAPING FABRICS

Black plastic and similar material used as a mulch should be put in place early in the season. Apply it several weeks before planting, to warm the soil. Landscaping fabrics can go on anytime before planting. Cut away holes for planting.

## ORGANIC LITTER

Organic mulches enrich your soil as they break down. They also provide the kind of environment that worms, friendly bacteria and other beneficial garden creatures thrive in, so there are benefits all round.

## ALUMINUM

Strips of aluminum-coated paper or heavy-duty aluminum foil put down between rows can be used as a mulch. As well as keeping weeds from germinating, they can confuse insect pests and discourage them from landing on your crops.

**WOOD CHIPS**

These make a long-lasting, weed-suppressing mulch. They're often used for paths and in permanent plantings, such as around your fruit trees and berry bushes. However, rain can wash small pieces away, leading to more work keeping areas near mulched beds clean.

A light-colored mulch such as straw reflects light and keeps soil cool. Dark-colored mulches help to warm the soil.

You will have to amend some types of organic mulch. For example, pine needles and leaves are acidic and should be neutralized with lime. (As a general rule, apply 5 pounds [2.2 kg] of lime per 100 square feet [9.3 sq m] to raise the pH of your soil 1 point. Sandy soils generally need less lime to raise the pH; clay soils need more.) If you use seaweed, rinse away the salt first. If you're uncertain of the nutrient value of a mulching material, have your soil tested annually so you'll know what changes are taking place.

## INORGANIC MULCHES

These mulches include those materials that don't improve soil, such as plastic or gravel. Gravel isn't practical in most vegetable gardens, but black plastic is widely used because it warms the soil early for the fastest crops. Landscaping fabrics are similar to black plastic but have tiny pores to let water and air in. Gardeners might find both black plastic and landscaping fabric expensive, but they can last several seasons if you remove and store them each autumn.

If you decide to use black plastic or similar landscaping fabrics, make sure you purchase the right width and length for your beds or rows. To determine the right width, measure across beds and rows then add at least 6 inches (15 cm) to each side. After you lay it out, anchor the sides with soil, rocks or boards. Cut away holes for planting. At the end of the season, remove and store it until next season, if it's still in good condition.

Part Three

# Planting
# Your Garden

# CHOOSING PLANTS AND SEEDS

Make a list of the plants you want to grow, along with an estimate of the number or amount of seed for each. Refer to your list when at the garden center or ordering from catalogs.

A STEP AHEAD
Punnets of healthy plants save you some time, which may justify their extra expense, especially if your growing season is short.

## BUYING PLANTS

When buying vegetable seedlings, look for healthy, green plants with lush foliage. Reject tall, leggy seedlings in favor of short, full plants. Upright, annual vegetables, such as bell peppers (capsicums), tomatoes or broccoli, that are planted individually, should be limited to one stem per pot or cell. An extra seedling may look like a bargain, but it's easy to damage both plants if you attempt to separate them, and the vigor

## FOOLPROOF VEGETABLES

There is really no such thing as a "foolproof" vegetable. They all need good soil preparation and regular care. But there are some relatively easy-to-grow crops that are good confidence builders for the novice gardener. Some of the most dependable are listed below, along with some growing hints.

**Bean, bush**  Pick regularly to prolong harvest.
**Bean, runner**  Needs a trellis.
**Beet**  Keep soil evenly moist.
**Garlic**  Plant autumn, harvest summer.
**Lettuce**  Best in cool weather.
**Onion**  Grow from young bulbs.
**Radish**  Sow in spring.
**Squash, summer**  Apply compost.
**Tomato, cherry**  Needs ample water.

## Miniature and Baby Vegetables

Experienced gardeners know that the biggest vegetables are not always the tastiest. In some cases, gourmet baby vegetables are full-sized cultivars harvested young. Others are naturally small. Try some of these.

**Beans**  Pick pods when ¼ inch (6 mm) wide; any cultivar.

**Beet**  Pull when root is about 1 inch (2.5 cm) in diameter; try 'Mini Gourmet', but any cultivar will do.

**Bell pepper (capsicum)**  Pick small peppers as needed; any cultivar.

**Carrot**  Pull when roots are colored; 'Mini Round', 'Tom Thumb'.

**Cauliflower**  Pick when heads are young.

**Corn**  Pick tiny ears 2 days after silks appear, or choose small-fruited cultivars; any sweet corn cultivar will do.

**Cucumber**  Pick when 2–6 inches (5–15 cm) long; any cultivar.

**Eggplant (aubergine)**  Pick up to 4 inches (10 cm) long; any cultivar.

**Garlic**  Pick while young before clove development. Serve as you would baby leeks or roast and squeeze onto bruschetta.

**Leek**  Can be picked while very young and cooked whole.

**Lettuce**  Harvest small, young leaves as needed; sow different cultivars together or choose leaf lettuce such as 'Oak Leaf' and 'Regency'.

**Melon**  Choose small-fruited cultivars; 'Bush Sugar Baby', 'Sugar Baby'.

**Onion**  Pull young for spring onions; pickling onions have small bulbs.

**Pea**  Pick when pods are 2–3 inches (5–7.5 cm) long; any cultivar.

**Pumpkin**  Choose small-fruited cultivars; 'Baby Blue', 'Golden Nugget'.

**Squash**  Pick at 4 inches (10 cm) or longer; 'Patty Pan', 'Green Buttons'.

**Tomato**  Choose small-fruited cultivars; 'Yellow Pear', 'Sweet Red'.

**Zucchini (courgette)**  Pick fruit at any size; 'Lebanese', 'Greenskin'.

Zucchini

Squash

of both will be reduced if you plant them together. Pots of vegetables such as cucumbers or pumpkins, which are usually planted in hills, should hold only a few small seedlings. Leafy crops, such as arugula (rocket) or leaf lettuce, aren't as fussy about spacing; they can be started, planted and harvested in clumps.

The soil in the seedling pots should be moist but not soggy. Roots should be well developed, but not so much that they've filled the pot. It's normal for a few threads of root to escape the pot, but avoid transplants with solid masses of tightly woven roots. Also check the seedlings for signs of insect pests or disease symptoms. The presence of beneficial insects, such as ladybugs, might indicate a recent pest problem, but it's better to take home the beneficials than the residue of pesticides. Look for webs, insect droppings or signs of damage, such as ragged holes or spotty leaves. Don't buy seedlings with discolored or wilted leaves. Look for identification labels, especially if you're unfamiliar with the seedling stages of vegetables. Closely related vegetables, such as broccoli, cauliflower and cabbage, look alike at this stage. If you're interested in a particular cultivar, shop early for the best selection or you might have to settle for unfamiliar cultivars. Most greenhouse

READY FOR ACTION
Keep your gardening kit in a handy carry-all and you won't need to search the house in your muddy boots.

growers have to limit how many cultivars they sow for space reasons. Consult a current seed catalog if you have to choose an unknown cultivar. A good nursery salesperson should be able to recommend the best for your garden.

Ask how the seedlings were grown. If you're strictly organic, look for growers who use starting medium, seeds, fertilizers and pest-control practices that conform to organic standards. If you can't find a source for organically grown seedlings and don't want to raise your own, you may have to settle for non-organic seedlings. At this stage, the

## CHOOSE STRONG PLANTS
Seedlings should look dark green and healthy. Avoid spindly plants that have not had enough light and those with discolored leaves. These have been stressed in some way and will not perform as well as they should.

COOK THEM QUICKLY
Steaming, stir-frying and microwaving do the best job of preserving the vitamins in your home-grown vegetables.

amount of synthetic materials imported to your garden is probably negligible. Also ask if the seedlings have been hardened off (gradually acclimatized to outdoor conditions). If they have been in a warm greenhouse or an air-conditioned super-market, you'll have to introduce them slowly to the outdoors (see page 65).

Once you get your seedlings home, make sure that you keep them watered if you are unable to transplant them to the garden immediately. Place them out of direct sun, keep a close eye on the weather and be ready to bring them indoors if a storm or frost threatens.

## Bareroot or Container Plants?

Depending on when and where you buy, your fruiting plants may be bareroot or growing in containers. Bareroot plants are sold when they're dormant (not actively growing), without any soil around the roots. This is the most practical way for mail-order nurseries to ship plants, but one disadvantage is that they are only available at certain times of year (usually late autumn and early spring). Bareroot stock must be planted as soon as possible after arrival.

Local nurseries most often sell their plants growing in containers. The disadvantages of container-grown plants are that they tend to be more expensive

BAREROOT PLANTS
Check that the roots and base of the plant are firm and healthy looking, with no unusual swellings (other than the graft union near the base of the trunk). Look for clean, evenly colored bark, free of suspicious holes.

than bareroot stock, and you'll have a much more limited selection. On the plus side, though, container-grown plants are available throughout the year and can be planted any time the ground isn't frozen. If you can't plant them right away, you can keep them growing in their pots until you're ready to set them in the ground. Container stock is quite easy to plant, and it tends to have a lower failure rate than bareroot stock.

## Don't Buy Problem Plants

Buying disease- and pest-resistant plants is important to the future health of your garden. But it's just as important to avoid buying plants that have problems right now. Otherwise, you might introduce serious problems, such as bacterial and viral diseases, that will affect all your crops. To reduce the risk, buy only from nurseries that offer certified disease-free plants. This means that the plants have been checked over and approved by nursery inspectors.

### Fast-Growers

In areas with a short growing season, fast-maturing crops are often the best chance for a good harvest. In long-season areas, use them for interplanting or succession planting. Here are a few to try: arugula (rocket), beans (bush types), beet, chicory (leafy types), Chinese cabbage, corn salad (lamb's lettuce, mâche), cress, kohlrabi, lettuce, mizuna, mustard, peas, radish, spinach, Swiss chard (silverbeet).

CHOOSE THE BEST
It may take a few seasons to find the varieties you prefer, but it's well worth the search.

The first thing to check when buying seeds is the date on the packet. Buy fresh seeds and buy only enough for the current year, unless you're able to store seeds under the proper conditions of low moisture and low temperature. Seeds are sold by weight or number of seeds. Check how much you're getting in each packet. Shopping around is time-consuming but worthwhile. Naturally, look for a reputable dealer because seeds can differ greatly in quality.

If you can find a source, it's even better to buy "virus-indexed" plants. These come from laboratories that test stock plants and grow only those that are virus-free. These laboratories sell young plants to commercial nurseries, who propagate and grow them under controlled conditions that prevent virus infection. Virus-free stock is available for most fruit trees, as well as for grapes, raspberries, blackberries and strawberries.

### CONTAINER VEGETABLES

If space is limited, consider using pots. Fill a suitable container with potting mixture (not garden soil, which will pack down too tightly after watering). Compact or dwarf cultivars are generally the best choice. Try some of these: bean (bush types), borecole, bell pepper (capsicum), carrot (short-rooted cultivars), corn salad (lamb's lettuce, mâche), cucumber (bush cultivars), eggplant (aubergine), lettuce, onion, pea (needs a trellis), radish, summer squash (bush cultivars), Swiss chard (silverbeet), tomato, watercress.

### CONTAINER-GROWN PLANTS

Check foliage is a bright, uniform green color. Check underneath leaves and at base of stems for insects or egg clusters hidden there. If you find a problem, send the plant back or don't buy it; you don't want to risk spreading pests or diseases to your other plants.

## STARTING SEEDS INDOORS

1. Take a tray with drainage holes and fill with a light, moist growing medium such as sifted compost. Press it firmly into the corners.

2. Level off the surface with a flat piece of wood, so the medium is ½ inch (12 mm) below the rim of the container and won't wash over the edge.

3. Mark furrows 2 inches (5 cm) apart, or sprinkle seeds evenly over surface. Space small seeds ½ inch (12 mm) apart, medium seeds 1 inch (2.5 cm) apart.

4. Firm surface by pressing seeds lightly with a smooth wooden block. Press gently so seeds are in contact with mix, but not so hard as to bury them.

5. Sieve a light layer of growing medium over surface of soil. Do not cover seeds that need light to germinate. Spray with a fine mist of water.

6. Label and cover container with glass or plastic wrap. Check daily for first sprouts. To prevent disease, remove cover when seedlings appear.

# Starting Seeds

Planting seeds indoors will get your seedlings off to a good start. Because you can control their environment, you can begin the new season earlier than when you plant outdoors.

## Containers

Start seedlings in just about any container that has holes for drainage. Seedlings started in their own pots won't require potting-up later. You can even purchase ready-to-use flats with cells for sowing single seeds. If you use containers such as peat pots or pellets, you can plant the pot along with the plant. These are a good choice for those vegetables that transplant poorly, such as cucumbers.

## Growing Medium

New seedlings need a light, moist medium for a quick start. Fill containers with moistened vermiculite, milled sphagnum moss, perlite or sifted compost Once true leaves have developed, the young plants will require extra nutrients. Water them with a liquid organic fertilizer, such as fish emulsion, at half strength. Gradually increase the dose to full strength. Alternatively, transfer seedlings to a potting blend with extra compost, or prepare a nourishing substitute by adding up to ½ cup (4 fl oz/125 ml) of dry, organic fertilizer to each 5-gallon (22.5 l) batch of homemade potting medium. Remember, the longer seedlings remain in pots, the more nutrients they need.

### SPECIAL HANDLING

Seedlings in peat pots need special care. Tear a hole in each side of the pot before you plant it, so that the roots can make their way out. Then, tear away the upper collar of the pot, because exposed peat will act like a wick, drawing the moisture up and away from the roots of the seedling. Plant as you would a normal seedling, but plant pot and all.

## TRANSPLANTING SEEDLINGS OUTDOORS

1. Transplant seedlings in early evening or on cool, overcast days to protect them from sun.

2. Gently slide each seedling out of its container, keeping the soil and rootball intact.

3. Holding gently, plant seedling in a hole slightly wider, but the same depth, as container.

4. Replace soil around roots first, fill hole level with bed, gently firm the surface and water.

## HARDENING OFF

At least 2 weeks before transplanting time, begin watering less frequently and withholding fertilizer. A week before you transplant, move the plants outdoors to a spot protected from strong light and wind. This allows young plants to adjust slowly to the extremes of temperature, wind and light. Gradually increase the time they spend outdoors. Within a week, they should be outdoors all the time. They'll need more water at this time, since sun and wind quickly dry the soil. Be prepared to bring them back indoors if a cold snap or storm threatens.

# Planting Outdoors

**NO WASTE**
Plant the seeds of leafy or root vegetables quite thickly and use the thinnings as tender, young additions to salads and stir-fries.

Some plants, such as beans, peas and root crops, do not transplant well. You'll get the best results by sowing these seeds directly into the garden.

## Sowing Seed

1. Planting dates vary among species and cultivars, so check your seed packets or a catalog. Ask local gardeners what is the expected date of the last frost for your area.

2. If you're planting in rows, mark them with wooden stakes at both ends before planting. Stretch a length of string down the row and use it as a guide to keep your rows straight while you plant. Transfer it from row to row as you go.

3. If you have raised beds, divide them into sections by plant cultivar, broadcast the seed over the appropriate section and label them, or simply sow your seed in rows across the raised bed.

4. Follow the spacing guidelines on the seed packet. Some packets indicate what length of row the package will sow. Most sowing recommendations are higher than necessary, to account for areas that are less than ideal. If conditions are good for germination, you may have to thin your seedlings later.

5. Cover seeds with soil to a depth two to three times the seed diameter, then firm them by pressing the soil lightly with the flat side of a rake or hoe.

6. The soil should stay moist but not soggy until your seeds begin to sprout. If you plant during a dry season, you may

have to water to ensure germination.
If the soil at the planting depth is moist
when you sow large seeds, they should
have sufficient moisture to germinate.
Fine seeds may need extra moisture. You
can cover the row with lengths of board
to retain moisture. Check the soil under
the boards frequently, and remove them
as soon as seeds sprout.

7. Once seedlings are growing well,
thin them to the final plant spacing. Pull
or snip off extras, leaving only the best.

8. Keep records of your plantings,
and record the location of each vegetable
species on a rough map.

ROOM TO GROW

Once your young plants are
well established, they may
need to be thinned. Pull
them out carefully, disturbing
the plants next to them as
little as possible, or snip
them off at soil level.

# Frost Protection and Extending the Season

Season extension means getting a head start in the spring, and prolonging production in autumn, thus squeezing a little more time into each growing season.

## Cold Frames

If you build your own cold frames, make the back taller than the front so that the glass roof slants at an angle of about 45 degrees, for the best light. A frame measuring about 4 feet (1.2 m) wide by 4 feet (1.2 m) long is a good size. It should be tall enough so your plants can grow in their pots or flats without touching the roof. Attach the roof at the back with hinges and prop it open with a piece of wood to allow for air circulation. Or the roof can simply sit on the frame and you can slide it open when you need to reduce the temperature inside the frame. It's best if the interior is painted white, to reflect light onto your plants.

Keep plants or seedlings in their pots or trays in the frame—you'll find that containers are easier to manage in the small space.

## Row and Plant Covers

These can be made from fabric or transparent plastic, and they provide protection from all but the hardest frosts at night. Lightweight row-cover fabric, made from spun-bonded polyester or

INDIVIDUAL PROTECTION
Covers such as this Wallo Water Protector will keep frost off special plants, but cones made of heavy-duty cardboard also work well.

COVER STORY
You can start growing in the garden earlier, and prolong your autumn harvest, if you use row covers to protect the tender plants from frosts.

### A COLD FRAME THROUGH THE FOUR SEASONS

In spring, harden off your seedlings in the cold frame before transplanting them out in the garden.

In summer, sow salad crops, such as spinach, for harvesting in autumn. The slats will keep the plants cool, but still let in sunlight.

In autumn, a cold frame will ensure the survival of your late-sown leafy crops, such as lettuce, until well after the first frost.

In winter, use your cold frame to give bulbs, such as golden shallots and garlic, their cold treatment before forcing them on.

## INTERPLANTING

The different growth habits and nutrient needs of lettuce and onions make them ideal candidates for interplanting. This way you get twice the yield from the same space.

## HARVEST MANAGEMENT

Successive sowings, about 10–14 days apart, of crops such as bush beans will provide you with a continuous harvest. As one planting finishes bearing, the next becomes ready to pick.

polypropylene, allows in water, light and air but keeps insects at bay. You can buy shaded or colored covers to reduce sunlight and heat in hot climates.

Plastic row covers will keep plants and soil warmer than fabric. Since heat builds up on sunny days, you'll need to vent plastic covers. Buy slitted plastic covers with built-in ventilation. To use, stretch plastic row covers over wire hoops inserted in the soil on opposite sides of the bed or row. You can buy the supports and covering together.

In a smaller garden, protect individual plants (instead of rows) from frost. Many different types of material are used to make plant covers (also

## Succession Planting

Succession planting means harvesting two crops from the same space in one season, by planting the second crop after you've harvested the first. Determine the length of your growing season by counting the days between the average date of the last spring frost and the average date of the first autumn frost. Then select two vegetables whose combined days to maturity fit that limit. Plant seeds or transplants of the first crop in early spring, then harvest them and replant with the second crop in midsummer. Between crops, prepare the soil as needed but avoid tilling. By midsummer, most weed seeds have germinated, and tilling will only bring more seeds to the surface. You can add compost before the second planting, or after planting, as a mulch. Timing is the challenge. Each crop must get off to a quick start and finish. Good choices for quick crops to grow in spring and autumn are: arugula (rocket), beets, carrots, collards, chicory, endive, kohlrabi, mustard greens, radish, shallots, spinach and Swiss chard (silverbeet).

### GOOD COMPANIONS

Artichokes and plants of the onion family are light feeders, so they will thrive in the same conditions.

known as cloches). Whatever you use, make sure the covering allows enough light and ventilation. Garden centers offer many choices. Or make your own protectors from plastic milk containers. Cut along three sides of the base so the base forms a flap that can be used to anchor it. Leave the top open during the day. Use until frost danger is past.

## Favorite Fruits and Nuts at a Glance

| CROP NAME | EXPOSURE | SOIL FERTILITY | HARDINESS | HEIGHT | SPREAD |
|---|---|---|---|---|---|
| Almond | Full sun | Average to fertile soil | Zones 6–9 | 15–30 feet (4.5–9 m) | 15–30 feet (4.5–9 m) |
| Apple | Full sun | Average soil | Zones 3–9 | 8–30 feet (2.4–9 m) | 8–30 feet (2.4–9 m) |
| Apricot | Full sun | Average to poor soil | Zones 5–9 | 8–24 feet (2.4–7.2 m) | 16–24 feet (4.8–7.2 m) |
| Blackberry | Full sun | Average to rich soil | Zones 5–9 | 4–7 feet (1.2–2.1 m) | 3–6 feet (0.9–1.8 m) |
| Blueberry | Full sun | Average to rich soil | Zones 3–9 | 2–15 feet (0.6–4.5 m) | 3–10 feet (0.9–3 m) |
| Cherry, sour | Full sun | Average to rich soil | Zones 4–8 | 8–20 feet (2.4–6 m) | 8–20 feet (2.4–6 m) |
| Cherry, sweet | Full sun | Average to poor soil | Zones 4–9 | 15–30 feet (4.5–9 m) | 15–30 feet (4.5–9 m) |
| Citrus | Full sun to light shade | Average to rich soil | Zones 8–10 | 10–30 feet (3–9 m) | 10–30 feet (3–9 m) |
| Fig | Full sun | Average soil | Zones 8–10 | 10–25 feet (3–7.5 m) | 10–25 feet (3–7.5 m) |
| Gooseberry | Full sun to light shade | Average soil | Zones 3–7 | 3–7 feet (0.9–2.1 m) | 3–7 feet (0.9–2.1 m) |
| Grape | Full sun | Average to rich soil | Zones 4–10 | 4–6 feet (1.2–1.8 m) | 8–15 feet (2.4–4.5 m) |
| Hazelnut | Full sun to light shade | Average to poor soil | Zones 2–9 | 6–70 feet + (1.8–21 m) + | 20 feet (6 m) |
| Kiwi | Full sun to light shade | Average to poor soil | Zones 7–9 | 4–6 feet (1.2–1.8 m) | 15 feet (4.5 m) |
| Mulberry | Full sun | Average soil | Zones 5–8 | 15–30 feet (4.5–9 m) | 10–20 feet (3–6 m) |
| Peach | Full sun | Average to poor soil | Zones 5–9 | 8–15 feet (2.4–4.5 m) | 10–20 feet (3–6 m) |
| Pear | Full sun | Average to poor soil | Zones 4–9 | 8–20 feet (2.4–6 m) | 8–20 feet (2.4–6 m) |
| Pecan | Full sun | Average to rich soil | Zones 6–9 | 50–150 feet (15–45 m) | 35–50 feet (10.5–15 m) |
| Plum | Full sun | Average to rich soil | Zones 4–10 | 8–20 feet (2.4–6 m) | 8–20 feet (2.4–6 m) |
| Raspberry | Full sun | Average to poor soil | Zones 3–9 | 4–6 feet (1.2–1.8 m) | 2–4 feet (0.6–1.2 m) |
| Strawberry | Full sun | Average to rich soil | Zones 3–10 | 10 inches (25 cm) | 1–2 feet (30–60 cm) |

A handy reference to 20 of the most popular fruits and nuts for planting in home gardens. Remember that some cultivars may have slightly different needs.

| BLOOM TIME | HARVEST TIME | USES AND STORAGE | POLLINATION |
|---|---|---|---|
| Early spring | Midsummer to autumn | Eat fresh; dry for storage | Cross-pollinated |
| Midspring | Midsummer to autumn | Eat fresh; keep for several weeks in refrigerator; or preserve | Cross-pollinated |
| Early spring | Early summer | Eat fresh; keep a week or two in refrigerator; dry; or preserve | Cross- and self-pollinated |
| Midspring | Midsummer | Eat fresh; keep a week or two in refrigerator; or preserve | Self-pollinated |
| Midspring | Mid- to late summer | Eat fresh; keep a few days in refrigerator; or preserve | Cross- and self-pollinated |
| Midspring | Early summer | Eat fresh; keep a few days in refrigerator; or preserve | Cross- and self-pollinated |
| Midspring | Early summer | Eat fresh; keep a few days in refrigerator; or preserve | Cross-pollinated |
| Varies | Varies | Eat fresh; keep a week or two in refrigerator; make into marmalade | Self-pollinated |
| Varies | Varies | Eat fresh; keep a few days in refrigerator; dry; or freeze | Self-pollinated |
| Midspring | Midsummer | Eat fresh; keep a week or two in refrigerator; or preserve | Self-pollinated |
| Midspring | Midsummer to autumn | Eat fresh; keep a week or two in refrigerator; or preserve | Self-pollinated |
| Early spring | Late summer to autumn | Eat fresh; keep for weeks in refrigerator; or freeze | Cross-pollinated |
| Midspring | Autumn | Eat fresh; keep for several weeks in refrigerator; or preserve | Cross-pollinated |
| Spring | Summer | Eat fresh; freeze; dry; or preserve | Self-pollinated |
| Early spring | Midsummer | Eat fresh; keep a week or two in refrigerator; or preserve | Self-pollinated |
| Midspring | Late summer to autumn | Eat fresh; keep for several weeks in refrigerator; or preserve | Cross-pollinated |
| Early spring | Autumn | Eat fresh; keep for several weeks in refrigerator; or dry | Cross-pollinated |
| Early spring | Midsummer | Eat fresh; keep a week or two in refrigerator; or preserve | Cross- and self-pollinated |
| Midspring | Midsummer to autumn | Eat fresh; keep a few days in refrigerator; or preserve | Self-pollinated |
| Midspring | Early to midsummer | Eat fresh; keep a few days in refrigerator; or preserve | Self-pollinated |

# Planting Fruits, Nuts, Berries and Vines

It's always exciting when planting day arrives. All the effort you've put into choosing the best cultivars, deciding where to put them and preparing the soil will pay off now as you put in your plants.

Alpine strawberry

## Autumn Planting

For those who live in a warm climate (Zones 6–10) autumn is a good time to plant most fruit and nut crops. Dormant, bareroot, mail-order plants will arrive in early to late autumn. Nurseries and garden centers may also offer container-grown plants through autumn.

If you live in Zone 5 or cooler and you have light, well-drained soil and winters that aren't severely cold, you can plant currants, gooseberries and hardy Concord grapes in autumn, but save the rest of your planting for spring.

In warm climates, the planting season extends well into winter. In temperate climates, bareroot apricots go in the ground from mid- to late winter. In warmer regions, blueberries and strawberries are best planted in winter.

## Spring Planting

In cool climates (Zone 5 and cooler), early spring is the best time to plant most fruits and nuts. Bareroot mail-order plants will arrive early, so prepare the planting site in autumn so it will be ready when your plants come. You'll want to get the plants in the ground

## PLANTING PINEAPPLES

Twist off any sideshoots or cut the crown of leaves off the top of the pineapple and let dry for a few days. Then plant the shoots or crowns about 1 foot (30 cm) apart in a warm, sunny position.

## STRAWBERRY BEDS

Set out your strawberries in rows that will allow easy access for cultivation and harvesting. Finish the job by applying a thick layer of organic mulch that will gradually break down and enrich the soil.

as soon as possible, so they will be well established before the heat and drought of summer. If you don't have the time to deal with your bareroot plants when they arrive or if the weather in your area is still dropping well below freezing at night, you may need to hold the plants indoors for a few days.

If you buy your plants locally, they'll most likely be growing in containers. While it's ideal to plant them early, container-grown fruit trees, shrubs or vines are much more forgiving of delays than bareroot plants, as long as you keep them well watered.

## PLANTING BAREROOT PLANTS

If you've never seen a bareroot plant before, you might be surprised when you unpack your box from the nursery. Bareroot plants are just what they sound

SEASONAL INTEREST
Choose dwarf or semi-dwarf fruit trees instead of purely ornamental trees if your space is limited. You will enjoy the display of flowers, followed by a season of harvest.

like—tentacle-like naked roots topped with bare branches or merely a single stem. They can look rather pathetic, but as long as you bought the plants from a reputable nursery and give them proper care, they will grow beautifully. (If you lose plants right after transplanting, which is not all that uncommon, contact the nursery for a refund or replacement.)

To get bareroot plants off to a good start:

1. When you're ready to plant, cut off any sickly, damaged or very long roots. Leave healthy roots alone. Give most fruit and nut plants, except blueberries, a preplanting booster by soaking their roots in a bucket of compost tea (see page 34). Soak the roots of strawberries and grapes for 20 minutes; soak bush and tree roots for 2 hours.

USING VERTICAL SPACE
Choose standard forms, such as this gooseberry, if your garden is small.

2. Dig a hole deep enough to hold the roots without curling them up at the ends. Slice into the walls of the hole with a spade to make them easy for roots to penetrate. Make a tall cone of soil in the center of the hole and firm it well.

3. Remove roots from compost tea, then dip them in a blend of 1 part bonemeal and 1 part powdered kelp. If the bacterial disease crown gall is a problem in your area, apply a preventive treatment of Agrobacterium radiobacter (sold as Galltrol-A and

FOR A SMALLER GARDEN
Dwarf cultivars, like this peach tree, do well in planters that are at least 2 feet (60 cm) wide and 3 feet (90 cm) deep.

---

## PLANTING

Dig a wide, shallow planting hole and slash the sides with the spade so roots can spread easily.

For bareroot plants, spread the roots over a cone of soil in the center of your planting hole.

With ballroot plants, set plant in hole so base of stem is level with the soil surface.

Fill hole, gently firm down soil and water with a fine spray to wet surrounding soil thoroughly.

Norbac 84). Dunk your bareroot fruit plants in it before planting to prevent later crown gall infection.

4. Put crown of plant (where the roots come together and shoots emerge) on top of the soil cone in the planting hole.

5. Check that the crown or graft swelling is level with the surface of the soil. If your soil tends to sink slightly as it settles, you may want to elevate the plant a little to adjust. If your plant sits too high or too low on the soil cone, lift it out, change the height of the cone and try again.

6. When you have the right crown or graft height, spread out the roots evenly over the soil cone. Holding the plant with one hand, fill in around the roots with the soil you removed from the hole. When the hole is half-filled, add some water so the planting site is thoroughly soaked; then finish filling the hole. Firm the soil gently and add a plant label.

### QUARTERING

To loosen a tight root ball, use a knife to make four deep cuts through the base of the ball. Spread the quartered root ball over a cone of good soil, fill the planting hole and water.

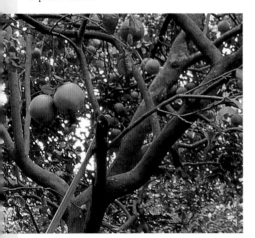

### SPACE-SAVER

This multi-graft citrus tree bears lemons, oranges, mandarins and grapefruit on the one tree, a huge saving in space and in the effort needed to look after four separate trees.

## PLANTS IN CONTAINERS

To remove a plant from a pot, squeeze the sides of a plastic pot to loosen, or invert a rigid pot and tap the rim gently, supporting the plant with your hand so that it doesn't fall out and break.

### Planting Aftercare

On year-old fruit trees, cut back the main trunk to about 2 feet (60 cm) in height to encourage it to develop new branches for later training. On hickories and walnuts, cut the young tree back by half, leaving several buds on the trunk to form new branches.

On bareroot fruit bushes, cut back up to half of the stems to compensate for the roots lost. Remove all but the base of the old canes from raspberries and blackberries to eliminate any diseases they may carry. And on grapes, remove all but the strongest stem to prepare the vine for future training.

On berries, remove all the flowers the first spring after planting to encourage good growth. Pinch off grape flowers for 2 years after planting.

## Planting Plants from Containers

1. Dig a hole the same depth as the pot, leaving the soil in the bottom of the hole undisturbed. If your soil is very heavy (clayey) or light (sandy), dig some composted pine bark or peat moss into the area around the planting hole.

2. Double-check that your plant will sit at the proper level. If you lay a stake across the hole and measure from the stake to the bottom of the hole with a stick, you can judge the right depth without having to lift the heavy plant in and out of the hole.

3. Remove the plant from its pot by putting one hand on the surface of the planting mix to support the top. Then put your other hand under the container, squeezing the sides gently to separate it from the roots. Turn the pot upside-down and slide the plant out.

4. If the plant has been growing in the pot for a long time, the roots will be matted on the outside of the root ball. Use a sharp knife to cut off matted parts. Loosen circling roots with your fingers.

5. Set the plant in the hole, spreading loose roots in different directions so each has its own space. Refill the hole with soil and water thoroughly.

Part Four

# Managing Your Garden

# Garden Care for Four Seasons

**PATIO BOUNTY**
Container-grown plants on even a tiny, sunny patio can produce a surprising harvest.

Being organized about your garden tasks reduces the work. Follow this simple guide to doing jobs at the right time and your crops will thrive, rewarding your efforts with abundant produce.

## WINTER

Winter is as important as any other season. The planning you do on long winter nights will help prevent problems later on. This is the time to decide what you want to grow and how much you are going to plant. As you search through seed catalogs, look for high-yielding cultivars that are insect- or disease-resistant, so you'll have fewer pest problems to cope with. Order seeds and save yourself a trip to the garden center later on. This is also a good time to plan your planting schedule.

## SPRING

The weather's getting warmer and your garden beds and soil are prepared (see page 28). But before you start digging and planting, take a few minutes to review the plans you made during the winter. Check your planting schedule to see what crops should go in first. Get out the seeds you ordered, or take your shopping list to the garden center and

### KEEPING RECORDS

Keep track of planting dates, fertilizer rates, pest problems and harvests. Some people make notes in a diary or on a calendar or create tables of garden data. As well as noting your garden's day-to-day progress, your records will also help you plan for greater success next year. For example, you can see how well different cultivars perform in your garden, or when space will be available for replanting. Update your records with each new season.

**POTAGER GARDEN**
A clump of eschscholzia adds a spot of vivid color to a mixed vegetable and herb garden.

**PLANNING PAYS OFF**
Think about where the shade will be so that taller plants don't rob smaller ones of precious sunlight. Mulching reduces the need for water and keeps weeds down.

buy the seeds, transplants and other supplies you need. Don't be tempted to buy extra plants or plants that aren't on your list. You'll either end up cramming the extras in with the others or digging new beds to accommodate them.

## SUMMER

This season is the time that your winter planning and spring planting pay off. As your vegetables and fruits mature in the warm summer weather, a little extra attention can keep yields high and routine maintenance minimal.

Mulches are the cornerstone of good gardening (see page 50). They help keep critical moisture in the soil and moderate temperature extremes for better root growth. They reduce weeding chores by smothering weed seeds and keep soil from splashing onto plants, which reduces the spread of soilborne diseases and keeps the produce cleaner. And as they break down, organic mulches release a balanced supply of plant nutrients and add organic matter to improve the structure of the soil. Mulches also save water, but not enough that you can forget about watering (see page 94).

## AUTUMN

As the lower temperatures arrive, many plants that took a break during the summer heat may make

**FRESH FOR THE TABLE**
You can pick your vegetables just before the meal.

**SUNNY CORNERS**
You'll be surprised at what a good supply of fresh vegetables can be produced, with forward planning, in even a tiny space, especially if it is sunny and sheltered.

new growth or set more fruit. Late-summer plantings of crops such as peas and lettuce can yield well into autumn. Once your crops are done for the season, spend a few minutes putting the garden to bed so that it will be ready for spring planting next season. In addition to making it look tidier during the winter, picking up dead plants and dropped vegetable matter eliminates hiding places for insect eggs and disease pathogens.

Check over your garden tools and have any that need sharpening attended to. Wash and dry your tools and apply a light coating of oil before storing them. While you're at it, pull up and clean off any metal or wooden stakes and store them so they don't rust or rot.

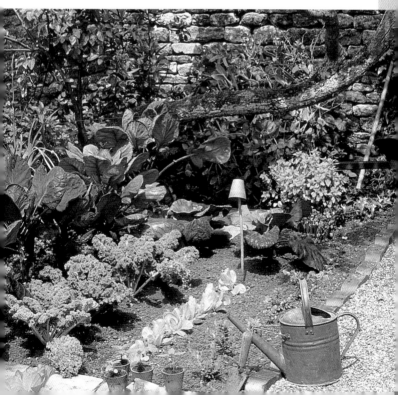

# MANAGING THE VEGETABLE GARDEN

Carrots and celery

## SPECIAL NEEDS

Some vegetables have more specific nutrient needs than just "more of everything." Cucurbits (cucumbers, melons and squash) require adequate magnesium. Garlic, onions, squash and tomatoes thrive with extra potassium and phosphorus but don't need much nitrogen. In fact, too much nitrogen will keep tomatoes from bearing fruit. To make sure your plants get just what they need, a soil test (see pages 28 and 29) will be invaluable. That way, you'll know if your soil is deficient or if it is adequately supplied with the necessary nutrients.

You can plunk a few tomato plants in a corner and get a few fruits. But if you want to get the best harvests you've ever had, it's worth preparing the site and maintaining your plants properly.

## PREPARING THE SOIL FOR VEGETABLES

In general, vegetables will thrive in normal, healthy garden soil with good drainage. Most grow best in a soil that is slightly acid or neutral (about pH 6.5–7.0). Vegetables that like the nutrient balance in alkaline soil include asparagus, melon, spinach and Swiss chard. If your soil is too acid or alkaline, you may need to adjust the pH by adding lime or sulfur.

Most vegetable crops will thrive in soils with a texture somewhere in the "loam" range: sandy loams, silt loams and even clay loams. Very loose, sandy soils with few rocks are ideal for root crops like carrots, beets and parsnips. Celery and members of the cabbage family, such as cauliflower, cabbage and broccoli, can handle wetter soils that are more on the clayey side. Of course, working in ample amounts of organic matter can make almost any soil suitable.

If you're starting a new site, strip off the existing sod, spread a 1-inch (2.5-cm) layer of compost over the area, and dig or till the top 6–8 inches (15–20 cm). If you've planted an existing garden with a cover crop or green manure, dig or till it in at least 2–3 weeks before planting. Or, if you mulched the soil for winter, rake off the mulch or work it in to let the soil warm up. If you're growing root crops, make sure you dig the soil deeply and

HEAD START
There's a small extra cost involved in buying young plants that are ready to be set out, and a more limited selection of cultivars to choose from, but you can save yourself a lot of time.

NATURAL CONTROLS
Growing flowers and herbs in your vegetable garden will help to attract beneficial, pest-eating insects. Few pests do enough damage to reduce your harvest noticeably. If you control pest insects without using poisons, you'll encourage beneficial insects that prey on them and keep their populations in check.

remove any rocks or clods that could impede good root development. Before planting, rake the soil to remove surface stones and clods.

## FERTILIZING

Many gardeners make a science out of fertilizing, but it doesn't have to be so complex. There are two approaches to fertilizing vegetables (well, three, if you count not fertilizing at all, which isn't very practical if you want good yields). The easiest way is to treat all your vegetables the same. Fertilize the vegetable garden each year, before planting, with a balanced material such as compost or a commercially available blend. For a midseason boost, side-dress with a dry fertilizer scratched lightly into the soil near the roots. Or give all of the plants a monthly dose of liquid seaweed or fish emulsion. The

**UNFINISHED BUSINESS**
If your bell peppers (capsicums) stop producing in midsummer, don't pull them up. They may set more fruit when the slightly cooler autumn weather arrives.

**SPACE SAVERS**
If space is limited, look for bush or compact cultivars of squash and other favorite crops. You'll get high yields from just a few plants in a small garden.

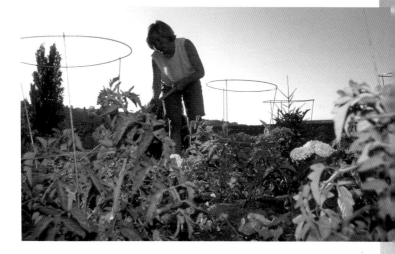

SIMPLIFY THE WORK
Plan your vegetable garden so that plants with similar water and nutrient needs are grouped together.

other approach is to fertilize each plant to meet its needs. This customized fertilizing is worth the trouble if you want to get extra-high yields or if you garden intensively (where closely spaced plants need extra nutrients).

## GETTING BETTER HARVESTS

**Beans** To get a steady supply of bush beans, plant successive crops at 7- to 10-day intervals. Or try pole beans—they grow tall, so you must set up a tripod of stakes for them to twine around, but they'll produce for a long season from a single planting and they're easy to pick.

**Broccoli** Look for cultivars like 'Packman' and 'Goliath' that will produce smaller side shoots after you harvest the main head.

**Carrots** Sow thickly and harvest the thinnings for eating each week.

**Corn** Plant successive crops every 7–10 days for a more even yield.

**Cucumbers** If space is limited and you want a high yield of cucumbers, choose bush cultivars to plant.

**Lettuce** If summer heat stops spring sowings early, try late-summer plantings for harvesting well into autumn.

**Peas** Like lettuce, peas may stop producing when summer's heat starts. Late-summer plantings will extend the pea season into autumn.

**Squash** Choose bush cultivars for a high yield from a small space.

# Easy-care Fruits and Berries

**BERRY DELIGHT**
Besides their white spring flowers, blueberries often produce outstanding autumn color, which makes them attractive as ornamentals.

Growing fruit is slightly more complicated than growing vegetables, but the rewards can make it all worthwhile. If you really want low maintenance, stick with the simplest fruit crops.

## BACKYARD BRAMBLES

Brambles, such as raspberries and blackberries, are easily grown, and plants can live as long as 10 years, so prepare the site carefully. They need full sun and should be planted far from wild relatives, which might carry disease. Choose a well-drained site or build a raised bed.

To save space and make harvesting easier, train brambles to a trellis. The double-armed T is an easy system. At either end of the bed, set in two vertical posts as tall as the mature plant will be. On each post, attach two horizontal bars, one in the middle and one at the top. Run a cord from the top corner of one crossbar to the top corner of the other. Repeat for the other side and for the lower crossbars. For easy access, remove the cords when it's time to prune.

## BLUEBERRY BASICS

Blueberry plants don't bear fruit until they're 3 or 4 years old, but if you're willing to wait, you can enjoy them as ornamentals in the meantime. All species

need a moist but loose-textured soil high
in organic matter. Most blueberries are
not self-fertile, so you'll need to plant at
least two, and preferably three, cultivars
that can cross-pollinate for good fruit set.

## STRAWBERRIES MADE SIMPLE

Early-summer strawberries produce just
the one big crop. Ever-bearing strawberries produce smaller spring and
autumn crops. Both types spread by
runners from the mother plant, with the

## LONG-SEASON HARVESTS

Spread your apple harvests
by choosing cultivars that
bloom at the same time (to
aid pollination), but mature
at different times. 'Liberty'
and 'Prima', for example,
will provide you with apples
from late summer until well
into autumn.

baby plants putting down roots. A space-saving planting method is the matted row system. Start with the plants in rows 4 feet (1.2 m) apart. Within the rows, space early-summer cultivars every 1½ feet (45 cm) and ever-bearing cultivars every foot (30 cm). For easier harvesting, limit the bed to three rows, leaving enough room at the front, back and sides for runners.

Pinch the flowers off early-summer plants the first year, so they put energy into their roots. For ever-bearing, pinch off flowers only until the start of summer. Throughout the season, let the runners fill in with new plants wherever they take root. In autumn, keep the plants

## PEACH AND NECTARINE

Be careful to choose cultivars that suit your climate. While excess cold is harmful, both of these fruit trees need some chilling if they are to flower properly. Don't plant in soil where a similar tree grew recently, as the decaying roots emit a chemical that can kill the new tree roots.

## ESPALIER TRAINING

While this takes patience and careful pruning, the result is beautiful, saving precious space in the garden and allowing unequaled access to the crop, be it apples, peaches, pears or whatever.

watered to increase the next year's crop. Mulch with straw to a depth of 2–3 inches (5–7.5 cm) in order to prevent winter damage.

The second summer after planting, rejuvenate the bed right after harvest by setting your lawn mower at 2½ inches (6 cm) and mowing over the whole bed. Rake up the debris, then narrow the width of each row to 1 foot (30 cm) by tilling or turning under the plants on the edges. Spread compost over the bed, and water the plants well to encourage new growth.

Depending on how healthy and productive your cultivar is, you can get 3 years or more of harvest. To ensure an ongoing supply, start a new bed in a different spot every 2–3 years. When you are finished with the first bed, dig it under and plant it with another crop until the new bed is exhausted.

FRESH IS BEST
Fig trees are very productive and generally easy to grow. They are seldom troubled by pests, except for birds. You may have to net your tree to keep the birds away.

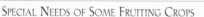

## SPECIAL NEEDS OF SOME FRUITING CROPS

**Apples**  Spray the leaves with fish emulsion just before the flower buds open. Later, spray leaves every 2 weeks through summer to provide micronutrients.

**Blueberries**  Adjust soil pH levels to fall between 4.5–5.2 for best growth. Blueberries have shallow roots that are easily damaged by cultivation, so mulch deeply instead.

**Grapes**  These are heavy feeders, so add colloidal phosphate to your compost before applying it around the vines. Test for potassium regularly and add as needed. Grapes do best in soil that has a pH of between 5.0–6.0.

**Peaches and nectarines**  These heavy feeders don't have extensive roots, so remove all sod from the root zone and keep the trees well mulched. Mix bonemeal or colloidal phosphate into the planting hole. Add potassium to the compost mulch. Spray the leaves with fish emulsion every 2 weeks through summer to supply micronutrients.

# EFFECTIVE WATERING

When rainfall is lacking, you'll need to provide water to keep your plants growing strongly and producing well. There are many different ways you can supply this water to your garden.

**DRIP IRRIGATION SYSTEMS**
Be careful if you design this type of system yourself—it's easy to make a mistake. You can eliminate errors by having a professional design the system, based on your garden plan. If the emitters wet only one side of a plant, the roots will grow lopsided.

### HAND WATERING
This is most useful for settling in seedlings and irrigating vegetables in containers or in very small gardens. It's also a handy way to spot-treat wilting plants until you can give a more thorough watering. Hand watering is not ideal for established plants, since it usually can't supply enough water to soak slowly into the soil.

### OVERHEAD WATERING
While sprinklers are common irrigation tools, they're not efficient. Only a small part of the water reaches the crops that need it. Sprinklers also provide an ideal environment for diseases that are spread on wet leaves.

### SOAKER HOSES
It's much more effective to provide water at ground level. Run a soaker hose (which leaks droplets or fine sprays of moisture along its length) next to a single-row planting or between a

Water enough to keep your plants growing, but not so much that roots become oxygen starved. For most soils, one good soaking is better than several shallow sprinkles. While hand watering is useful to revive wilting plants, there are better long-term options.

## CONSERVING WATER

Group vegetables with low, medium and high water needs and water sections individually.

Use a rain barrel to catch water off your roof and siphon it to your garden with a length of hose.

Cover soil with organic mulch, which holds water like a sponge.

Control weeds that rob your plants of water.

Protect your plants from drying winds.

double-row planting. This will moisten the planting area without benefiting nearby weeds. Weave or loop flexible rubber or plastic soaker hoses in and out among clumps of plants. Canvas and rigid rubber hoses work best when run in straight lines.

## DRIP IRRIGATION

These have a customized network of hoses or pipes engineered to carry a specific amount of water to any given place in the garden. They use special emitters that let the water seep out to the rooting area of each plant or plant grouping, soaking the soil deeply.

# Pruning Primer for Fruits and Berries

Pruning is probably the most daunting part of fruit-tree care for novices. It takes practice, and you will probably make a few mistakes, but as plants are very forgiving, these are rarely fatal.

## Making the Right Pruning Cuts

Each pruning cut you make affects the plant differently and helps you to direct its growth. With just two different kinds of cuts, you can shape practically any fruiting plant as you wish. Once you understand these two cuts, you're well on your way to pruning success.

Thinning cuts open the tree to sunlight. They are especially valuable for rejuvenating older, overgrown fruit trees,

PRUNING BASICS
A pruning saw, a very sharp budding knife and hand pruners are the absolute basics. Substantial gloves will save your hands from accidental damage. The narrow blade of the pruning saw gives good access to tight spaces.

A VERY USEFUL TOOL
Branch loppers have long handles that extend your reach significantly. They can cut branches up to 1 inch (2.5 cm) in diameter.

## Removing Large Branches

1. Make a cut halfway through from underneath, about 1 foot (30 cm) from the trunk.

2. Make the next cut from above, about 1 inch (2.5 cm) farther out; the branch will break off.

3. Finish with a clean, straight cut just outside the branch base (the collar).

### CLEAN CUTS

Clippers, shears and pruners are handy for cutting back vines and clump-forming weeds. Such plants are effectively weakened by having to use their reserves of nutrients to replace the foliage you have cut off.

## A THINNED TREE

Thinning removes a branch where it arises from another branch, the trunk or the ground. Use thinning cuts to shorten overly long branches, clear out crowded growth, remove a branch that crosses or rubs another, or take out dead and diseased wood.

where you want to remove a number of smaller branches and suckers and leave the larger branches. To thin a too-long or poorly placed branch, cut it back to the ground, to a side branch or to a shoot that's aimed in an uncrowded or desired direction. If you cut back to the trunk or to another branch, make the cut outside the slanted branch collar that forms a swelling at the base of the branch.

Heading cuts remove shoot tips, encouraging buds farther back on the stem to sprout. You can choose the best new shoots to become main branches on a young tree or to provide productive new growth on older trees (especially peaches and nectarines). In most cases, it's best to make a heading cut just above a bud to avoid leaving a stub.

## CHOOSING PRUNING TOOLS

A few good tools will make your pruning sessions easier. Here's the basic tool collection you'll need to maintain your fruiting trees, shrubs and vines, along with some tips on how to use them.

### THE KINDEST CUT

If you prune and train your young fruit trees carefully, you can eliminate the need to take out large branches later on. This is a big help, since removing big branches leaves wounds that are easy marks for pests and diseases. But if disease, damage or some other dilemma requires you to remove a large branch, see the three-step approach on page 97, or hire a professional arborist to do the job for you—for your safety and the health of your tree.

Hand pruners (also called pruning shears or secateurs) are used for cutting twigs less than ½ inch (12 mm) in diameter. Loppers (basically hand pruners with very long handles) are useful for cutting stems up to about 1 inch (2.5 cm) in diameter, depending on the model you buy. The long handles make pruning thorny-stemmed plants much more pleasant, since your hands will be farther away from the thorns.

Pruning saws are perfect for cutting branches larger than 1 inch (2.5 cm) in diameter, especially in tight spaces. Pole pruners are handy if you need to prune branches farther than your normal reach. They have either shear-type blades or a saw blade (or sometimes both) on a pole 4–6 feet (1.2–1.8 m) long.

HAND PRUNERS
Choose the "bypass" kind, with two curved blades that cut like scissors; they cut more cleanly than the straight-edged blade-and-anvil types. If you are cutting back thorny brambles, blackberries, raspberries or gooseberries, look for cut-and-hold bypass shears that hang onto the trimmings so they're easy to pull out.

# DEALING WITH PESTS AND DISEASES

The best pest controls are specific, safe, easy and effective. If your garden plants are bothered by pests, choose control methods that target the pests and not other organisms.

## PROPER IDENTIFICATION

This is the first step toward successful pest control. Consult a book on how to identify garden pests, or submit insect or disease samples to a local Cooperative Extension Service. Then select controls that are environmentally safe.

## RESISTANCE

One of the easiest ways to avoid problems is to choose cultivars that are designed to resist the pests that plague your vegetables. Plant breeders have developed an array of new cultivars that are able to defend themselves against specific diseases and insect pests. Find out which conditions could be a problem and look for resistant cultivars in catalogs and garden-supply stores.

## WEEKLY INSPECTION

Check leaves, flowers and stems for signs of insects or pathogens at least once a week. In large stands, examine three to five plants at three different locations. Become familiar with insect life cycles so you'll recognize resting (egg and cocoon) and active (larva and adult) stages.

**SAFE CONTROLS**
Colorado beetle larvae (top), which attack potato foliage, and aphids (bottom) can be knocked off your plants with a forceful jet of water. Or pick off these and other pest insects by hand early on cool mornings, when they are sluggish.

## COMMON VEGETABLE PESTS AND DISEASES

| PEST | DAMAGE | PREVENTION AND CONTROL |
|---|---|---|
| Snails and slugs | Seedlings eaten, irregular holes in leaves. | Place shallow containers of beer in garden, or trap pests under boards. |
| Aphids | Foliage wilted or curled, deformed buds and flowers. | A short, sharp spray of water from the hose will dislodge them. Spray with insecticidal soap. |
| Cabbageworms | Leaves eaten. | Use row covers. Spray or dust with BT. |
| Carrot fly | Carrot roots eaten. | Rotate carrot plantings. Use row covers. Plant crops in late spring to minimize the damage. |
| Cutworms | Plant stem chewed at soil surface. | Place cardboard or metal cutworm collars around the stem of the plants. Sprinkle moist bran mixed with BTK on the soil surface in the evening. Add parasitic nematodes to the soil at least a week before planting. |
| Leaf miners | Winding or large, blotchy lines on leaves, especially those of beets, spinach and tomatoes. | Use row covers. Pick off and destroy infected leaves. Control adults with yellow sticky traps or a pyrethrin/rotenone mix. |
| Squash borer | Holes in base of stem, wilting leaves. | Use row covers until flowers appear. |
| European corn borer | Tunnels in corn stalks and ears. | Use pheromone lures and sticky traps. |
| Beetles (flea, Mexican bean, Japanese, cucumber) | Chewed foliage. | Eliminate weeds. Use row covers. Spray with garlic or pyrethrin. |
| Two-spotted mite | Discoloration and bronzing of the foliage. | Use a garlic or pyrethrin/rotenone spray. |

| DISEASE | DAMAGE | PREVENTION AND CONTROL |
|---|---|---|
| Powdery mildew | Downy patches on foliage. | Provide good air circulation. Control weeds. Spray foliage with compost tea. |
| Damping-off | Seedlings weaken and collapse because of decay at soil line. | Start seeds in well-drained mix. Avoid overwatering, crowding and poor air circulation. Disinfect reused pots and flats. |
| Rust | Rust-colored powder on the leaves. | Plant resistant cultivars. Provide good air circulation. Remove infected leaves. |
| Wilt (Fusarium and Verticillium) | Leaves yellow, plant gradually wilts. | Rotate crops. Plant resistant cultivars. Destroy infected plants. |

# Dealing with Weeds

**TIMING IS CRUCIAL**
The annual and biennial weeds in this field reproduce by setting abundant seeds. Preventing them from flowering is one key to controlling them.

A weed is any plant growing where you don't want it. What plant it is doesn't matter, but where it is does. Although any plant can be a weed, some plants are considered weeds more often than others.

## PLAN A WEED-CONTROL STRATEGY

To control your lawn and garden weeds effectively and efficiently, you need to use the right technique at the right time. This requires an essential piece of knowledge: How long do your particular weeds live?

## ANNUAL WEEDS ARE SPREAD BY SEED

Annual weeds, such as lamb's-quarters *Chenopodium album*, live an entire life within a year; they sprout from seed, grow, flower, set seed and die. Most annuals start this cycle in the spring and finish by autumn. Winter annuals sprout in autumn, grow a few inches tall, then go dormant until early spring. In spring, they resume growing and set seed by early- to midsummer. Winter annuals, such as common chickweed *Stellaria media*, are the first weeds you'll see in the spring.

One part of controlling annuals is never to let them set seed. If the original plants die without making more seed, they won't be back the following year. Unfortunately, seeds from previous years' weeds can survive in the soil for many years, and new weed seeds may drift

## WEEDS AS HOSTS

Some weeds harbor harmful insects or diseases. If you control the weeds you reduce the risk of their associated problems. For example, weeds of the nightshade (Solanaceae) family, such as horsenettle and black nightshade, shelter insects that will attack your tomatoes, potatoes and eggplants (aubergines); and bishop's weed *Ammi majus* often shelters carrot rust flies.

## LET'S GET PHYSICAL

Pulling up annual weeds is very effective if the soil is damp enough to release the roots. Dispose carefully of any that reroot easily, such as purslane *Portulaca oleracea*, so that you get maximum return from your crop.

in on the wind or be carried in on clothing or fur. For these reasons, the other half of controlling annual weeds involves mulching and other techniques to prevent those seeds from sprouting.

## BIENNIALS TAKE TWO YEARS

For biennial weeds, such as bishop's weed *Ammi majus*, the seed-to-seed cycle spreads over 2 years. These weeds

sprout from seed in the spring or
summer, then usually grow into a
ground-hugging circle of leaves called
a rosette. The leaves produce sugars that
move down to the roots and are stored
as starch. Next spring, the plant uses
the stored food energy to send up a
flowering stalk, which may or may not
have leaves. The plant flowers, sets
seed, then dies.

You have two main options with
biennial weeds: Dig out the rosette—root
and all—in the first year; or, if the weed
isn't too visible or crowding other plants,
wait until the second year and cut the
plant down to the ground. If you wait
until the weed is just about to flower, the
plant will have used up most of its stored
energy and will be unlikely to return.

## Perennials Are Persistent

Wild garlic *Allium vineale*, kudzu vine
*Pueraria lobata* and other perennial
weeds live for 3 years or more. Like
biennials, perennials store carbohydrates

### Dig in the Dark

If you're determined
to till but also want
to keep weeds to a
minimum, consider
tilling your garden
after dark. It sounds
crazy, but researchers
have had remarkable
success with this
technique, reducing
weed cover by 70 to
80 percent. It seems
that exposure to just
a few seconds of light
is all some weeds
need to germinate.
If you till only when
it's dark, many of
the seeds will be
reburied without being
triggered to sprout.
Dig any time between
1 hour after sunset to
1 hour before sunrise.

COLD FRAMES
While generally used to give
seedlings a headstart, frames
are also effective in keeping
weeds from sharing the
water and nutrients you have
provided for the benefit of
your salad greens.

to fuel early growth the next spring. That food energy may be stored in a taproot, in spreading underground stems called rhizomes or in spreading aboveground stems called runners or stolons. Or it may be in a tuber (like a potato) or a bulb (like an onion).

Some perennials, such as dandelions *Taraxacum officinale*, reproduce only sexually—by setting seed from fertilized flowers. But some also reproduce non-sexually, by a process called vegetative reproduction. New plants can sprout from rhizomes and stolons. Tubers have "eyes" that produce new plants. And bulbs multiply, giving rise to new bulbs that can each become a plant. You can think of this vegetative reproduction as a type of self-cloning for plants.

Perennial weeds are generally the most difficult to control. Carbohydrates stored in their taproots, rhizomes, tubers or bulbs give them a strong start each spring, as well as the power to grow again if their leaves are lost or damaged. Just preventing seed formation on perennials is not enough to get rid of them; you must either dig up all of the underground structures or force them to use up their food reserves by repeatedly removing their aboveground growth.

Each time you remove the stems and leaves, the plant must draw on stored carbohydrates to send up new growth. Because the new growth soon starts to photosynthesize more food for the plant, frequent weeding—every 7 to 14 days— is best. If you can't weed that often through the spring and summer, weed before flowering and again later in the season. Perennials build up their food reserves in late summer and autumn to prepare for the next year's early growth. Cut them down until they are too weak to survive winter.

SUSTAINED ATTACK
Mowing an area repeatedly until the new sprouts stop shooting can help control both biennial and perennial weeds. The roots may be too depleted to survive winter.

INVASIVE PLANTS
Weeds can be a big problem at the edges of the vegetable garden, where grasses and a variety of weeds may creep in. A mowing strip will help, but the best way to deal with these weeds is by hand, giving them regular attention before they can take over.

# CONTROLLING WEEDS IN THE VEGETABLE GARDEN

While prevention can go a long way toward reducing weeds, a few are sure to pop up during the season. When they do sneak past your defenses, you have several ways to get rid of them.

## HAND-PULLING AND HOEING

When it comes to killing weeds among your crops, the tried-and-true methods are pulling them out by hand or hacking them down with some type of blade (usually a hoe). You can also try flaming them, if you take care not to damage the vegetable plants nearby, but don't be fooled into thinking that one weeding will get you through the season.

The secret to control is persistence. Take a little time each week and pull up weeds as they emerge. Weaken perennial weeds by forcing them to use up food stores to regrow. And no weed should ever get the chance to set seed. Best of all, you'll use less time and energy weeding a little each week than you would if you waited until the weeds were a tall, menacing, seed-filled mess.

## SMOTHERING WEEDS

Weeds like the same things as your vegetables: light, water and nutrients. If you're willing to leave part of the garden unplanted for a season, you can deprive

COMPETITION
A smother crop is a plant that grows well when crowded. By growing close together, smother crops choke out weeds. If you have a really bad weed infestation, you may have to take the vegetable garden out of production for a year to let the smother crop do its job.

## HAND-WEEDING
There's nothing so discouraging to weeds as a constant personal attack.

## RAISED BEDS
Weeds are easier to control when the bed is raised, as lawn grasses are less invasive. Also, hand-weeding in a raised bed is easier because it places much less strain on your back.

the weeds of all three with a smother crop. Such a crop must do its work before or after the vegetable season.

A smother crop of a winter annual grass such as winter wheat *Triticum aestivum* covers the soil in the autumn as well as in early spring, but you can turn it under early enough for it to break down (2–4 weeks before you plan to plant). Other effective smother crops include grasses, such as annual rye *Lolium multiflorum* and winter rye *Secale cereale*, as well as some broad-leaved plants, such as buckwheat *Fagopyrum esculentum*. Plant buckwheat in spring, turn it under before it goes to seed, then follow it with another buckwheat crop in summer and winter wheat in autumn.

If your vegetable garden backs onto a fence, don't plant right against the fence. Use a mulch along the fence or create a barrier with black plastic or cardboard and check regularly for invasive weeds.

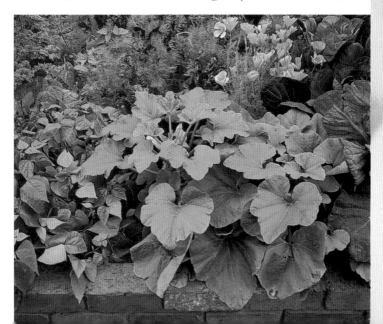

# Controlling Weeds in the Fruit Garden

Unlike a vegetable garden, which you replant each year, fruit plantings are relatively permanent, so make sure the area is as free of weeds and weed seeds as possible before you start planting.

## Strawberries

Strawberries send out runners to produce new plants, so any mulch you use must be sparse enough to let the runners reach the soil. Straw is a popular choice, as are pine needles. Spread the mulch about 1 inch (2.5 cm) thick. Pull out any weeds as they emerge through the mulch. Add another 1–2 inches (2.5–5 cm) of mulch in the autumn to protect the plants during the winter.

## Berry Bushes and Brambles

A hoe and about 4 inches (10 cm) of mulch are your best tools for keeping down weeds around berry bushes and brambles (such as raspberries and blackberries). You'll especially appreciate the long handle on your hoe if you grow bramble cultivars with thorns. Training brambles to a post-and-wire trellis will make weed control easier.

## Fruit Trees

Your fruit trees are probably already surrounded by one of the best weed-control materials: grass. Even commercial orchards have returned to growing grass between the rows of trees because it

AUTUMN SWEETNESS
Mulch under grape vines to control weeds. Once the vines are well established, reduce the water supply and keep the soil dryish.

If berry vines are supported on wires, it is much easier to keep the weeds down among them. Once the area around the plants is cleared, apply a layer of mulch to discourage regrowth and to conserve moisture.

stops the soil from washing or blowing away and competes well against weeds. Remove the grass in a 2-foot (60-cm) ring around the base of each tree to make mowing simpler and reduce the chance of damaging the trunk with the mower. Mulch the bare area with a good layer of straw, compost, pine needles or some other organic mulch. Keep it away from the trunk and rake it away in autumn to keep rodents from nesting in it.

## CLEAN FRUIT

Besides keeping the weeds down, a good layer of mulch around your strawberries will keep the fruit from coming in contact with the soil.

Part Five

# Plant
# Directory
# ~
# Vegetables

## *Abelmoschus esculentus*

HARDINESS
Zones 5 and
warmer.

DAYS TO MATURITY
50–60 frost-free
days.

COMMENTS
Cultivars include
'Annie Oakley',
'Clemson Spineless'
and 'Emerald'.

# OKRA (GUMBO)

THE ESSENTIAL INGREDIENT IN GUMBO,
OKRA IS ALSO ADMIRED FOR ITS LOVELY,
HOLLYHOCK-LIKE FLOWERS. IT THRIVES
IN HOT WEATHER.

**Position** Plant in full sun in fertile
and well-drained soil; pH 6.5–7.5.

**Cultivation** Sow seed when frost
danger is past and the soil is warm.
Prewarming the soil with black
plastic mulch will speed up
germination. In cooler areas, start
seed indoors in individual pots
2–4 weeks before the last frost
and set out when the weather is
settled. Set out or thin to stand
12–15 inches (30–37.5 cm) apart.
Grows quickly in warm weather
and needs both food and water;
irrigate in dry spells and give it
compost tea or fish emulsion once
a month.

**Pests and diseases** Little troubled by
pests, but aphids are a sign of water
stress. In cool areas, okra will not
bear as prolifically as in warm
climates. Red-podded cultivars, such
as 'Burgundy', are often the most
prolific producers.

**Harvesting and storage** Clip or
pinch off young pods when they
are 1–4 inches (2.5–10 cm) long
and still soft. Larger pods will be
woody. Harvest daily in warm
weather. Okra freezes well.

**Special tips** Blossoms are edible.

*Allium* spp.

HARDINESS
All Zones for green (spring) onions; Zones 3 and warmer for bulb onions, but choose cultivars to suit the day length.

DAYS TO MATURITY
60–115 days from transplanting. Green (spring) onions from sets can be harvested in as few as 35 days.

COMMENTS
More mature plants can withstand severe frost.

# ONION

A STAPLE FOR MANY CENTURIES, THE BULB OF THE VERSATILE ONION PROVIDES PLENTY OF GOOD EATING IN LITTLE GARDEN SPACE.

**Position** Plant in full sun in well-drained soil that is rich in humus; pH 6.0–7.5.

**Cultivation** For summer harvest, sow indoors 3–4 months before last spring frost and set out 3–4 inches (7.5–10 cm) apart a month before last frost. For onions to store, sow thickly a month before the last frost and thin to 3–4 inches (7.5–10 cm) apart. For quicker crops or in colder areas, grow onions from small bulbs called "sets," available at garden centers or by mail. Plant sets 1 inch (2.5 cm) deep and 2 inches (5 cm) apart, pulling every second one when ready for use as green (spring) onions. Grow onions in beds or small patches to maximize yield in small spaces. Keep well weeded because they are easily shaded out. Irrigate and fertilize with fish emulsion or compost tea to encourage good early growth, which will determine eventual bulb size.

**Pests and diseases** Garden-grown onions have few pest or disease problems. Where onion maggots are troublesome, use row covers supported by hoops to prevent egg-laying by the onion maggot fly. Rotate onions and their relatives with other crops. Cold weather may

# *Onion* continued

Bulbing onion cultivars can be pulled before the bulbs have begun to form and used as green (spring) onions.

prevent bulb formation, but failure to form bulbs more often indicates use of an unsuitable onion cultivar. Bulb formation is triggered by day length. Long-day cultivars are best in areas farther from the equator; short-day types in areas closer.

**Harvesting and storage**  Pull green (spring) onions and onions for fresh use as needed. For storage onions, wait until most tops have fallen over, then knock over any upright stalks with a rake. Pull the onions 1–2 days later and let them dry on the ground. (In wet weather, dry them on open mesh or shallow trays in a well-ventilated place.) Use onions with thick, green stems immediately; they will not store. When onions are thoroughly dry, braid the tops and hang in a cool, dry place or clip off the tops and store bulbs in mesh bags or slat-sided boxes.

**Special tips**  For space-saving green onions, sow several seeds in one pot and transplant later as a clump.

**Related plants**

**Potato onion *A. cepa*, Aggregatum Group**  Also called multiplier onion. Forms a cluster of underground bulbs. Usually harvested the second year after planting. Eat the larger bulbs and replant the smaller ones.

**Pickling onion *A. cepa***  Also called pearl onion. Cultivars produce small

Red onions are also called Italian or Spanish onions. These red-skinned cultivars are often sweeter than types with white or yellow skins.

bulbs that are cooked or pickled whole. Try 'Snow Baby' and 'Early Aviv'.

**Red (Italian or Spanish) onion *A. cepa*** Cultivars include 'Bennie's Red', 'Rossa di Milano' and 'Red Florence' (elongated shape).

**Slicing onion *A. cepa*** Refers to mild-flavored onions grown for fresh use. Most store poorly. Grow Vidalia types (such as 'Texas Grano') in warmer areas, and Walla Walla types (such as 'Walla Walla Sweet') in colder ones.

**Spanish onion *A. cepa*** Large bulbs with mild flavor, usually with yellow or white skin. In favorable climates, bulbs can weigh up to 5 pounds (2.5 kg).

**Egyptian onion *A. cepa*, Proliferum Group** Also called tree onion, top onion or catawissa onion. Edible, but strongly flavored. Instead of flowers, it produces a curious-looking head of small onion bulbs, some of which can be planted in spring or autumn to produce the next year's crop.

**Welsh onion *A. fistulosum*** Also called ciboule, Japanese bunching onion or green (spring) onion. Does not form a bulb, but rather a slender, white stalk.

# *Allium cepa* Aggregatum Group

ALLIACEAE

HARDINESS
All Zones; can be planted in autumn in Zones 6 and warmer.

DAYS TO MATURITY
120–150 days; or pull earlier to eat as green (spring) onions.

COMMENTS
Will withstand moderate frost. Named cultivars are not generally available; most suppliers offer generic French (or golden) shallots.

# SHALLOT

A RELATIVE OF THE ONION, THE SHALLOT PRODUCES SMALL, FIRM BULBS THAT KEEP LIKE GARLIC BUT ARE MUCH SWEETER AND MILDER IN FLAVOR.

**Position** Plant in full sun in well-drained soil that is rich in humus. Shallots will tolerate all but the most acid soil.

**Cultivation** Shallots do not grow from seed but from bulblets or "sets." Plant 2–4 weeks before the last spring frost, 1 inch (2.5 cm) deep and 4–6 inches (10–15 cm) apart. Keep cultivated or mulch and water regularly to encourage strong early growth. Each set will divide and produce eight to 10 shallots. Where climate permits, autumn planting will produce larger shallots the following summer.

**Pests and diseases** To avoid root maggots, do not plant where shallots or their relatives, such as onions or leeks, have grown the previous year. Dry conditions or poor soil produces scrawny shallots. Work in plenty of compost or well-rotted manure and water regularly.

**Harvesting and storage** When the tops are nearly dry, pull out the plants and dry the bulbs in a well-ventilated, sunny area. Store by hanging in a cool, dry place, or clip off the stems and store the bulbs in mesh bags.

# *Allium porrum*

HARDINESS
Zones 3 and
warmer; grow as
a winter vegetable
in mild areas.

DAYS TO MATURITY
70–105 days in
the garden.

COMMENTS
'King Richard'
and 'Titan' are
early leeks;
'Carina' and
'Alaska' are good
for overwintering.
"Baby" leeks can
be harvested
earlier.

# LEEK

THIS ONION RELATIVE IS GROWN FOR ITS
STOUT, FLAVORFUL STEM. IT HOLDS WELL IN
THE GROUND FOR LATE HARVESTING.

**Position** Plant in full sun in loose,
very rich, well-drained soil;
pH 6.0–7.5.

**Cultivation** Start seed indoors up to
12 weeks before last spring frost.
Transplant from seed flats to small,
individual pots when large enough
to handle. This produces larger
transplants and better leeks. Set out
after frost, 6 inches (15 cm) apart,
in a trench 6 inches (15 cm) deep
or in holes made with a hoe handle
or dibble, covering all but 1 inch
(2.5 cm) or so of the leaves. Keep
well weeded. As leeks grow, fill in
the trench gradually or, if planted
on level soil, "hill" them by drawing
soil up around the stems. This
produces a longer white stem,
which is the edible part. You can
also use a deep mulch to blanch
the stems. Keep the soil moist,
especially early in the season.

**Pests and diseases** To avoid damage
by root maggots, do not plant leeks
where other members of the onion
family have grown the previous
year. Short, tough stems indicate
either a lack of moisture or soil
fertility or inadequate hilling.

**Harvesting and storage** Dig up or
pull out leeks when they are large
enough for use. Before a hard

# *Leek* continued

Feed your leeks regularly to ensure that their growth is unchecked and that they will have plump, tender stems.

freeze, mulch the bed heavily to keep it diggable through winter. Harvest overwintered leeks before spring growth begins. Pack leeks in damp sand or peat moss and store in a cool place. Harvested leeks stored in this way will keep for 6–8 weeks.

**Special tips** Young plants will tolerate light frost; mature ones, severe frost. Cultivars include 'Carina' (large, thick stem, matures in late autumn, very cold-tolerant); 'Splendid' (long, thin, tender stem, produces high yields); 'Titan' (long, thick stem, grows quickly).

### Related plants

**Asian leek *A. tuberosum*** Also called Chinese leek, Chinese chives or garlic chives. A hardy perennial grown for its mildly garlic-flavored leaves, which are used in stir-fries and soups. The spring flowers are also edible. Named cultivars are not generally available.

**Chives *A. schoenoprasum*** A popular herb that can be grown in a pot or as an edging for the vegetable garden. The long, cylindrical leaves are usually cut and used as a flavoring or garnish. The mauve flowers are also edible and make a pretty garnish.

# *Allium sativum*

HARDINESS
Zones 3 and
warmer; must be
prechilled before
planting to form
bulbs in warmer
climates.

DAYS TO MATURITY
120–150 days for
spring plantings;
autumn plantings
are harvested the
following summer.

COMMENTS
Crush and soak
garlic to make an
effective garden
spray for insects.

# GARLIC

GARLIC IS AN EASY-TO-GROW AND
REWARDING CROP. PLANT IT IN AUTUMN
TO HARVEST THE FOLLOWING SUMMER.

**Position** Plant in full sun or partial
shade, but bulbs will be smaller in
partial shade. Likes well-drained,
fertile soil that is rich in humus;
pH 6.0–7.0.

**Cultivation** Best planted in autumn,
2–4 weeks before first frost. Plant
individual cloves, pointed end up,
1–2 inches (2.5–5 cm) deep and
4–6 inches (10–15 cm) apart.
Deeper planting is best where
frequent freezing and thawing may
cause heaving (when the soil lifts
due to temperature changes and
plants are dislodged from their

roots). Apply fish emulsion or
compost tea in spring to encourage
vigorous growth. Keep the bed
cultivated or mulched. Irrigate until
tops begin to brown, then withhold
water to let the plant dry naturally.

**Pests and diseases** Little troubled
by pests, but reduce threat of root
maggots by not planting where
garlic or its relatives, such as onions
and shallots, have been planted the
previous year. Humid conditions at
harvest may induce neck rot. Use
these heads immediately or freeze,
as they do not keep well.

**Harvesting and storage** Use spring
shoots and flower stems chopped
in salads and dips, as you would

# *Garlic* continued

The soft drying stems of garlic plants are easy to braid in the traditional way. The braided bunches are then hung up to finish drying out.

chives. Pull mature garlic plants when about 75 percent of the foliage is brown; tie in bundles and dry in a dark, well-ventilated place. Braid for storage or clip stems and store in mesh bags in a dry, cool area. Freeze peeled cloves; thaw slowly before using.

**Special tips** Pot garlic heads or cloves and grow indoors for wintertime use as greens.

### Related plants
**Elephant garlic *A. ampeloprasum***
Elephant garlic is milder and has larger heads (up to a pound [500 g]) than other types of garlic. Plant deeper than garlic, up to 4 inches (10 cm) deep.

**Hard-neck garlic *A. sativum*, var. *ophioscorodon*** Also called serpent garlic, top-setting garlic or rocambole. Prized in oriental cuisine, it produces a coiled flower stem. Remove the stem to direct growth to the roots. Cloves are large and form in a single ring around a central, woody stem. Cultivars include 'Russian Red' and 'Chet's'.
**Soft-neck garlic *A. sativum*** The standard commercial type, also called artichoke garlic. Cloves form in an overlapping pattern, like the scales of an artichoke. More productive than hard-neck types, but the cloves are smaller. Cultivars include 'French Silverskin' and 'California Early'.

# *Amaranthus tricolor*

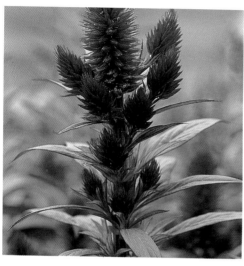

HARDINESS
Zones 4 and
warmer, but needs
some protection
in colder areas.

DAYS TO MATURITY
Requires 40–55
frost-free days,
although thinnings
can be harvested
earlier.

COMMENTS
Other common
names include
Chinese spinach,
Joseph's-coat, leaf
amaranth, tampala
and vegetable
amaranth.

# AMARANTH

GROW AMARANTH FOR ITS NUTRITIOUS
LEAVES, WHICH CAN BE EATEN BOTH RAW
IN SALADS AND COOKED AS GREENS.

**Position** Prefers heat and full sun.
Not fussy, but prefers soil rich in
humus; pH 6.0–7.0.

**Cultivation** Sow seed after frost,
when soil has warmed. Barely cover
and keep moist until germinated. In
short-season areas, start amaranth
indoors 4 weeks before last frost
date. Water freely and thin to
18 inches (45 cm) apart.

**Pests and diseases** Protect plants
from flea and cucumber beetles
with row covers, or spray with a
garlic infusion. Rotate plantings to
avoid stem rot from soilborne
diseases. In cooler climates, it may
require soil-warming plastic mulch.

**Harvesting and storage** Harvest
whole plants as thinnings; pick the
young, tender leaves from mature
plants. Harvest frequently to
encourage new growth. Can be
frozen in the same way as spinach.

**Special tips** Plant away from
cabbage-family plants or cucumbers
to reduce pest damage; or plant
adjacent to those crops to serve as
a "trap crop." There are no named
cultivars, but oriental seed
companies often carry natural
variants with light green, dark green
or red-striped leaves.

*Apium graveolens* var. *dulce*

# CELERY

IT ISN'T EASY TO GROW, BUT WITH A LITTLE ATTENTION TO ITS NEEDS, CELERY DOES BEAUTIFULLY IN THE BACKYARD.

**Position** Plant in full sun in moisture-retentive, rich soil, with adequate calcium and plenty of well-rotted manure or compost worked in; pH 5.5–7.5.

**Cultivation** Start seed indoors 4–6 weeks before the last spring frost. Germination and seedling growth are slow. Keep seedlings watered and do not expose to temperatures below 55°F (13°C), which can cause plants to bolt to seed. Set plants out when the weather is well settled (about a month after the last frost),

10–12 inches (25–30 cm) apart. Because the roots are relatively shallow, do not allow the soil to dry out; feed the plants with compost tea or fish emulsion at least once a month. If desired, you can blanch celery before harvest by slipping a bottomless paper bag over the plant and tying it in place, or by putting wide boards on edge on both sides of the celery row and holding the boards in place with stakes. The idea is to keep the sun off the stems. This whitens them and keeps them from becoming tough, although self-blanching cultivars are available. Excessive heat, lack of moisture or low soil fertility will also result in tough, stringy celery.

# *Celery* continued

HARDINESS
Zones 5 and
warmer, except
where temperatures
in early summer
drop below 55°F
(13°C). Autumn
and winter crop
in mild areas.

DAYS TO MATURITY
80–105 days.

COMMENTS
Young plants
cannot tolerate
frequent falls in
temperature below
55°F (13°C); mature
plants withstand
severe frost.

Single stems of 'Improved Utah' can be picked as needed to give
a continuous harvest of small quantities of celery for 2–3 months.

**Pests and diseases** Rotate plantings
with other crops to avoid blight
problems. Handpick off parsleyworms or celeryworms (green
caterpillars with yellow and
black bands).

**Harvesting and storage** Cut celery
for immediate use just below soil
level. In cooler areas, harvesting
can be extended if plants are
protected by an insulating mulch
of straw and covered with opaque
white polythene. However, before
a hard freeze, pull up the entire
plant and roots, and store, packed
in dry leaves or straw, in a cool
cellar or garage.

**Special tips** Plant celery in well-
manured beds, three or four plants
abreast and 10–12 inches (25–30 cm)
apart. Dense growth will shade out
weeds and automatically blanch the
celery. Cultivars include 'Improved
Utah' and 'Tendercrisp', both green
cultivars, while 'Stokes Golden
Plume' is a yellow celery. 'Giant
Red' has stalks tinged with red,
while 'Lathom Self-Blanching' has
been bred to resist bolting to seed.

*Apium graveolens* var. *rapaceum*

HARDINESS
Zones 5 and
warmer. Use as an
autumn and winter
crop in mild areas.

DAYS TO MATURITY
110–120 days;
can withstand
increasingly severe
frost for the last
30–45 days.

COMMENTS
Cultivars include
'Large Smooth
Prague', which is
widely available.

# CELERIAC

IN SALADS, SOUPS AND STEWS OR AS A
COOKED VEGETABLE, THE ROOT OF CELERIAC
HAS ALL THE FLAVOR OF CELERY.

**Position** Plant in full sun in rich,
moisture-retentive soil, with
adequate calcium and plenty of
well-rotted manure or compost
worked in; pH 5.5–7.5.

**Cultivation** Start seed indoors
6–8 weeks before last spring frost
and set out, 10–12 inches
(25–30 cm) apart, when the threat
of frost is past. Celeriac can be
direct-seeded, but it germinates
slowly and can be overtaken by
weeds. Keep bed well weeded and
watered. Apply compost tea or fish
emulsion at least once a month.

**Pests and diseases** Rotate plantings
of celeriac and celery with other
crops to avoid the blights to which
they are both vulnerable. Handpick
off celeryworms or parsleyworms
(green caterpillars with yellow and
black bands). Inadequate moisture
will yield small, tough, fibrous roots.

**Harvesting and storage** Harvest the
turnip-like root when large enough
for your needs. Harvest all plants
before the ground freezes; cut stems
close to the roots and store like
turnips (see page 155) in damp
sawdust or sand in a cool place.

**Special tips** Other common names
include celery root, German celery,
knob celery, turnip celery.

# *Arachis hypogaea*

**HARDINESS**
Zones 7 and warmer, but may produce light crops in Zones 5–6.

**DAYS TO MATURITY**
110–120 frost-free days.

**COMMENTS**
Other common names include goober, groundnut and pindar. Cultivars include 'Jumbo Virginia', 'Spanish' and 'Tennessee Red'.

# PEANUT

NOT A NUT BUT A PROTEIN-RICH MEMBER OF THE LEGUME FAMILY, THE PEANUT CAN BE ROASTED, BOILED OR MADE INTO A SAUCE.

**Position** Plant in full sun in loose, well-drained soil rich in humus and with adequate calcium; pH 5.8–6.2.

**Cultivation** In warmer climates, sow seed 1 inch (2.5 cm) deep and 3 inches (7.5 cm) apart after last spring frost when soil is warm, and thin to 1 foot (30 cm) apart. In cooler areas, start in individual pots 4–6 weeks before last frost and set out, 1 foot (30 cm) apart, in soil that has been prewarmed with black plastic mulch. Plant whole shells, or remove shell first, taking care not to damage the papery skin.

Keep weeded. Do not mulch; if plastic mulch is used to warm soil, it must be removed when the peanuts flower. Stems bearing fertilized flowers dive into soil around the plant, and a peanut forms at the end of each stem.

**Pests and diseases** Little troubled.

**Harvesting and storage** Dig up plants when frost has killed the foliage. Hang by the roots in a well-ventilated place until the pods have completely dried. Roast shelled nuts, or roast them in the shell by soaking clean pods in salted water for several hours, then heating in a 300°F (150°C) oven until completely dry and crisp (about 1 hour).

# *Arctium lappa*

**HARDINESS**
All Zones, although the eventual length of the root will depend on the length of the growing season.

**DAYS TO MATURITY**
120 days or more.

**COMMENTS**
Other common names include gobo and nagau pong.

# BURDOCK

MILDLY BITTER AND AN EXCELLENT ADDITION TO SOUPS AND STEWS, BURDOCK IS A NUTRITIOUS ROOT VEGETABLE.

**Position** Plant in full sun. Requires deep, well-prepared soil, as the roots can grow to 2 feet (60 cm) or more in length; pH 6.0–7.3.

**Cultivation** Sow seed in spring for an autumn harvest, or in late summer for overwintering. Thin the plants to 2–3 feet (60–90 cm) apart. Cultivated burdock looks much like its relative, the common burdock *A. minus*, with large, heart-shaped leaves, but it can grow to 8 feet (2.4 m) tall. Cultivate shallowly until the plant is large enough to shade out weeds.

**Pests and diseases** Burdock is rarely troubled by pests. In rocky or heavy soil, roots may fork or become deformed, making harvesting difficult. Planting in raised beds will help to avoid this problem.

**Harvesting and storage** Harvest after autumn frosts, or leave roots in the ground for spring harvest. Burdock stores well in a cool cellar if you treat it in the same way as you would turnips or carrots (see pages 155 and 180 respectively).

# *Armoracia rusticana*

HARDINESS
All Zones, but
best in Zones 5
and warmer.

DAYS TO MATURITY
150–180 days in
first year where the
season permits;
otherwise, first
harvest is in the
second year.

COMMENTS
Severe frost will
kill horseradish
leaves but will not
damage the roots.
Young leaves of
horseradish can be
added to salads.

# HORSERADISH

HORSERADISH IS A HARDY PERENNIAL
GROWN FOR ITS ROOTS, WHICH ARE GRATED
FOR USE AS A TANGY CONDIMENT.

**Position** Plant in full sun in well-
drained, deep and preferably light
soil; pH 6.0–7.0.

**Cultivation** Plant this invasive
vegetable in a bottomless bucket
sunk into the soil. Plant root
divisions in spring, 2 inches (5 cm)
deep and 12–18 inches (30–45 cm)
apart. Weed or mulch after the
leaves appear above the ground.
Even soil moisture encourages rapid
growth and large roots.

**Pests and diseases** Flea beetles
sometimes attack but rarely do

more than cosmetic damage. Avoid
growing in heavy, shallow or stony
soil. May be difficult to eradicate or
move once established—new plants
grow from root bits left in the soil.

**Harvesting and storage** Dig up roots
when 12–15 inches (30–37.5 cm)
long, up to 2 inches (5 cm) thick
and fairly smooth. Dig up as
needed until the ground freezes.
Store whole roots in sand or
sawdust in a cool place.

**Special tips** Pack smaller roots in
sawdust and save for planting next
year. Cut tops flat and bottoms at
an angle, so you put them in the
ground right-side up, so producing
straighter and more uniform roots.

# ASPARAGUS

THIS CLASSIC SPRING VEGETABLE REQUIRES WELL-PREPARED SOIL WITH HIGH FERTILITY. A WELL-MAINTAINED PATCH CAN YIELD ABUNDANTLY FOR DECADES.

**Position** Avoid low-lying areas subject to heavy dew and morning fogs, to reduce the possibility of rust. Prefers full sun, but will tolerate some shade. Likes fertile, well-drained soil; will tolerate slightly alkaline pH (6.5–6.8) and saline soils.

**Cultivation** Grow from seed started indoors or in an outdoor seedbed; or hasten the first harvest by using year-old crowns. Dig a trench 8 inches (20 cm) deep in well-composted and well-limed soil.

Place the crowns in the trench 15 inches (37.5 cm) apart, fanning the roots in all directions. Cover with soil to half the depth of the trench. When foliage peeks above ground level, finish filling the trench with soil. Mulch or cultivate shallowly and irrigate during dry spells. Keeping the foliage healthy and lush after harvest is critical to the next year's crop. Each autumn, cut back the dead ferny foliage and mulch heavily with compost or straw-rich manure. Early each spring, rake off all but 1–2 inches (2.5–5 cm) of mulch to let the spears emerge.

**Pests and diseases** Asparagus rust can be a serious problem in damp

# Asparagus continued

HARDINESS
Zones 3 and warmer; asparagus grows best in areas where the soil freezes in winter.

DAYS TO MATURITY
Gardeners used to wait until the third year to take a first small harvest of asparagus; newer hybrid cultivars can be picked sparingly for 1–2 weeks in the second year. A mature patch can be harvested for as long as 10 weeks.

A dense stand of ferny fronds (left) grows up after you stop harvesting the emerging spears. The foliage helps the plants to build up the nutrients needed for the next crop.

locations; use rust-resistant cultivars. Reduce damage from asparagus beetles, which overwinter in garden debris and emerge in spring to feed on the young spears, by burning or hot-composting the old asparagus foliage and cultivating the asparagus patch shallowly before applying the autumn mulch. Perennial weeds and grasses can be troublesome in the asparagus patch. Be sure the area is free of perennial weeds before planting, and mulch or cultivate to stay ahead of them.

**Harvesting and storage** Carefully cut the spears at ground level or simply snap them off, leaving any woody stem behind. Harvest while the tips of the spears are still tightly closed; in warm spring spells, this may mean daily harvesting. Bottle or freeze excess spears. A mature patch, say 5 years old, can yield 1 pound (500 g) or more of asparagus per foot (30 cm) of row.

**Special tips** In heavy soils, plant in raised beds to improve drainage. Lay crowns at ground level, rather than in trenches, and mound the soil over them. Cultivars include 'Jersey Centennial', a high-yielding hybrid; 'Martha Washington' and 'Mary Washington', rust-resistant old favorites; and 'Viking KB3', which is recommended for extremely hot or cold climates.

*Atriplex hortensis*

HARDINESS
All Zones.

DAYS TO MATURITY
40–50 days;
thinnings can be
harvested sooner.
Will withstand
moderate frost.

COMMENTS
Other common
names include
French spinach,
mountain spinach
and sea purslane.

# ORACH

THE VIVID FOLIAGE OF RED ORACH MAKES
IT AN ATTRACTIVE ADDITION TO BOTH
ORNAMENTAL AND VEGETABLE GARDENS.

**Position** Plant in full sun. Not fussy,
but prefers fertile, well-drained soil;
pH 7.3–8.0.

**Cultivation** Sow seed 4–6 weeks
before the last spring frost; thin to
stand 8 inches (20 cm) apart, using
the thinnings in salads. Like
spinach, orach bolts to seed quickly
in hot weather; unlike spinach, it
will germinate and grow in warm
weather. For an extended harvest,
keep the flower heads pinched out.
Frequent small plantings will assure
plenty of young, tender leaves in
spring, summer and autumn.

**Pests and diseases** Little troubled by
pests. Pull bolting plants, as they
can grow to 6 feet (1.8 m) or taller
when in flower and may self-sow,
becoming a weed problem.

**Harvesting and storage** Pick the
succulent, young leaves as needed.

**Special tips** Red orach *A. hortensis*
var. *rubra* (shown above) holds its
color during cooking and is striking
in salads and as a garnish. Named
cultivars are not generally available,
but seed companies offer variants
based on leaf color, usually dark
green, light green or red.

# *Basella alba*

**HARDINESS**
Zones 7 and
warmer.

**DAYS TO MATURITY**
120–150 frost-free
days, but some
leaves can be
harvested earlier.

**COMMENTS**
Cultivars include
'Rubra', which has
red-veined leaves
and red stems.
Other common
names include
Ceylon spinach
and Indian spinach.

## SPINACH, MALABAR

A VINING PLANT NATIVE TO TROPICAL
AFRICA AND ASIA, MALABAR SPINACH
HAS GLOSSY LEAVES THAT ARE USED IN
THE SAME WAYS AS SPINACH.

**Position** Plant in full sun, near
a fence or trellis, in moist soil that
is rich in humus; pH 6.0–7.5.

**Cultivation** Start seed indoors up to
8 weeks before the last frost and set
out after frost danger is well past. In
warmer areas, seed can be planted
*in situ*. Alternatively, grow from
stem cuttings. Likes heat and grows
slowly if at all until the temperature
is to its liking. Set out plants 3 feet
(90 cm) apart and provide a fence
or trellis to support them. Water
well in dry weather.

**Pests and diseases** Little troubled by
pests. In warm climates, Malabar
spinach can spread to 30 feet (9 m)
in a season, overrunning small
gardens, but a spread of 6–10 feet
(1.8–3 m) is more common.

**Harvesting and storage** Pick the
fresh leaves as needed; in ideal
weather it regrows rapidly.

**Special tips** Malabar spinach grows
quickly and can be treated as an
annual climber in cooler areas. Try
growing it as an ornamental cover
over a trellis, arch or pergola, using
the leaves as required.

*Beta vulgaris* subsp. *cicla*

**HARDINESS**
Zones 3 and warmer; grow as a winter vegetable in mild areas.

**DAYS TO MATURITY**
50–60 days; thinnings can be harvested sooner.

**COMMENTS**
Other common names include leaf beet, silverbeet. Cultivars include 'White King', 'Fordhook Giant', 'Rhubarb Chard' (a red-stemmed cultivar).

# SWISS CHARD

VIGOROUS AND EASY TO GROW, A SINGLE PLANTING OF SWISS CHARD CAN PROVIDE A FULL SEASON OF FRESH LEAVES. USE IT AS YOU WOULD SPINACH, OR PLANT IT IN THE FLOWER GARDEN FOR ITS VIVID COLOR.

**Position** Plant in full sun or, in warm areas, partial shade. Not fussy, but prefers rich, well-drained soil; pH 6.0–6.8.

**Cultivation** Sow 1–2 weeks before last spring frost. Plant ½ inch (12 mm) deep and firm the soil with the back of a hoe. Thin to stand 8–12 inches (20–30 cm) apart, using the thinnings in salads or transplanting them to new beds. Cultivate, and water regularly to keep your plants growing strongly.

**Pests and diseases** Little troubled by pests. Row covers will deter flea beetles. Swiss chard is fairly drought tolerant, but water stress results in tough stems.

**Harvesting and storage** Pick the large outer leaves by pulling stems from the base with a slight twist. Leave the center to sprout new leaves. Leaves are usually cooked separately from the wide inner rib, which is often steamed and eaten like asparagus. You can freeze the leaves as you would spinach.

**Special tips** Swiss chard is attractive and has a neat growing habit. Interplant it with flowers for an ornamental and edible border.

# *Beta vulgaris* subsp. *vulgaris*

**HARDINESS**
Beets thrive in almost any climate, but where summers are hot (Zones 8 and warmer), grow them as an autumn, late winter and early spring crop.

**DAYS TO MATURITY**
55–70 days in the garden, or sooner if you grow quick-maturing cultivars such as 'Little Egypt' after starting seedlings indoors.

# BEET

DON'T WASTE BEET LEAVES—THEY ARE DELICIOUS. STEAM OR LIGHTLY FRY IN OIL AS YOU WOULD SPINACH, OR USE THE YOUNG LEAVES RAW IN SALADS.

**Position** Plant in full sun in well-drained, rich, neutral soil, free of stones. If soil is heavy or shallow, grow only round cultivars; long-rooted ones may be deformed or tough at maturity; pH 6.0–7.5.

**Cultivation** Beet seeds are compound—each "seed" actually contains as many as a half-dozen seeds. For this reason, many gardeners sow beets sparingly to reduce thinning tasks. But because beets are known for spotty germination, other gardeners sow them heavily to assure a full stand. The middle course is a moderately heavy seeding after first soaking the seeds in tepid water for several hours to encourage germination. Plant 1 inch (2.5 cm) deep and 2–4 inches (5–10 cm) apart, about 1 month before the last spring frost. Firm the seedbed well with your feet or the back of a hoe. Thin the young plants when they are 2–3 inches (5–7.5 cm) tall. Beets are among the few root vegetables that can be transplanted, so you can move any excess seedlings to another spot, taking care not to double over the taproot when transplanting. The thinnings can also be used as salad greens. Beets tend to

# Beet continued

All types of beet can be served raw or cooked. Start harvesting when the beets are about 1 inch (2.5 cm) in diameter.

become woody and tasteless when left in the ground too long; small monthly sowings will give you a continuous supply of tender, sweet beets for the table. The exceptions are cultivars bred for the root cellar, such as 'Lutz Winter Keeper'. Plant these in midsummer, at least 2 months before the first autumn frost (or in the spring if your growing season is short), and leave in the ground until a hard frost threatens. Beets need regular watering to keep them tender and to prevent interior discoloring that results from uneven soil moisture.

**Pests and diseases** Row covers will thwart flea beetles and leafminers.

Discourage the disease leafspot by not growing beets where they or their relatives, such as spinach and chard, have been grown in the previous year. Beets do poorly in hot weather and dry soil; if your summers are scorchers, grow beets in the cool seasons, including winter in mild-climate areas.

**Harvesting and storage** Harvest greens as soon as they are large enough for use. Harvest beets as "babies" when they are 1 inch (2.5 cm) or more in diameter; check by gently probing the soil at the plant's base. When removing the tops, leave 1 inch (2.5 cm) of stem attached to the roots to prevent

'Golden Beet', with its golden orange flesh, adds a gourmet touch to salads. Grate or julienne the flesh, which, like that of all beets, is rich in folic acid and vitamin C.

bleeding. Cook with stems attached and cut away the stems before serving. Pull beets for storage before a hard frost, cut tops close to the roots, and store in sand or sawdust in a cool place. Beets can also be bottled or pickled.

**Special tips** Grow small-rooted cultivars, such as those bred as specialty "baby beets," in a cluster without thinning. Plant two or three seeds together, each cluster 6 inches (15 cm) apart, and harvest when the beets reach eating size.

**Related plants**

**Cylindrical beet _B. vulgaris_ subsp. _vulgaris_** Tapered roots, up to 7 inches (17.5 cm) long and 2 inches (5 cm) in diameter. Hill the crowns to keep the topmost part of the root from being exposed and toughened. 'Cylindra' and 'Formanova' are popular cultivars. They are easy to peel and slice into uniform pieces for pickling or bottling.

**Golden beet _B. vulgaris_ subsp. _vulgaris_** Sweet and tender-fleshed, but golden orange in color. Prized for its unusual color, which does not "bleed" when cooked as red beets do. Plant golden beets more thickly than other types because they tend to germinate poorly. Cultivars include 'Golden' and 'Burpee's Golden'.

*Brassica napus* Napobrassica Group BRASSICACEAE

**HARDINESS**
Zones 3 and warmer; grow as a winter vegetable in mild areas.

**DAYS TO MATURITY**
90–110 days. Will withstand severe frost.

**COMMENTS**
Other common names include swede, swede turnip and yellow turnip.

# RUTABAGA

A FAVORITE IN SCANDINAVIAN COUNTRIES, RUTABAGA IS A RUGGED GARDEN VEGETABLE THAT SHRUGS OFF THE COLD AND OTHER ADVERSE CONDITIONS.

**Position** Plant seed in full sun in fertile, well-drained soil. Will tolerate heavy soil better than most other root vegetables; pH 5.5–6.8.

**Cultivation** Sow 12–14 weeks before first autumn frost and thin to stand 4–6 inches (10–15 cm) apart. Cultivate early; the large leaves will quickly grow to shade out weeds.

**Pests and diseases** Rotate rutabaga and other root crops to avoid root maggots. Protect young plants from flea beetles with row covers; larger plants may suffer cosmetic damage, but that will not affect the yield.

**Harvesting and storage** Pull rutabagas when they are large enough for use. The greens are also edible. Harvest all roots before a hard freeze and store in damp sand or sawdust in a cool place. Rutabagas can be waxed to prevent wrinkling during storage. Trim the root and crown and dip them briefly in a pot of water with a layer of melted paraffin on top.

**Special tips** Cultivars include 'Altasweet' and 'Laurentian'. Rutabagas that reach maturity in hot weather can be tough.

# *Brassica oleracea* Acephala Group

HARDINESS
Zones 3 and warmer; use as a winter vegetable in mild areas.

DAYS TO MATURITY
65–80 days, but thinnings can be harvested earlier and used as table greens. Young plants withstand light frost; mature ones, severe frost.

COMMENTS
Cultivars include 'Champion', 'Georgia Blue Stem' and 'Vates'.

# COLLARD

A CABBAGE RELATIVE, COLLARD IS AMONG THE MOST NUTRITIOUS OF GARDEN GREENS.

**Position** Plant in full sun in fertile, moist soil with adequate calcium; pH 6.5–6.8.

**Cultivation** Sow seed in early spring and thin to 1½ feet (45 cm), or transplant as you would cabbage. Spring-planted collards, if well cared for, will keep producing past the first frost, but you can also plant in midsummer for an autumn crop only. Tolerates summer heat, but prefers cool weather, so mulch to keep the soil cool. Keep moist and apply fish emulsion or compost tea once a month for lush growth.

**Pests and diseases** Protect young plants from flea beetles and cabbageworms with row covers. Rotate collard and other cabbage-family members to avoid soilborne diseases. Direct-seeding too thickly may result in crowded and spindly plants. Thin gradually, first to 6 inches (15 cm), then 1 foot (30 cm), then 1½ feet (45 cm).

**Harvesting and storage** Harvest leaves as needed from bottom of plant, leaving the crown to sprout new leaves. Harvest crown before hard freeze for tender "baby collards." Freeze for winter use.

**Special tips** It can tolerate heat but is tastier after frost.

*Brassica oleracea* Acephala Group BRASSICACEAE

HARDINESS
All Zones; may
overwinter in areas
as cool as Zone 6.

DAYS TO MATURITY
55–65 days, but
thinnings can be
harvested sooner.

COMMENTS
Cultivars include
'Red Russian', a
noncurly cultivar
with purplish stems
and leaves, 'Dwarf
Blue Curled Vates'
and 'Winterbor'.
Common names
include borecole
and colewort.

# KALE, CURLY

HARDY AND NUTRITIOUS, CURLY KALE
PROVIDES TASTY GREENS LATE IN THE
SEASON, EVEN UNDER A BLANKET OF SNOW.

**Position** Plant in full sun in fertile
and well-drained soil, with adequate
calcium; pH 6.5–6.8.

**Cultivation** Direct-seed 4–6 weeks
before the last spring frost, about
½ inch (12 mm) deep. Thin to
1–1¼ feet (30–37.5 cm) apart; use
the thinnings in salads. Cultivate
shallowly or mulch to control
weeds. Tolerates heat but prefers
cool soil. Plant autumn crop
6–8 weeks before first frost, or later
to overwinter. Give fish emulsion or
compost tea liberally once a month
to encourage lush leaf growth.

Leaves toughen with age. Keep
plant well picked; plant an autumn
crop for a second harvest of tender
leaves. Kale is sweeter after frost.

**Pests and diseases** Use row covers
to protect young plants from flea
beetles and cabbageworms, or use
BT, a microbial insecticide, to
control cabbageworms. Rotate kale
and other cabbage-family plants to
avoid soilborne diseases.

**Harvesting and storage** Pick leaves
as needed from base of the plant;
new ones will sprout from top.

**Special tips** Young plants will take a
light frost; mature ones, severe frost.

## *Brassica oleracea* Botrytis Group

HARDINESS
Zones 3 and warmer. Use as spring and autumn crops in cool-spring areas, and as a winter crop in mild climates.

DAYS TO MATURITY
50–120 days.

COMMENTS
Cultivars include the attractive 'Purple Head Improved' (left). The color fades during cooking.

# CAULIFLOWER

CAULIFLOWERS ARE HEAVY FEEDERS THAT REQUIRE PLENTY OF WATER. THE HEADS OF WHITE VARIETIES MUST BE PROTECTED FROM THE SUN (BLANCHED) TO KEEP THEM WHITE.

**Position** Plant in full sun in rich, well-drained soil with plenty of calcium, and ample amounts of well-rotted manure or compost worked in; pH 6.0–7.0. A light dressing with lime will be necessary if the soil is too acidic. This will also reduce the likelihood of club root infection.

**Cultivation** Start spring crops indoors and do not set out too early; severe frost can cause the plant to form a "button" instead of a full-sized head. Space plants 1½–3 feet (45–90 cm) apart, and mulch to keep the soil cool. Start autumn crops 90–120 days before the autumn frost; set out when seedlings are 4–5 weeks old. Keep cauliflower growing steadily with plenty of water and one or more applications of fish emulsion or compost tea. When heads appear, use a clothespin to clip several large leaves together over the head to shade it and keep it white, or remove a large lower leaf and lay it over the developing head. "Self-blanching" cultivars grow their own "shading" leaves, but may still need help from you if high heat wilts the protective leaves. Cauliflower cultivars have also been bred

# *Cauliflower* continued

Try planting aromatic herbs, such as pennyroyal, peppermint, sage and thyme, near your cauliflowers. It may help to deter insect pests.

to cater for various climates. For instance, where long, hot summers are the norm, choose early-maturing types to prevent the occurrence of problems, such as leaves forming among the curds, or the curds forming loose heads.

**Pests and diseases** Control cabbage-worms with row covers, or a dose of BT, a microbial insecticide. Do this early, as it is difficult to control worms when they have become established inside the developing head. Row covers will also deter flea beetles on young plants; older, vigorous plants can withstand flea beetle attack. Rotate cabbage-family plantings to avoid soilborne diseases. In humid areas, heads may discolor during blanching due to excess moisture. Clip or tie the leaves together loosely to keep sunlight off the head, but do not cut off the circulation of air.

**Harvesting and storage** Cut heads before the curds begin to coarsen and separate. Cool weather may slow head development. When harvesting, leave a few leaves around the head to avoid breaking it. Cauliflower keeps, refrigerated, for up to 2 weeks. It can also be broken up into segments before being plunged into boiling water, refreshed in cold water and then frozen or used for making pickles.

As an interesting change, try growing some of the cauliflowers with colorful, more open heads that do not need to go through the blanching process.

**Special tips** Young plants will withstand a light frost; mature ones, moderate frost. 'Snow Crown' and 'Rushmore' are early cultivars; longer-season cultivars include 'Snowball Elite' and 'Andes'.

### Related plants

**Green cauliflower *B. oleracea*, Botrytis Group** A specialty cauliflower with yellow-green, rather than white, curds. Green cauliflower, like purple cauliflower, is easier to grow than the white cultivars, since it does not require blanching. Popular cultivars include 'Alverda'.

**Mini cauliflower *B. oleracea*, Botrytis Group** Grow minis if space is limited, or if family needs dictate. They have smaller curds, measuring 4 inches (10 cm) across. Up to five can be grown in the space taken by one cauliflower of the usual size.

**Purple cauliflower *B. oleracea*, Botrytis Group** Like a cauliflower in habit, but it has looser flower heads, like broccoli. Purple cauliflower is milder and more tender than broccoli. The head has a deep purple cast, which disappears during cooking. No blanching is required. Cultivars include 'Purple Head Improved', 'Violet Queen' and 'Burgundy Queen'. The attractive purple flower heads can be used as a garnish or to add color to salads.

*Brassica oleracea* Capitata Group

# CABBAGE

VALUED FOR THOUSANDS OF YEARS BECAUSE
OF ITS HARDINESS AND STORAGE LIFE,
CABBAGE CAN BE GROWN ALMOST
ANYWHERE, ALTHOUGH IT IS SUBJECT TO
ATTACK BY PESTS.

**Position** Plant in full sun. Any soil
texture, provided it is well drained
and fertile; pH 6.0–6.8.

**Cultivation** Grow as a spring and
autumn crop in most areas, or as a
winter crop where temperatures
rarely drop below freezing. Avoid
plantings that will mature in hot,
dry weather. Start spring crops in
a cool place indoors 6–8 weeks
before the last spring frost and set
out 4 weeks before the last frost.
Give seedlings plenty of light and

withhold fertilizer to discourage
spindly growth. Set plants 1–1½ feet
(30–45 cm) apart, depending on
expected head size. In cool-summer
areas, you can plant successive crops
every month, ending with a storage-
type cabbage about 2 months
before autumn frost. Summer
plantings may fail in warmer
climates. Heavy mulch will help to
retain moisture and keep the soil
cool. Cabbage prefers rich soil; add
compost or rotted manure before
planting and apply fish emulsion or
compost tea a month after planting.

**Pests and diseases** Use row covers
or BT, a microbial insecticide, to
control cabbageworms. Aphids are

HARDINESS
Zones 3 and
warmer, with soil-
cooling mulch in
hotter climates.
Use as a winter
vegetable in
mild areas.

DAYS TO MATURITY
60–110 days.
Young cabbage
plants will with-
stand light frost;
mature ones more
severe frost.

COMMENTS
Cabbage is an
excellent source of
calcium in the diet.

Standard cabbage types (above) form a tighter head than the Savoy cabbage (left), which has puckered or crinkled leaves. Savoy cabbage is also milder and sweeter.

a sign of heat or water stress; hose them off with a strong water spray or spray the plants thoroughly with insecticidal soap. Rotate cabbage-family plantings to avoid soilborne diseases. To avoid head splitting, use a shovel to sever roots on one side of the plant when the head is fully formed. This slows maturity and helps the cabbage to "hold" without splitting.

**Harvesting and storage** Harvest early cultivars as needed, as they do not store well. Harvest storage-type cabbage before a hard freeze and store, roots and all, in dry leaves in a cold cellar or garage. Can be pickled or made into sauerkraut.

**Special tips** Cut early and midseason cabbage high on the plant, leaving as many loose lower leaves as possible. As many as six small cabbages, called "cabbage sprouts," will form on the stem, providing a delicious second harvest. Grow cabbages with plants that won't compete for calcium.

**Related plants**
**Flowering cabbage *B. oleracea*, Acephala Group** This is actually a kale, rather than a cabbage. The flowering cabbage forms a loose head or rosette of colorful green and red, white or magenta leaves. It differs from flowering kale in that the leaves are smooth-edged rather

Red cabbage makes excellent coleslaw and soup, and is pretty enough to grow in the flower garden. Marigolds and aromatic herbs planted nearby may help to deter pests.

than frilly or ruffled. Both types are edible but are grown chiefly as ornamentals for autumn color (cool temperatures are needed for the striking colors to develop fully). Good cultivars are 'Osaka' hybrids (flowering cabbage) and 'Nagoya' hybrids (flowering kale).

**Pointed head cabbage** *B. oleracea*, **Capitata Group** Forms a cone-shaped head. It is quick-maturing, and has been popular for centuries. Cultivars include 'Early Jersey Wakefield', 'Greyhound' and 'Trumpet F1 Hybrid'.

**Red cabbage** *B. oleracea*, **Capitata Group** Attractive blue-purple leaves and red-purple heads with white veining. Cultivars include 'Ruby Perfection Hybrid', 'Red Acre' and 'Red Rookie'.

**Round head cabbage** *B. oleracea*, **Capitata Group** Globe-shaped or flattened round heads. Early cultivars include 'Darkri', 'Polar Green' and 'Emerald Acre'. Midseason cultivars include 'Stonehead' and 'Copenhagen Market'. Late or storage cultivars include 'Late Flat Dutch' and 'Danish Ballhead'.

**Savoy cabbage** *B. oleracea*, **Capitata Group** Puckered, crinkly, light green or blue-green leaves. Heads are often less tight than smooth-leaved cabbage, but the flavor is superior. Cultivars include 'Savoy King' and 'Savoy Ace'.

## *Brassica oleracea* Cymosa Group

HARDINESS
Zones 3 and
warmer; grow as
a winter crop in
mild areas. Where
springs are cool,
grow as a spring
and autumn crop;
otherwise, does
best in autumn.

DAYS TO MATURITY
70–95 days.

COMMENTS
Calabrese broccoli
(left) is perfect for
small gardens.
It produces new
sprouts over a
long period.

# BROCCOLI

VIRTUALLY UNKNOWN IN HOME GARDENS
50 YEARS AGO, BROCCOLI IS NOW A
COOL-WEATHER FAVORITE.

**Position** Full sun. Well-drained soil
with plenty of calcium; pH 6.7–7.2.

**Cultivation** Start spring seedlings
indoors, about 2 months before the
last spring frost. Set out hardened-
off transplants in the garden a
month before the last frost. Space
plants 1–2 feet (30–60 cm) apart;
wider spacing will yield larger
heads. Cultivate or mulch and keep
the soil evenly moist. Lack of water
will stress the plant, which may fail
to head or may become vulnerable
to insect pests. Sow autumn crops
directly about 90 days before the

first autumn frost, or transplant
about 60 days before frost.

**Pests and diseases** Use cardboard or
metal "collars" to deter cutworms.
Row covers will thwart flea beetles,
cabbageworms and root maggots.
Spray or dust with BT, a microbial
insecticide, if cabbageworms are a
problem. To avoid soilborne
diseases, don't plant broccoli and
other cabbage-family plants in the
same spot more than once every
3 years. In some areas, spring
broccoli bolts to seed prematurely
at the onset of hot weather. Choose
quick-maturing cultivars and expect
spring-grown broccoli heads to be
smaller than those grown in autumn.

A cool-weather favorite, broccoli is now known to be a valuable addition to the diet, and is thought to provide protection against a number of ills, including some cancers.

**Harvesting and storage** Harvest broccoli heads when they have reached maximum size but before the tight, green flower buds begin to loosen and show yellow. Spring crops are best harvested once, with as much of the edible stem as possible. Cut autumn broccoli heads with less stem attached, leaving as much of the plant intact as possible so that it will produce smaller sideshoots or "florets," which you can harvest until there is a hard freeze. After picking, broccoli freezes well.

**Special tips** A small planting of Chinese cabbage nearby will draw flea beetles away from broccoli.

**Related plants**

**Chinese broccoli *B. oleracea*, Alboglabra Group** Also called Chinese kale, kaai laan or gai lan. Similar to calabrese broccoli, but the buds and leaves are lighter green and sweeter. The stems and young leaves are also eaten steamed or stir-fried. More heat-tolerant than standard broccoli.

**Purple broccoli *B. oleracea*, Cymosa Group** Identical to green broccoli except that the head has a distinct purplish cast, which disappears during cooking.

**Romanesco broccoli *B. oleracea*, Cymosa Group** Unusual conical heads of pale green, peaked florets that resemble little rocket ships.

This variety of purple broccoli is striking even in the flower garden but, unfortunately, the color fades during cooking.

The crunchy texture is more like cauliflower than broccoli. Requires wider spacing—up to 3 feet (90 cm)—and a longer growing season than most standard broccoli. In most areas it is planted in late spring for autumn harvest.

**Calabrese broccoli** *B. oleracea*, **Italica Group**  Also called Italian broccoli, asparagus broccoli, or sprouting broccoli. Does not form a large central head but a profusion of smaller, looser heads or "sprouts." Cut when about 4 inches (10 cm) long, with surrounding small leaves, and use like regular broccoli. The plant will produce new sprouts over a long period.

**Broccoli raab** *B. rapa*, **Ruvo Group**  Also called rapini or rapine; this vegetable is prized in Italy. It is usually blanched, then chopped and fried in olive oil with garlic. The glossy, dark green leaves are harvested along with the flower buds and stems. Spring crops may bolt to seed quickly; autumn plantings usually produce three or more harvests of flower shoots and leaves.

# *Brassica oleracea* Gemmifera Group

# BRUSSELS SPROUTS

INDIVIDUAL BRUSSELS SPROUTS LOOK LIKE
TIGHTLY WRAPPED MINIATURE CABBAGES.

**Position** Plant in full sun in
well-drained and fertile soil, with
adequate calcium levels; pH 6.0–6.8.

**Cultivation** Require a long growing
season and are best when matured
in cool weather. Short-season
vegetable gardeners can set out
transplants when they sow other
spring crops; in other areas, wait
until late spring. Space plants about
2 feet (60 cm) apart and keep
weeded or mulched. Pinch off top
leaves to encourage side growth.

**Pests and diseases** Rotate with
non-cabbage-family crops to avoid
soilborne fungal and viral diseases.
Use row covers to deter cabbageworms, flea beetles and root
maggots, or BT, a microbial
insecticide, for cabbageworms.
Water well and grow in fertile soil
to reduce vulnerability to aphids.

**Harvesting and storage** Harvest the
lower sprouts by breaking off the
leaf below and snapping off the
sprout. Sprouts higher up will
continue to grow. Entire stalks can
also be harvested. Harvest anytime
until early winter to complete
harvest before the ground freezes.

**Special tips** Sprouts keep for several
weeks on the stalk if you pull up
the whole plant and keep it cold.

# *Brassica oleracea* Gongylodes Group

BRASSICACEAE

HARDINESS
Zones 3 and
warmer. Grow in
mild areas as a
winter vegetable,
and in most areas
to harvest in spring
and autumn.

DAYS TO MATURITY
38–55 days.

COMMENTS
Cultivars include
'Early Purple
Vienna' (purple-
skinned cultivar),
'Early White
Vienna' and 'Grand
Duke Hybrid'.

# KOHLRABI

BOTH THE SWOLLEN, TURNIP-LIKE STEM AND
THE LEAVES OF KOHLRABI ARE EDIBLE, AND
THEY ARE OFTEN COOKED TOGETHER.

**Position** Plant in full sun in fertile
and well-drained soil with adequate
calcium; pH 6.0–7.0.

**Cultivation** Direct-seed 2–4 weeks
before the last spring frost or start
indoors 6–8 weeks before last frost
and set out 6 inches (15 cm) apart.
Use thinnings of direct-seeded crops
as salad greens. Mulch or cultivate
to control weeds. Set out autumn
crops from transplants, or direct-seed
2 months before autumn frost.

**Pests and diseases** Use row covers
to protect the young plants from
flea beetles and cabbageworms,
or control cabbageworms with BT,
an insecticide. Rotate kohlrabi and
other cabbage-family plants to avoid
soilborne diseases. Keep watered or
mulched and avoid plantings that
will mature in hot weather, which
produces tough, woody kohlrabi.

**Harvesting and storage** Harvest the
entire plant when swollen stem is
about 2 inches (5 cm) in diameter.
Overgrown kohlrabi can be woody.
Best eaten fresh, but will keep for
2 weeks in the refrigerator.

**Special tips** Will withstand a light
frost. Thin raw slices are a good
low-calorie nibble, with a crunch
like stir-fried water chestnuts.

## *Brassica rapa* Chinensis Group

# CABBAGE, CHINESE

NUTRITIOUS AND FAST-GROWING, CHINESE CABBAGE CAN BE ADDED TO STIR-FRIES, OR EVEN EATEN FRESH IN SALADS. IT IS A GOOD SOURCE OF DIETARY CALCIUM.

**Position** Likes to be planted in full sun in well-drained soil that is rich in humus; pH 6.0–6.8.

**Cultivation** Head-forming types of Chinese cabbage quickly go to seed in warm weather or if seedlings are exposed to severe frost, so plant quick-maturing cultivars for early crops. Transplants poorly in spring, but can be moved successfully in peat pots. Direct-seed after the last frost; thin to stand 1 foot (30 cm) apart. Set autumn crops from transplants or direct-seed 2–3 months before the first frost, and give wider spacing, up to 2 feet (60 cm) apart. Transplant or direct-seed leafy types from spring through late summer, thinning to 6–12 inches (15–30 cm) apart, depending on the cultivar.

**Pests and diseases** Use row covers to protect from flea beetles.

**Harvesting and storage** Harvest spring crops before warm weather. Harvest autumn cabbages before a hard freeze; will keep in a cool cellar for several weeks if trimmed and wrapped in newspaper.

**Special tips** Plant Chinese cabbages at the base of your pea trellises,

Cook fast-growing choy sum (facing page) and bok choy (above) only briefly so you can fully enjoy their delicate flavor.

where they will get some shade and be sheltered from the wind.

### Related plants

**Bok choy *B. rapa*, Chinensis Group** Also called pak choi, Ching-Chiang cabbage or Chinese chard. A leafy Chinese cabbage with spoon-shaped, light green to blue-green leaves and thick, crisp stems, favored for stir-fries. Popular cultivars include 'Mei Qing Choi' and 'Joi Choi'.

**Michihli cabbage *B. rapa*, Pekinensis Group** Head-forming cabbage. Tall-growing, cylindrical in shape. Cultivars include 'Jade Pagoda' and 'Michihli'.

**Napa cabbage *B. rapa*, Pekinensis Group** Head-forming, barrel-shaped, and larger than Michihli types, this type grows up to about 10 pounds (4.5 kg). Early cultivars include 'Springtime' and 'Blues', and late ones include 'China Pride' and 'Wintertime'. 'Lettucy Type' is a Napa cultivar with a loose, open top, like romaine (Cos) lettuce.

**Choy sum *B. parachinensis*** Similar to bok choy, but the leaves are thick, glossy and dark green. Named cultivars are not generally available, but seed suppliers may offer variants.

## *Brassica rapa* Japonica Group

HARDINESS
All Zones; grow as
a winter vegetable
in mild climates.

DAYS TO MATURITY
40 days; the
thinnings can be
harvested earlier.
Will withstand a
moderate frost.

COMMENTS
Cultivars include
'Tokyo Beau',
'Tokyo Belle'.
Other common
names include
Japanese mustard
and kyona.

# MIZUNA

MILDER THAN MOST MUSTARDS AND EASY
TO GROW, MIZUNA ADDS DASH TO SALADS
AND STIR-FRIES, OR IT CAN BE COOKED IN
THE SAME WAY AS OTHER GREENS.

**Position** Plant in full sun. Not fussy,
but best in light, well-drained soil;
pH 5.8–6.2.

**Cultivation** Sow 2–4 weeks before
last spring frost, or 6–8 weeks
before first autumn frost as an
autumn crop. Thin to stand
4–6 inches (10–15 cm) apart, using
thinnings in salad. Irrigate to
promote rapid growth.

**Pests and diseases** Row covers will
protect young plants, especially
spring crops, from flea beetles.

Mizuna can become strong-flavored
in hot weather. Avoid plantings that
will mature during hot spells, or
use as cooked greens then, rather
than in salads.

**Harvesting and storage** Leaves will
grow to 12–14 inches (30–35 cm);
cut when 4–6 inches (10–15 cm)
long for best salad greens. Harvest
as needed with scissors about
1 inch (2.5 cm) above the crown;
the plant will sprout new leaves.
Four or five harvests are possible.
Or harvest whole plants for cooking.

**Special tips** Seeds packaged as
"cutting mix" contain mizuna along
with other lettuce and spicy salad
greens. Eat as mixed baby leaves.

# Brassica rapa Rapifera Group

HARDINESS
All Zones; grow as
a winter vegetable
in mild climates.

DAYS TO MATURITY
35–60 days.
Turnips can with-
stand light frost.

COMMENTS
Cultivars include
'Tokyo Cross
Hybrid', 'Purple-
Top White Globe',
'Seven Top' (grown
for greens) and
'Golden Ball' (with
yellow flesh).

# TURNIP

GROWN BOTH FOR ITS TENDER LEAVES AND
FOR ITS CRISP ROOT, TURNIP HAS THE BEST
FLAVOR AND TEXTURE IN COOL WEATHER.

**Position** Plant in full sun in loose,
deep soil that is rich in humus;
pH 5.5–6.8.

**Cultivation** Sow ½ inch (12 mm)
deep 4–6 weeks before last spring
frost. Thin to stand 3 inches
(7.5 cm) apart; use thinnings as
fresh or cooked greens. Sow your
autumn crop 8–10 weeks before
first autumn frost. Water regularly
for fast growth in spring, because
turnips bolt to seed in hot weather.

**Pests and diseases** Use row covers
to protect from flea beetles. Reduce
root maggot damage, especially in
spring crops, by not planting where
other root crops have grown the
preceding year. Turnips that mature
in hot weather may be fibrous or
strong-flavored. For spring crops,
choose quick-maturing cultivars.

**Harvesting and storage** Pull turnips
as needed, as 1-inch (2.5-cm) wide
"babies" up to 3–4-inch (8–10-cm)
roots. Larger turnips can be woody.
Turnips are more tender than other
root vegetables and are damaged by
hard frost. Store roots in damp sand
or sawdust in a cool place; freeze
leaves as you would spinach.

**Special tips** Avoid overhead
watering to prevent mildew.

*Brassica rapa* Rapifera Group

HARDINESS
All Zones; grow as
a winter vegetable
in mild areas.
Can survive low
temperatures.

DAYS TO MATURITY
90 days.

COMMENTS
Named cultivars
are not generally
available. Tyfon's
other common
names include
Holland greens.

# TYFON

A MILD-FLAVORED CROSS BETWEEN TURNIP
AND CABBAGE, TYFON IS A FROST-HARDY,
QUICK-GROWING GREEN THAT IS COOKED IN
THE SAME WAY AS SPINACH.

**Position** Plant in full sun or partial
shade. Not fussy, but prefers rich,
well-limed soil; pH 6.0–7.0.

**Cultivation** Sow ½ inch (12 mm)
deep 4–6 weeks before last spring
frost, 8–10 weeks before first
autumn frost, or later as a winter
vegetable in mild areas. Thin to
stand 4–6 inches (10–15 cm) apart;
use thinnings as salad or cooking
greens. Or grow unthinned if you
plan to harvest leaves by shearing.
Water regularly to encourage
abundant leafy growth.

**Pests and diseases** Use row covers
to protect plants, especially spring
crops, from flea beetles. Avoid
plantings that will mature in hot,
dry weather. Like its cabbage-family
relatives, tyfon bolts quickly in heat.

**Harvesting and storage** Pick fresh
leaves as needed, or harvest by
cutting with garden shears or
scissors, leaving 1 inch (2.5 cm)
above the crown to resprout. In
cool weather, a planting should
provide several cuttings, about a
month apart. Freeze leaves as you
would kale or spinach.

**Special tips** In most climates, a light
row cover will extend your harvest
well into the winter.

*Brassica* spp.

HARDINESS
All Zones; grow as
a winter vegetable
in mild areas.

DAYS TO MATURITY
40–50 days;
thinnings can be
harvested earlier.
Will withstand
moderate frost.

COMMENTS
As the weather
gets hotter, so do
the leaves of
mustard plants.

# MUSTARD

MUSTARD IS GROWN MAINLY FOR ITS SPICY
SEEDS, WHICH ARE GROUND OR LEFT WHOLE
TO PRODUCE A POPULAR CONDIMENT. THE
LEAVES OF SOME VARIETIES ADD A DELICIOUS
ZING TO SALADS.

**Position** Plant in full sun. Not fussy,
but prefers light, well-drained soil;
pH 5.8–6.2.

**Cultivation** Sow 2–4 weeks before
the last spring frost or 6–8 weeks
before the first autumn frost. Thin
to stand 4–6 inches (10–15 cm)
apart, adding the thinnings to salads
or soups. Irrigate, especially during
dry spells, to promote rapid growth.

**Pests and diseases** Rarely troubled
by pests. Good air circulation

prevents mildew. Bolts to seed
quickly in hot weather. Avoid
plantings that will mature in hot,
dry weather; grow as an autumn
crop in warm-spring areas.

**Harvesting and storage** Pick leaves
as needed from the outside of the
plant, allowing new leaves to sprout
from the center. Tender leaves do
not store well in the refrigerator.

**Special tips** Cut off the flower stalk
as soon as it makes its appearance
in the center of the plant. This will
prolong your harvest of leaves,
which can be mixed with cress in
the traditional "mustard and cress"
combination salad. However, if you
are growing this crop for its black

# *Mustard* continued

The striking purple-red leaves of red mustard *B. juncea* var. *foliosa* add color to salads, but use sparingly, as the bite can be startling to diners unfamiliar with mustard leaves.

seeds, leave the flowers undisturbed until the seeds are set and ripened. Always harvest your seed crops in dry weather.

**Related plants**

**Black mustard *B. nigra*** Has edible leaves, but is grown chiefly for its seed, which is used to produce a traditional spicy condiment.

**Brown mustard *B. juncea* 'Crispifolia'** Large, curly or frilled green leaves, usually grown for greens. Other cultivars include 'Green Wave' and 'Southern Curled'.

**Rape *B. napus*** Grown mainly as an oilseed crop. Rape is also grown by organically minded gardeners, who make use of the way its strong tap roots break up heavy clay soils; they also grow it to dig in as a green manure crop to help in the control of nematodes.

**Red mustard *B. juncea* var. *foliosa*** Broad, flat leaves with red or purple coloring, very spicy. Cultivars include 'Osaka Purple' and 'Red Giant'.

**White mustard *B. hirta*** The seeds are ground for a condiment; less pungent than black mustard.

# *Capsicum annuum*

HARDINESS
Zones 4 and
warmer.

DAYS TO MATURITY
55–80 days from
transplanting for
green peppers;
15–20 days more
for mature, fully
colored peppers.

COMMENTS
Scientific studies
show that planting
marigolds nearby
reduces the
number of aphids
on bell peppers.

# BELL PEPPER (CAPSICUM)

BELL PEPPERS ARE CRISP AND JUICY WHEN
GREEN, BUT SWEETER WHEN ALLOWED TO
RIPEN TO RED, YELLOW OR ORANGE.

**Position** Plant in full sun in light,
well-drained soil, not overly rich;
pH 6.0–7.0.

**Cultivation** Start seeds indoors
6–8 weeks before last spring frost.
Do not overwater pepper seedlings,
as they are vulnerable to root rot.
Set out 10–15 inches (25–37.5 cm)
apart when frost danger is well past
and the soil has warmed. In colder
areas, prewarm the soil with black
plastic mulch. Young bell peppers
will tolerate cool spells but will not
thrive until warmer weather arrives.
Cultivate shallowly; do not mulch

until the soil is thoroughly warm.
Too much nitrogen will produce
lush foliage and few peppers, but
an application of fish emulsion or
compost tea when the plants are
in flower can help to increase the
yield. Magnesium is critical; in
magnesium-poor soils, scatter
1 teaspoon of Epsom salts around
the base of each plant. Irrigate in
dry spells. Bell peppers, particularly
thick-fleshed sweet peppers, are
prone to blossom-end rot if they
become drought-stressed.

**Pests and diseases** Do not plant
where pepper or other nightshade
family members, such as tomatoes
and eggplants (aubergines) have

# Bell pepper continued

Essential to many Asian and Mexican dishes, hot peppers come in many sizes, shapes and degrees of "heat." Wear gloves when cutting up and avoid contact with eyes.

been grown in the preceding 2 years. Protect young plants from cutworms with cardboard or foil collars. Keep bell peppers away from corn plantings to reduce earworm damage to the fruit. Sunscald can cause dry, sunken patches on the fruit. Plant more closely, keep watered and grow cultivars with good leaf canopies to avoid fruit damage.

**Harvesting and storage**  Pick immature or green peppers when they are large enough for use. Leave some fruit on the plant to mature. Fully ripe peppers will be yellow, orange or red, depending on the cultivar. Pick mature peppers when 50–75 percent colored; they will finish ripening in 1–2 days at room temperature. When frost threatens, harvest all the remaining fruit. Fresh peppers will keep for 2 weeks or more if stored at around 55°F (13°C) (a refrigerator is too cold), or freeze them for winter cooking. Freeze or pickle thick-fleshed hot peppers, such as jalapeño and hot cherry; dry thin-fleshed ones, such as cayenne.

**Special tips**  Hot peppers and sweet peppers may cross-pollinate. Plant them well away from each other, especially if you intend to save the seed. Bell peppers are attractive plants of bushy habit that can be

Less juicy than bell peppers, frying peppers retain their shape and flavor well during cooking. They may drop their flowers in the heat, so provide shade during hot spells.

interplanted in the flower garden. They can also be successfully grown in containers. Handle hot peppers with care—the capsaicin they contain will burn sensitive tissues, such as the eyes and mouth.

### Related plants

**Hot peppers** *C. annuum*, **Longum Group** Also called chili peppers. Hot peppers come in a wide variety of shapes, sizes and degrees of "heat." The milder cultivars include 'Ancho' or 'Poblano', a large, mildly hot pepper that is often served stuffed. Medium-hot peppers include jalapeño and 'Hungarian Wax'. Fiery peppers include cayenne and Thai peppers. Hot weather intensifies the flavor and heat.

**Pickling peppers** *C. annuum*, **Conoides Group** Usually small, thin-fleshed peppers with a cone shape, borne upright on the plant. 'Sweet Pickle' is ornamental, with red, orange, yellow and purple fruits on the same plant. The long and thin 'Pepperoncini' is an Italian favorite, usually picked when green but turning red at maturity.

**Sweet peppers (bell)** *C. annuum*, **Grossum Group** Blocky in shape and thick-fleshed, these peppers are most often used fresh in salads and relish trays or for stuffing. Most cultivars turn red or yellow when

# *Bell pepper* continued

These small pickling peppers, which ripen to red, yellow and orange, also provide a lovely contrast in color in the salad bowl.

fully ripe; purple and "chocolate" peppers are colored at their immature stage and turn red when fully ripe. Popular cultivars include 'Ace' (red at maturity), 'Orobelle' (yellow), 'Jupiter' (red), and 'Oriole' (orange).

**Sweet peppers (other)** *C. annuum,* **Grossum Group** Frying peppers, also called Italian, ramshorn, Cubanelle or banana peppers, have elongated fruit up to 1 foot (30 cm) long. They are generally thinner-fleshed than bell peppers and hold their shape and flavor better in cooked dishes. Cultivars range from dark green to light yellow when immature and ripen to red, orange or yellow; they include 'Biscayne' (pale green, ripens red), 'Sweet Banana' (yellow, ripens red), 'Bullhorn' (yellow, ripens orange) and 'Gypsy' (yellow, ripens red). Pimento peppers, also called cheese peppers, are thick-fleshed and flattened in shape. Excellent when fresh and the best pepper for roasting. Popular cultivars of pimento include 'Super Red Pimento' and 'Yellow Cheese'.

# *Chrysanthemum coronarium*

HARDINESS
Zones 2 and
warmer; use as a
winter vegetable
in mild areas.

DAYS TO MATURITY
45 days, but
thinnings can be
harvested earlier.
Tolerates light to
moderate frost.

COMMENTS
There are no
named cultivars,
but some seed
companies offer
variants based on
leaf size and shape.

## CHRYSANTHEMUM, GARLAND

THE AROMATIC, EDIBLE LEAVES OF THE
GARLAND CHRYSANTHEMUM ARE POPULAR
IN ORIENTAL CUISINES, EITHER STIR-FRIED OR
DROPPED INTO SOME OF THE CLASSIC SOUPS.

**Position** Avoid hot, dry areas. Not
fussy, but prefers fertile, moist soil;
pH 6.0–6.7.

**Cultivation** Direct-seed about ½ inch
(12 mm) deep in early spring or
autumn and thin to 4–6 inches
(10–15 cm). Use the thinnings in
stir-fries, soups or salads.

**Pests and diseases** Little troubled by
pests, but to avoid leaf diseases,
don't plant where flower garden
chrysanthemums (now more
correctly called dendranthemas)

have been grown. Hot weather and
inadequate moisture can cause
premature bolting to seed. The
flowers, however, are attractive.

**Harvesting and storage** Harvest
whole plants or side leaves as
needed, but avoid planting in hot
weather, as the leaves become
disagreeably bitter. Garland
chrysanthemum "cooks down" in
the pot, so several plants may be
needed for a soup.

**Special tips** Remove flower buds to
prolong the harvest of leaves. Other
common names include crown
daisy, edible chrysanthemum,
shungiku and tong ho choi.

*Cichorium endivia*

**HARDINESS**
Zones 4 and warmer; grow as a winter vegetable in mild areas.

**DAYS TO MATURITY**
80–100 days.

**COMMENTS**
Escarole (left) cultivars such as 'Full Heart Batavian' are easy to find. Curly- or fringed-leaved cultivars of endive, also called frisée, include 'Salad King', 'Giant Fringed Oyster' and 'Traviata'.

# ENDIVE AND ESCAROLE

IN WARM AREAS GROW ENDIVE AND ESCAROLE BETWEEN TOMATOES, WHERE THEY WILL APPRECIATE THE SHADE.

**Position** Full sun or partial shade in warm areas. Prefers fertile, well-limed, well-drained soil; pH 5.5–7.0.

**Cultivation** In cool-spring areas, start indoors 8 weeks before last frost and set out a month before last frost, 10–12 inches (25–30 cm) apart. Cover plants if a hard frost threatens. In warmer areas, they're best as autumn crops, started in midsummer and set out 2 months before first autumn frost, or even later in mildest areas. They can be blanched by inverting a pot or box over the plant, or by tying the outer leaves together at the top. In humid areas, blanching by tying may cause the inside leaves to rot.

**Pests and diseases** Provide good air circulation to avoid molds. Control slugs with shallow pans of beer set in the soil. Water well and provide shade in hot spells to prevent brown, crisp ends on endive leaves.

**Harvesting and storage** Cut entire head at base in the morning while dew is still on plant. Rinse; wrap in paper towels, then in a plastic bag. Keeps up to 2 weeks refrigerated.

**Special tips** Broadleaf endive is known as escarole. See "Forcing chicory" page 166 for Belgian endive.

# *Cichorium intybus*

HARDINESS
Zones 3 and warmer; only leafy types grow in the coldest areas; they also grow as a winter crop in mild areas. Some cultivars can be planted in autumn for spring harvest in areas as cool as Zone 5.

DAYS TO MATURITY
40–130 days, depending on type. Leafy types, such as cutting chicory (left), grow fast.

# CHICORY

THE LEAVES OF CUTTING CHICORY IMPART A TANGY FLAVOR TO GREEN SALADS. CUT THE LEAVES FROM THE PLANT AS NEEDED.

**Position** Full sun. Well-drained, moderately fertile soil; pH 6.0–6.5.

**Cultivation** Direct-sow after frost or set out as transplants, 8–12 inches (20–30 cm) apart. Sow or transplant the autumn crop 2 months before first frost. Avoid plantings that will mature during hot weather. Keep well watered to avoid bolting to seed. Modern cultivars of head-forming chicories do not require cutting back to form heads.

**Pests and diseases** Chicory is little troubled by pests. Keep the soil moist to avoid interior browning of head-forming types. Head-forming types are inconsistent; many plants will produce only leaves or loose rosettes, despite the best conditions.

**Harvesting and storage** Harvest leaves of leafy types as needed. Cut head-forming types as needed when the heads are firm (plants will hold in the garden for several weeks). Harvest chicories grown for their roots before a hard frost.

**Related plants**
**Cutting chicory *C. intybus*** Also called catalogna, leaf chicory or Italian dandelion. It is grown for its leaves, which vary in shape from dandelion-like to smooth or

Heading chicory, which is popular in Europe broiled, roasted or served in salads, grows faster than loose-leafed types, but more slowly than endive.

rosette-like, and in color from light to dark green and also red-tinged. Some can be cut and left to resprout for continued harvest. Cultivars include 'Rouge di Verone', 'Catalogna', 'Elodie' and 'Bionda'.

**Forcing chicory** *C. intybus* Also called witloof and Belgian endive. Cut initial head in autumn, then dig up roots, trim to 8 inches (20 cm), and bury upright in moist sand or peat. Kept in complete darkness at 50–60°F (10–15°C), the roots will produce small pale sprouts or "chicons" in about 3 weeks. Cultivars include 'Witloof Improved'.

**Heading chicory** *C. intybus* Also called radicchio or Italian chicory. Red-tinged leaves surround a small,

red head with white veining, resembling red cabbage. Older cultivars, such as 'Rossa di Treviso', may require cutting back to 1 inch (2.5 cm) in midsummer to form heads in autumn. Modern cultivars form heads without cutting back. Cultivars include 'Adria', 'Giulio' and 'Rossa di Verona'. 'Pan di Zucchero', or sugarloaf, makes large heads similar to romaine (Cos) lettuce.

**Root chicory** *C. intybus* Also called coffee chicory or Sicilian chicory. Has edible leaves, but is usually grown for its large roots, which you can dig up in autumn, dry, and grind. This is infused to make a coffee-like beverage. Cultivars include 'Magdeburgh'.

# *Crambe maritima*

HARDINESS
Zones 4 and
warmer.

DAYS TO MATURITY
Grown from seed,
sea kale will not
provide a harvest
until the third year.
After that, harvest
annually in spring.

COMMENTS
Tolerates salty
environments
very well.

# KALE, SEA

GROW SEA KALE FOR THE TENDER SHOOTS
THAT EMERGE IN SPRING. YOU CAN BLANCH
AND EAT THESE LIKE ASPARAGUS.

**Position** Plant in full sun or partial
shade in rich, well-drained, slightly
alkaline soil; pH 6.0–7.0.

**Cultivation** Best started from
divisions, but specialty suppliers
usually stock only seeds. Plant
about six seeds in mounds 2–3 feet
(60–90 cm) apart, 2–4 weeks before
last spring frost. Thin to three or
four plants per hill. In colder areas,
mulch over winter.

**Pests and diseases** Rarely troubled
by pests. Sea kale roots tend to rise
to the surface. Cover exposed roots
with soil each autumn to prevent
winter-kill and to increase shoot
production the following year.

**Harvesting and storage** In late
winter, before the first shoots
appear, invert a large clay pot or
basket over the mound. To speed
shoot emergence, mulch around the
pot with straw or dry leaves. Check
periodically for shoots, and cut
them with a knife below the soil
surface when they are 6–8 inches
(15–20 cm) long. Cut third-year
plants for 1–2 weeks; harvest older
plants for 3–4 weeks. Remove the
pot when the harvest is finished.

**Special tips** Top-dress with compost
or well-rotted manure each spring.

*Cucumis sativus* CUCURBITACEAE

# CUCUMBER

THESE HEAT-LOVING PLANTS CAN BE GROWN ON A TRELLIS OR FENCE TO SAVE GARDEN SPACE. THEY ARE COOL AND REFRESHING IN SALADS, BUT THEY CAN ALSO BE PICKLED.

**Position** Plant in full sun, in a site with good air circulation, in light soil with well-rotted manure or compost worked in; pH 6.0–7.0.

**Cultivation** Cucumbers dislike cold soil, so wait for 3–4 weeks after the last frost to direct-seed or transplant them into the garden. Indoors, sow seed in peat pots 2–3 weeks before you plan to set them out, or presprout in a moist paper towel and plant into soil that has been warmed by covering with a sheet of black plastic mulch. Thin plants to

stand 1–1¼ feet (30–37.5 cm) apart in rows, or plant in "hills" (each with four or five plants) about 4 feet (1.2 m) apart. Mulch, or keep cultivated until plants begin to vine. Cucumbers need ample food and water; irrigate during dry spells and give them fish emulsion or compost tea once a month. Where the growing season permits, plant successive crops 6 weeks apart. Support on a trellis or fence.

**Pests and diseases** Use row covers to protect young plants from cucumber beetles, but remove the covers when the plants bloom. Trellising will improve air circulation and reduce the risk

HARDINESS
Zones 4 and
warmer.

DAYS TO MATURITY
48–70 frost-free
days, slightly less
for gherkins or
baby pickles.

COMMENTS
Spiny amaranth
*Amaranthus
spinosus* plants
standing among
cucumbers may
attract and trap
black cutworms
away from your
cucumbers.

Keep picking your cucumbers to encourage the vines to keep producing fruit. Try finely
chopping the flesh, draining, and combining with Greek yogurt, garlic and mint.

of mildew. Do not grow cucumbers
or their relatives, such as squash
and melons, in the same spot more
often than once every 3 years.
Sudden collapse of cucumber plants
indicates wilt disease, which is
spread by cucumber beetles.
Straw mulch may help to deter
beetle attack, and some cultivars
are less vulnerable to the beetles.
Successive plantings will extend the
harvest even where these beetles
are troublesome.

**Harvesting and storage** Cucumbers
are best picked small, at 3–4 inches
(7.5–10 cm) for pickling types and
6–8 inches (15–20 cm) for slicers.
A yellowish tinge at the blossom

end indicates overmaturity. Pick
often, especially during hot spells,
to encourage continued fruiting.
Pickle your excess cucumbers.

**Related plants**
'Burpless' cucumber *C. sativus*  Also
called Lebanese cucumber or
oriental cucumber. Cultivars include
'Sweet Slice', 'Burpless Hybrid' and
'Japanese Long Pickling'.
**Gynoecious cucumber *C. sativus***
This cultivar was bred to produce
only female flowers, which greatly
increases the yield per plant.
Gynoecious cucumbers require
another cucumber cultivar to
pollinate them (seeds of a pollinator
are included with packets of

# Cucumber continued

If you choose high-yielding bush cultivars, you will need only a small space to put in a few cucumber plants in order to maintain a good supply for the table.

gynoecious cucumbers). They also need higher soil fertility to support the higher yields. Cultivars include 'Saladin Hybrid' and 'Early Pride'.

**Pickling cucumber *C. sativus*** The fruits are also called gherkins or cornichons. Although all cucumbers can be pickled, some cultivars were selected for this purpose because of their small size, crispness or small seed cavity. They are often lighter green than slicing cultivars, with soft "spines" on the fruit. Suitable cultivars include 'Picklebush', 'Vert de Massy' and 'Bush Baby'.

**Serpent cucumber *Trichosanthes cucumerina* var. *anguina*** Also called snake gourd or club gourd.

A popular vegetable in Asian countries. The long, thin fruits will curve and coil on the ground, but grow straight if the vine is trellised.

**Slicing cucumber *C. sativus*** These cultivars are generally grown for fresh or salad use, rather than pickling, and are usually longer, smoother and darker green than the pickling types. Cultivars include 'Straight Eight', 'Spacemaster' and 'Marketmore'.

# *Cucurbita pepo*

## SQUASH, SUMMER

SUMMER SQUASH GROW QUICKLY, SO PICK
THE FRUITS EVERY FEW DAYS, WHILE THEY
ARE YOUNG AND TENDER.

**Position** Plant in full sun in
well-drained soil rich in humus;
pH 6.0–6.5. Needs good circulation.

**Cultivation** Sow when all danger
of frost is past, or start indoors in
individual pots 2–3 weeks before
last frost and transplant carefully to
avoid breaking roots. Space bush
types 1½–2 feet (45–60 cm) apart;
vining types need wider spacing,
up to 4 feet (1.2 m), and should
be planted in hills, with three or
four seeds to a hill. Cultivate or
mulch. Squash benefits from plenty
of compost or rotted manure.

**Pests and diseases** Use row covers
to protect young squash plants from
cucumber beetles and squash
borers; remove covers when the
plants bloom. Radishes or basil
interplanted with squash helps repel
beetles and squash bugs. Do not
plant where squash or its relatives,
such as melon and cucumber, have
grown the preceding year. Good air
circulation helps prevent mildew.
However, if plants are attacked by
mildew, spray foliage thoroughly
with a mild baking soda solution
(1 teaspoon to 1 quart [1 l] of
water). You can reduce the chance
of many squash diseases by planting
resistant cultivars. A straw mulch
will help to deter insects and keep

'Gold Rush', an attractive yellow-skinned zucchini (courgette). The fruit forms behind the flower, which gradually collapses as the fruit swells and grows.

the soil moist, which is essential for healthy fruit. Dust foliage with wood ashes to deter insect pests. Fruit that is not pollinated turns black and rots before reaching picking size. This often happens early in the season, before male blooms appear, or in cool spells, when pollinating insects are less active.

**Harvesting and storage** Pick summer squash small for best flavor. Harvest every few days to encourage more fruiting. Cut squash off with a sharp knife and handle carefully, as the skin bruises easily. Freeze or pickle excess fruit. For stuffing, pick blossoms in early morning, before they have been pollinated.

**Special tips** Successive plantings of just a few plants, sown a month apart, will extend the picking season in areas where squash often succumb to insects and disease. Vining types of summer squash can be grown up a trellis to save space.

**Related plants**

**Pattypan squash** *C. pepo* **var.** *melopepo* 'Early White Bush', 'Peter Pan Bush Scallop'.

**Yellow squash** *C. pepo* **var.** *melopepo* 'Seneca Prolific' and 'Butterstick' (straightnecks), or 'Golden Crookneck' and 'Pic-n-Pic Hybrid'.

**Zucchini** *C. pepo* **var.** *melopepo* 'Aristocrat' (dark green), 'Gold Rush' (yellow), 'Cocozelle' (striped).

# *Cucurbita pepo* var. *pepo*

HARDINESS
Zones 4 and
warmer.

DAYS TO MATURITY
100–115 frost-free
days. For use as
homegrown jack-
o'-lanterns in short-
season areas, grow
a cultivar such as
'Autumn Gold',
which is orange
even when
immature.

COMMENTS
Pumpkin vines like
to sprawl, but can
be gently pushed
back into place.

# PUMPKIN

AS FAMILIAR AS FALLING LEAVES IN AUTUMN,
THE HANDSOME PUMPKIN MAKES FINE PIES
AND BAKED DISHES, AS WELL AS JACK-O'-
LANTERNS FOR HALLOWE'EN.

**Position** Plant in full sun. Not fussy
about soil texture, but likes a fertile
soil; pH 6.0–7.0.

**Cultivation** Sow in hills 4–5 feet
(1.2–1.5 m) apart, two or three
seeds to a hill, after the last spring
frost. In short-season areas,
start your pumpkins indoors in
individual pots 2–3 weeks before
the last frost. Set out carefully to
avoid disturbing the roots. A good
shovelful of compost or well-rotted
manure in each hill will boost
growth. Mulch or cultivate until

the plants begin to vine. The
pumpkin plant's broad leaves will
shade out most weeds. If garden
space is limited, try growing some
of the space-saving extra small,
bush-type pumpkins.

**Pests and diseases** Row covers will
help to deter cucumber beetles and
squash borers, but remove them
when the plants bloom to allow
pollination. Straw mulch also helps
to deter cucumber beetles. Prevent
mildew by providing good air
circulation. Plants that collapse
before setting fruit are probably the
victims of the squash borer. Those
that collapse before the fruit ripens
may be infected with a wilt disease

# *Pumpkin* continued

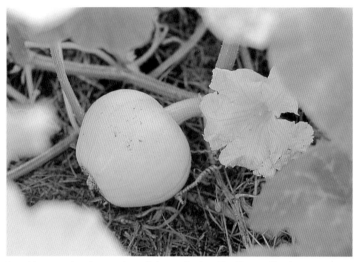

Pumpkins come in a huge variety of sizes and colors. The flowers, like those of other kinds of squash, can be stuffed, lightly fried and eaten.

spread by cucumber beetles. Cover the plants until they bloom to reduce the risk of crop loss.

**Harvesting and storage** Harvest pumpkins when they are fully colored and their shells are hard, or after light frost has killed the vines. Store in a cool, dry area. Pumpkins keep for several months but lose flavor in long storage. The cooked flesh freezes well, however. Cultivars meant for cooking, such as 'Small Sugar', taste better than large field pumpkins.

**Special tips** If you want to win the big-pumpkin contest, cultivate plants such as borage and lemon balm near your pumpkin patch to attract bees. Research shows that pumpkins pollinated by numerous bees form larger fruits. A crop of beans, peas or clover in the pumpkin patch will enrich the soil for next year's crop.

**Related plants**

**Japanese pumpkin *C. mixta*** Also called Hokkaido squash or Chinese pumpkin. This variety has a green skin and dark orange, moist, sweet flesh. While not suitable for carving, it has a superb flavor.

# *Cucurbita* spp.

HARDINESS
Zones 4 and
warmer.

DAYS TO MATURITY
85–110 frost-free
days.

COMMENTS
The flesh of the
fast-growing 'Gold
Nugget' (left) is
rich in flavor.

## SQUASH, WINTER

AROMATIC PLANTS, SUCH AS NASTURTIUM OR
MINT, MAY HELP REPEL PESTS FROM SQUASH.

**Position** Plant in full sun, in an area
with good air circulation. Prefers
rich, well-composted, well-drained
soil; pH 6.0–6.5.

**Cultivation** Sow 1–2 weeks after
the last spring frost, 1½–2 feet
(45–60 cm) apart in rows or in hills
4–5 feet (1.2–1.5 m) apart with
three or four plants in each hill. In
short-season areas, start indoors in
individual pots 2–3 weeks before
planting and set out in soil that has
been prewarmed with black plastic
mulch. Transplant carefully to avoid
damaging the roots. Mulch to hold
in the soil moisture.

**Pests and diseases** Use row covers
to protect young plants from
cucumber beetles and squash
borers, but remove when plants are
in bloom. Straw mulch will help to
deter insects, as will interplantings
of radishes or basil. Provide good
air circulation to avoid mildew.
Do not plant where squash or its
relatives, such as cucumbers and
melons, have been grown in the
preceding year. Mildew can be a
serious problem, especially in late-
summer damp spells. Plants may be
killed, or weakened too much to
ripen fruit. At the first sign of
mildew, spray foliage thoroughly
with a mild baking soda solution
(1 teaspoon to 1 quart [1 l] water).

# Squash, winter continued

'Sweet Dumpling' is a small and attractive squash that requires no curing before storage. Squash flowers can be stuffed, fried lightly and served as an entrée.

**Harvesting and storage** Harvest when the shell is hard enough that it cannot be dented with a finger-nail. Harvest all fruit as soon as light frost has killed the vines; any more than a light frost will shorten storage life. Leave on the ground to "cure" in the sun for 10–14 days, but cover the fruit if frost threatens. This curing sweetens the flesh and toughens the skin for storage. Wipe the skin with a cloth dipped in a weak bleach solution to prevent rot. Store in a cool, well-ventilated place.

**Related plants**

**Acorn squash *C. pepo* var. *pepo***
Also called pepper squash. Acorn-shaped, usually dark green to near black. Sweet, moist, orange flesh. High-yielding, usually five to seven fruits per plant. Try 'Ebony Acorn', 'Table Queen', 'Swan White' and 'Cream of the Crop' (white-skinned with off-white flesh).

**Delicata squash *C. pepo*** Also called sweet potato squash. Oblong fruits striped green and ivory, 8 inches (20 cm) long and 3 inches (7.5 cm) in diameter. Orange flesh. Doesn't need curing. Cultivars include 'Delicata' and 'Sugarloaf'.

**Spaghetti squash *C. pepo*** Also called vegetable spaghetti. Oval-shaped, with buff or light yellow skin and pale orange-yellow flesh. Bake, then scrape out the flesh with a fork (it separates into pasta-like

The vegetable marrow squash, also called Lebanese zucchini, is commonly eaten while small and immature, but can be left on the vine to attain its full size.

strands). Serve topped with tomato sauce. Cultivars include 'Vegetable Spaghetti' and 'Orangetti Hybrid'.

**'Sweet Dumpling' squash** *C. pepo* Flattened, round fruit, 3–4 inches (7.5–10 cm) in diameter, with pale orange flesh and striped skin.

**Vegetable marrow squash** *C. pepo* var. *pepo* There are bush forms, but most cultivars are trailing vines that can be trellised. Pick at 8–12 inches (20–30 cm) and use like summer squash or eggplant (aubergine). Cultivars include 'Cousa'.

**Buttercup squash** *C. maxima* Dark green and blocky, with a "button" or small turban at the blossom end. Orange-fleshed fruits that keep well. The Japanese kabocha squashes are

similar. Cultivars include 'Sweet Mama' and 'Honey Delight'.

**'Gold Nugget' squash** *C. maxima* A quick-maturing winter squash with round, orange fruits. A bush-type plant good for small gardens.

**Hubbard squash** *C. maxima* Also called blue hubbard. Large, warty fruits, usually one or two to a vine, with hard rind. An excellent keeper. Nonstringy flesh can be cooked, puréed and frozen. Cultivars include 'New England Blue Hubbard' and 'Hubbard Improved Green'.

**Butternut squash** *C. moschata* Small seed cavity with a thick neck of solid, orange flesh. An excellent keeper. Cultivars include 'Waltham Butternut' and 'Ponca'.

*Cynara cardunculus*

# CARDOON

THIS THISTLE-LIKE PLANT, A RELATIVE OF THE
GLOBE ARTICHOKE, IS GROWN CHIEFLY FOR
ITS STALKS, WHICH ARE BLANCHED AND USED
MUCH LIKE CELERY.

**Position** Plant in full sun in
well-drained, fertile soil with
ample moisture; pH 6.0–7.0.

**Cultivation** Start seedlings indoors
if season is short; otherwise, direct-
seed 1–2 weeks before the last
frost. Thin to 2 feet (60 cm) apart.
A month before autumn frost, or
earlier if the plant is large enough,
tie the leaf stalks together and wrap
the plant with burlap or heavy
paper to exclude sunlight and
whiten the stalks. Stalks will be
fully blanched in 3–4 weeks.

**Pests and diseases** Few pests trouble
this formidable-looking plant.
Provide good drainage to prevent
crown rot.

**Harvesting and storage** Harvest
blanched stalks as needed until a
hard freeze threatens, then bank the
plant with earth or straw to prolong
your harvest into winter. You can
also dig up and eat the main roots.

**Special tips** Where growing seasons
are short, cardoon plants may not
reach their full height but will still
supply usable stalks. Will withstand
light frost.

# *Cynara scolymus*

HARDINESS
Zones 8–9, mild coastal climates; in Zones 5–7 with special winter care.

DAYS TO MATURITY
May produce edible buds in the first year but the first harvest is more likely to be in the second year. In warm climates, buds appear in late spring; where cooler, in summer.

COMMENTS
'Green Globe' is widely available.

## ARTICHOKE, GLOBE

THIS PLANT IS GROWN CHIEFLY FOR ITS LARGE, EDIBLE FLOWER HEADS, BUT THE YOUNG SUCKERS CAN ALSO BE BLANCHED OR STEAMED AND EATEN LIKE ASPARAGUS.

**Position** Plant in full sun with protected exposure. Prefers rich, well-drained soil; near-neutral pH.

**Cultivation** Start seed indoors in late winter and transplant in late spring, when soil has warmed thoroughly. Can reach 5 feet (1.5 m) or more in height; space seedlings 2 feet (60 cm) apart in the row and allow 3 feet (90 cm) or more between rows. Be generous with compost or manure. Water deeply and mulch between the rows.

**Pests and diseases** Little troubled by insect pests but is susceptible to crown rot. Well-drained soil is essential. Do not allow mulch to smother the crown. In Zones 7 and colder, winter-kill is the chief problem. Cut the plant back in late autumn and protect over winter by inverting a basket or box over the crown and mulching deeply.

**Harvesting and storage** Cut the buds before the scales have begun to open, with 1 inch (2.5 cm) of stem still attached.

**Special tips** Side-dress with blood meal or other high-nitrogen fertilizer in early spring.

*Daucus carota* **subsp.** *sativus*

# CARROT

THE NUTRITIOUS CARROT IS A POTENT ALLY
IN YOUR BODY'S FIGHT AGAINST ILLNESS.

**Position** Plant in full sun in deep,
light soil without stones or other
obstructions. In heavier or shallow
soil, plant round or half-long
cultivars. Improve clay soil with
organic matter; pH 5.5–6.8.

**Cultivation** Sow the first crop in
early spring, after threat of severe
frost is past. Seed is very small; mix
half-and-half with fine sand to help
avoid overseeding. Plant a scant
½ inch (12 mm) deep and firm the
seedbed gently with the back of a
hoe. Mark the row well; carrots
are slow germinators and may not
appear for 3–4 weeks. Or drop a

radish seed every 2 inches (5 cm)
into the row with your carrot seeds
to help mark it. Radishes germinate
quickly and will also help break up
any soil-crusting that could smother
the more delicate carrot seedlings,
which look like fine blades of grass.
Keep the soil evenly moist until the
carrots are up. Thin to 2–3 inches
(5–7.5 cm) apart. Plant successive
crops every few weeks until
3 months before autumn frost.
Weed carrots carefully during their
growing period. Do not overwater
as continually wet soil causes rot.

**Pests and diseases** Use row covers
to deter carrot rust flies, which lay
eggs at the base of carrot plants.

HARDINESS
Zones 3 and
warmer. Plant
early-maturing
types in cold areas.

DAYS TO MATURITY
50–70 days. Will
tolerate light frosts.

COMMENTS
Early-maturing
'Parmex' and
'Planet' suit heavy
soils. 'Minicor' and
'Scarlet Nantes' do
well in moderately
deep soils. Long
'Imperator' and
'Gold Pak' suit
deep, light soils.

Short carrot cultivars, such as 'Early Horn' (above), do well in containers. The longer Nantes or Amsterdam-type cultivars (facing page) are grown in deeper soils.

The larvae feed on the roots. Crops planted after late spring and harvested before late summer often escape damage without protection. Rotate carrot plantings to avoid bacterial diseases. Twisted roots point to inadequate thinning. Forked roots often mean that the seedbed was not fine enough. Hairy roots indicate excessive fertility. Do not use fresh manure or high-nitrogen fertilizer on carrot beds. Splitting occurs when heavy rain follows a dry period.

**Harvesting and storage** Carrots are ready to eat when fully colored. Pull when the ground is moist to avoid breaking roots, or dig with a garden fork. Harvest autumn crops before the ground freezes, or earlier if shoulders (root tops) appear above the ground. Dry in the sun and store, packed in dry leaves or straw, in a cool, moist place. To spread the harvest, carrots can be harvested while they are still young.

**Special tips** Cover newly seeded carrot rows with boards or black plastic for 3 weeks, then remove. This preserves soil moisture and prevents sprouting of weeds ahead of the slower-germinating carrots. Never step on the carrot seedbed. If space is limited, grow carrots in the ornamental garden. Their brilliant feathery tops are pretty in a border.

*Eruca sativa*

**HARDINESS**
All Zones.

**DAYS TO MATURITY**
40 days, although thinnings can be harvested earlier.

**COMMENTS**
Other common names include roquette, rucola and rugula.

# ARUGULA (ROCKET)

THE TENDER LEAVES OF THIS EUROPEAN GARDEN FAVORITE ADD A NUTTY, PEPPERY BITE TO SALADS AND SANDWICHES.

**Position** Plant in full sun as well as half-day sun or partial shade. Avoid hot, dry positions. In mild climates, grow as a winter vegetable. Not fussy, but prefers fertile, moist soil; pH 6.0–7.0.

**Cultivation** Direct-seed as early as possible in spring. Light frost will not harm the seedlings. Thin to 8 inches (20 cm) apart, using thinnings in salads.

**Pests and diseases** Cover with row cover to deter flea beetles. Sown too late, spring-planted arugula will bolt to seed in warm weather before reaching a harvestable size. In cold climates, sow seed indoors and set out as soon as the ground can be worked. An autumn crop, direct-seeded or set out as seedlings 1–2 months before the first frost, will stand longer without bolting. Try making successive plantings a week apart.

**Harvesting and storage** Pick large leaves from the bottom of the plant. New leaves will sprout from the center crown. Weekly picking should yield eight to 12 large leaves per plant. Use fresh; do not freeze.

**Special tips** Add the flowers of bolting plants to salads.

# *Foeniculum vulgare* var. *azoricum*

**HARDINESS**
Zones 4 and warmer; grow as a winter vegetable in mild areas.

**DAYS TO MATURITY**
65–90 days.

**COMMENTS**
Tolerates light frost. Cultivars include 'Zefa Fino' and 'Romy'. Other common names include finocchio.

# FENNEL, FLORENCE

FLORENCE FENNEL IS GROWN CHIEFLY FOR ITS ENLARGED LEAF BASES, WHICH HAVE AN INTRIGUING FLAVOR OF LICORICE.

**Position** Plant in full sun in fertile, well-drained soil; pH 6.5–7.0.

**Cultivation** In cool-spring areas, direct-seed spring crop 2–4 weeks before last frost and thin to stand 8–10 inches (20–25 cm) apart. Transplants poorly. Since it bolts to seed quickly in hot weather, start seedlings in warmer areas in peat pots or individual pots a month before last frost; do not let roots outgrow the pots before setting out. Sow small, successive crops where the season permits; avoid plantings that will mature in hot, dry weather.

Autumn crops are easier to transplant; set out 2 months before first frost. Keep weeded and mulched; water during dry spells.

**Pests and diseases** Handpick off celery- or parsleyworms, which are green caterpillars with black and yellow stripes. Florence fennel becomes woody when overmature. Plant small, successive crops to prolong your harvest.

**Harvesting and storage** Cut the entire plant below the base of the bulb. Use fronds as seasoning for fish. Fennel does not freeze well.

**Special tips** Use the ripe seed of bolted plants in salads.

*Glycine max*

HARDINESS
Zones 5 and
warmer.

DAYS TO MATURITY
65–120 frost-free
days.

COMMENTS
Seed companies
sometimes offer
variants by seed
color, usually
yellow, green
or black.

# SOYBEAN

ONE OF THE OLDEST FOOD CROPS, THE
NUTRITIOUS SOYBEAN IS WIDELY USED IN
ORIENTAL CUISINES, EITHER FRESH OR
PREPARED AS TOFU, SOY SAUCE OR MISO.

**Position** Plant in full sun in light,
well-drained soil; pH 6.0–7.0.

**Cultivation** Sow after frost danger
is past, 1 inch (2.5 cm) deep and
2 inches (5 cm) apart. Keep
cultivated until plants grow large
enough to shade out weeds. Water
is critical when plants are in flower.

**Pests and diseases** Less troubled by
pests than other beans. Rotate
plantings of soybean and its legume
relatives, such as beans and peas.
May not mature for use as a dried

bean in short-season areas, but
some cultivars can be grown for
use as fresh beans.

**Harvesting and storage** Harvest for
fresh use when beans are plump
and tender. Bottle or freeze fresh
beans. For dry soybeans, pull the
plants when most of the foliage has
died and hang them to finish drying
in a well-ventilated place. Shell and
store as you would any dried bean.

**Special tips** 'Envy' and 'Hakucho
Early' are short-season cultivars,
primarily for using fresh. 'Panther'
and 'Black Jet' need a longer
season and are grown primarily
for use as dried beans.

# *Helianthus tuberosus*

HARDINESS
All Zones.

DAYS TO MATURITY
110–150 days for
a spring-planted,
first-year crop.
Autumn-planted
crops are ready
the next autumn.

COMMENTS
'Fuseau' is a
smooth-skinned
yam type; 'French
Mammoth White'
is a traditional
knobby tuber;
'Sugarball' is a
round tuber.

## JERUSALEM ARTICHOKE

THE JERUSALEM ARTICHOKE IS A HARDY
PERENNIAL VEGETABLE. IT PRODUCES TASTY
POTATO-LIKE TUBERS.

**Position** Plant in full sun or partial
shade. Plant away from other
garden beds, as most cultivars are
perennial in all Zones and many are
invasive. Not fussy, but prefers
loose, fertile soil; pH 6.0–6.5.

**Cultivation** Plant pieces of tuber
6–8 weeks before the last spring
frost or in autumn. Plant in the
same way as potatoes, each piece
with one or more "eyes," 3 inches
(7.5 cm) deep and 1–1½ feet
(30–45 cm) apart in rows or beds.
Mulch or weed early; plants will
grow quickly and shade out weeds.

**Pests and diseases** Rarely troubled
by pests and diseases. Difficult to
eradicate once it is established, but
diligent harvesting each year will
keep the bed under control.

**Harvesting and storage** Mulch the
bed to keep the ground diggable
after a hard freeze. Jerusalem
artichokes do not store well, so
dig as needed. Cook them as you
would potatoes.

**Special tips** Plants can withstand
moderate frost; freezing does not
damage tubers. Other common
names include sunchoke.

*Ipomoea aquatica*    CONVOLVULACEAE

HARDINESS
Zones 7 and
warmer.

DAYS TO MATURITY
100–120 days.
It grows poorly
in cool seasons
and will not
withstand frost.

COMMENTS
Named cultivars
are not generally
available. Oriental
seed suppliers may
offer variants based
on growth habit or
leaf size.

# SPINACH, WATER

A MEMBER OF THE MORNING GLORY FAMILY,
WATER SPINACH IS A PERENNIAL WHEN
GROWN IN ITS NATIVE SUBTROPICS.

**Position** Plant in full sun or partial
shade in rich, constantly moist soil;
pH 5.5–6.5.

**Cultivation** Start the seed indoors
and set out after frost danger is well
past. Allow plenty of space as this
plant sends out runners and roots
at the leaf nodes, quickly growing
into a clump. Keep the soil quite
moist, as water spinach is really a
semi-aquatic plant.

**Pests and diseases** Not generally
troubled by pests. Water spinach
needs day temperatures higher

than 72°F (22°C) to grow quickly.
Do not plant too early.

**Harvesting and storage** Pick young
leaves and shoots for use in salads,
stir-fries or cooked dishes.

**Special tips** You can eat both the
young leaves and the shoots. Other
common names include swamp
cabbage and kankon.

# *Ipomoea batatas*

HARDINESS
Zones 5 and
warmer.

DAYS TO MATURITY
90–120 frost-free
days.

COMMENTS
Wait until the soil
is thoroughly warm
before mulching
heat-loving plants,
such as sweet
potato, otherwise
you are keeping
the underlayer
of soil cold.

# SWEET POTATO

SWEET POTATOES ARE A WARM-WEATHER
CROP THAT PRODUCE TASTY AND NUTRITIOUS
TUBEROUS ROOTS. THEY CAN BE COOKED IN
THE SAME WAY AS POTATOES.

**Position** Plant in full sun in loose,
well-drained soil that is not too rich;
pH 5.5–6.5.

**Cultivation** Plant from growing
shoots or "slips," which are
available by mail order or at many
garden centers. Plant after frost
danger is well past. With a rake,
make a ridge of soil 6–10 inches
(15–25 cm) high and 6–8 inches
(15–20 cm) wide. Plant the slips
into the ridge about 12 inches
(30 cm) apart. Mound the soil onto
the ridge at least once before the

vining plants make further
cultivation impossible. Keep the
newly set slips watered until they
begin to grow. After that, irrigate
sweet potatoes only during
extended dry spells. Although sweet
potato is a perennial, it is usually
grown as an annual in cooler
climates. The stems sprawl across
the garden bed and tend to grow
roots at leaf nodes, many producing
more tubers, so don't be tempted to
trellis your plants or keep the stems
off the ground. Allow plenty of
space for a bountiful crop.

**Pests and diseases** Use certified
disease-free slips. Rotate plantings
and keep soil organic matter high

# Sweet potato continued

The leaves of sweet potato look very similar to those of its close relative, morning glory *Ipomoea purpurea*.

to reduce nematode damage. Deer love the tender leaves and shoots; if they are a problem in your area, you may need to fence off your sweet potatoes.

**Harvesting and storage** Dig up sweet potatoes before frost or as soon as the vines have been killed by a light frost. Left in the ground, they will spoil. The tuberous roots are very tender, so dig and handle them carefully. Cure them for 10–14 days in a warm, fairly humid area, and store where the temperature does not fall below 55°F (13°C). With proper storage, they will keep for 6 months or

more. You can also cook the roots and freeze the pulp.

**Special tips** Sweet potatoes are divided into dry-flesh and moist-flesh types. The latter are often called "yams," although they are not botanically related to yams. The cultivars 'Georgia Jet', 'Vardeman' and 'Centennial' are moist-flesh sweet potatoes. Dry-flesh cultivars, which keep better, include 'Orlis' and 'Yellow Jersey'.

*Lactuca sativa* ASTERACEAE

**HARDINESS**
All Zones; grow as a winter vegetable in mild areas.

**DAYS TO MATURITY**
40–90 days. The young leaves and thinnings can be harvested earlier. Leaf lettuces mature most quickly, followed by bibb and romaine (Cos).

**COMMENTS**
The iceberg lettuce (left) forms a crisp, cabbage-like head.

# LETTUCE

HEAD LETTUCES REQUIRE A LONGER SEASON THAN SOME OTHERS. THE YOUNG PLANTS WILL WITHSTAND LIGHT FROST OR MODERATE FROST WITH PROTECTION.

**Position** Plant in full sun in cool weather, partial shade in warm weather. Prefers fertile, well-drained soil; pH 6.0–6.8.

**Cultivation** Sow the seed of leafy types directly in the ground a month before the last frost. Barely cover the seeds and firm the soil with the back of a hoe. Start head-forming types indoors 6–8 weeks before the last frost and set out, 8–10 inches (20–25 cm) apart, 1–2 weeks before last frost. Leave leaf lettuces unthinned for "baby"

salad greens and pick at about 21 days, or thin to encourage large-leaved plants. Sow or transplant successive crops until a month before the first frost, ending with a cold-tolerant cultivar such as 'Winter Density'. Grow summer-maturing crops in partial shade, or cover with a lath frame to shield them from the midday sun. Cultivate shallowly or mulch; water frequently, especially during hot spells, as the stress of a water shortage can cause them to bolt, running to seed prematurely. Water at ground level, rather than spraying with the garden hose, because damp foliage encourages various rots. For best results when growing these quick-to-mature

# *Lettuce* continued

The cultivar 'Little Gem' forms a neat little heart. These and other similar attractive varieties can be planted as an edible border around your flower beds.

vegetables, provide a regular, light application of a nitrogen fertilizer, compost tea or fish emulsion to ensure that growth is not checked in any way.

**Pests and diseases** Quick-growing lettuce seldom has pest problems, but rotate crops to avoid soilborne diseases. Control slugs by trapping them in shallow pans of beer set flush with the soil surface. Bitter leaves suggest heat and water stress, or simply overmature lettuce. Plant small crops at frequent intervals, 7–10 days apart, for a continuous supply.

**Harvesting and storage** Harvest as needed for fresh use. Cut unthinned leaf lettuce with scissors 1 inch (2.5 cm) above roots, leaving the plants to resprout for a second harvest. Cut larger whole plants at soil level. Harvest lettuce in the morning, when it is juicy and crisp.

**Special tips** Many of the varieties that can be cut leaf by leaf for the salad bowl make attractive additions to the flower or vegetable garden border and are decorative enough to grow in containers on a sunny terrace or apartment balcony. If your family is small or your needs are limited, look for packets of seeds that contain a mixture of varieties. These are often sold under the name of "Mesclun lettuce mix."

Many of the crinkly, red-leafed cultivars of lettuce make a welcome addition of both color and texture to a bowl of mixed salad greens.

Lettuce germinates poorly at temperatures above 80°F (27°C). Prechill seed before sowing, or start summer crops in a cool place.

### Related plants

**Bibb lettuce** *L. sativa* Also called Boston, butterhead or cabbage lettuce. Forms loose heads of soft, folded leaves. Cultivars include 'Buttercrunch', 'Dark Green Boston', 'Sangria' (red-tinged leaves) and 'Tom Thumb' (miniature bibb).

**Iceberg lettuce** *L. sativa* Also called crisphead or cabbage lettuce. Forms a tight head of crisp-textured leaves. Prefers a long, cool growing season. Cultivars include 'Great Lakes' and 'Ithaca'.

**Leaf lettuce** *L. sativa* This is the quickest and easiest-to-grow member of the lettuce clan. It can double as an ornamental garden edging. It is also called cutting lettuce. Instead of heads, it forms loose leaves that can be harvested while quite small. Cultivars include 'Black Seeded Simpson', 'Red Sails', 'Salad Bowl' and 'Oak Leaf'.

**Romaine lettuce** *L. sativa* Also called Cos lettuce. Forms an upright, elongated head of crisp, ribbed leaves. Has a better heat tolerance than does iceberg. Cultivars include 'Parris Island', 'Valmaine' and 'Rosalita' (a red-leafed cultivar). This variety is the one preferred for the famous Caesar salad.

*Lactuca sativa* var. *augustana*

HARDINESS
Zones 3 and
warmer. In colder
areas, harvest the
leaves only if the
stalk takes too long
to develop.

DAYS TO MATURITY
45 days for leaves
(thinnings can be
harvested earlier);
90 days for stalks.
Tolerates light frost.

COMMENTS
Named cultivars
are not generally
available.

# CELTUCE

CELTUCE HAS LETTUCE-LIKE LEAVES AND
CELERY-LIKE STALKS. WHEN COOKED, IT
TASTES LIKE A CROSS BETWEEN SUMMER
SQUASH AND ARTICHOKE.

**Position**  Plant in full sun in well-
drained soil; pH 6.0–6.7. Otherwise
not fussy.

**Cultivation**  Sow in early spring
and again in midsummer. Best if
matured in cool weather. Seeds are
small; sow thinly and cover lightly.
Thin to 1 foot (30 cm) apart,
using the thinnings with other
salad greens.

**Pests and diseases**  Usually free from
pests and diseases. Water frequently
to delay the leaves becoming bitter
and to help keep the central stalk
tender. Warm weather induces the
plants to bolt to seed, which also
toughens the stalk.

**Harvesting and storage**  Pick the
leaves as needed. Use young leaves
in salads and cook older ones. Cut
the stalk at its base and peel for use
as a raw or boiled vegetable, or in
stir-fries and soups.

**Special tips**  Other common names
include asparagus lettuce.

# *Lagenaria siceraria*

HARDINESS
Zones 5 and
warmer.

DAYS TO MATURITY
90 frost-free days
for mature gourds;
a shorter period for
immature, edible-
sized fruits.

COMMENTS
Other common
names are cucuzzi,
po gua and yugao.
Other types of
*L. siceraria* include
calabash, dipper
gourd and
sugar trough.

# GOURD, BOTTLE

ALTHOUGH EDIBLE, BOTTLE GOURDS ARE
COMMONLY GROWN AS ORNAMENTALS.

**Position** Plant in full sun in
well-drained, rich soil; pH 6.0–6.5.
Provide good air circulation.

**Cultivation** Plant after frost danger
is past. Sow two or three seeds to
a hill and site hills 6 feet (1.8 m)
apart, or sow more closely if you
can train the vine to a trellis or
fence. Mulch or keep weeded. If
allowed to sprawl, the vining plant
will eventually shade out weeds. It
is drought-tolerant, but irrigate for
larger and more numerous fruits.

**Pests and diseases** Use a trellis to
improve air circulation and lessen
mildew problems. Rotate plantings
of gourds and their relatives, such
as squash and melons. In short-
season areas, pinch off flowers after
the plant has set several fruits, to
ensure maturity before frost.

**Harvesting and storage** Pick young
fruits and cook as you would
summer squash. For use as a
birdhouse, dry the mature gourd
until the seeds inside rattle. Wax
the gourd to preserve it.

**Special tips** Hang up dried gourds
for birdhouses. Cut an entrance for
the birds by drilling many small
holes close together, then scrape out
the center and dry out the gourd.

*Lens culinaris*

HARDINESS
Zones 5 and
warmer.

DAYS TO MATURITY
120–150 days.

COMMENTS
Named cultivars
not generally
available.

# LENTIL

A STAPLE IN MEDITERRANEAN CUISINES, THE
PROTEIN-RICH RED LENTIL IS A RELATIVE OF
THE PEA AND IS NEARLY AS EASY TO GROW.

**Position** Plant in full sun in light,
well-drained soil; pH 5.8–6.2.

**Cultivation** Sow 1–2 weeks before
last spring frost, about 1 inch
(2.5 cm) deep and 3–4 inches
(7.5–10 cm) apart. Plants have
tendrils, like peas, but grow only
about 1⅓ feet (40 cm) tall and do
not need a trellis. Weed or mulch
and irrigate during dry spells until
the pods begin to dry, then
withhold water to hasten drying.

**Pests and diseases** Avoid mildew by
providing good air circulation. If
weevils are a problem, do not grow
where beans or peas have grown in
the preceding year. Rainy or humid
weather may cause mature seeds to
sprout or rot in their pods. Pull
plants when most of the foliage has
died and hang up by the roots in
a well-ventilated place to finish the
drying process.

**Harvesting and storage** Harvest as
you would dried bean varieties, but
do not remove from pods until you
are ready to use. Freeze well-dried
pods for several hours to avoid
potential weevil problems, and store
in airtight cans or jars.

**Special tips** Lentils keep better if
they are left in their pods.

*Lepidium sativum*

HARDINESS
Zones 2 and
warmer; grow as a
winter vegetable in
mild areas.

DAYS TO MATURITY
21–35 days.
Will withstand
severe frost.

COMMENTS
Other common
names are curly
cress and
peppergrass.
Named cultivars
are not generally
available.

# CRESS

QUICK AND EASY TO GROW, CRESS ADDS A
SPARK TO SALADS OR IS A PRETTY GARNISH.

**Position** Plant in full sun or partial
shade in soil that is moist and rich
in humus; pH 6.0–7.0.

**Cultivation** Sow thickly in rows in
early spring, 4–6 weeks before the
last frost. Barely cover and firm the
soil with the back of a hoe. Sow
successive small plantings every
7 days until 2 weeks after last frost.
Later plantings may bolt to seed in
summer heat. Sow autumn crop
2–4 weeks before the first frost.

**Pests and diseases** Do not grow
where members of the cabbage
family have been grown in the

preceding year. Row covers will
help to deter flea beetles. Hot
weather and inadequate supplies
of water will cause cress to bolt to
seed prematurely.

**Harvesting and storage** Cut with
shears just above the crown and let
the plants resprout for two or three
more cuttings.

**Special tips** Upland cress *Barbarea
verna* is also called American cress,
scurvy grass or cressy greens. It
has a spicy flavor like watercress
(see page 202). It forms a small
rosette of dark green, rounded
leaves, which can be harvested
whole or leaf by leaf. Sow as
above and thin to 6 inches (15 cm).

## *Luffa acutangula* and *L. cylindrica*          *Cucurbitaceae*

HARDINESS
Zones 5 and warmer.

DAYS TO MATURITY
80 days for immature, edible fruits. Up to 150 days for fully mature fruits.

COMMENTS
Common names include Chinese okra, dish cloth vine, loofah and vegetable sponge.

# LUFFA

LUFFA PRODUCES SQUASHLIKE FRUITS THAT ARE EDIBLE WHEN YOUNG. ITS MATURE FRUITS ARE DRIED AND USED AS SPONGES.

**Position**  Plant in full sun, near a fence or trellis, in rich, well-drained soil; pH 6.0–6.5.

**Cultivation**  In warm areas, plant after last frost, two to three seeds in hills about 6 feet (1.8 m) apart, or closer. In colder areas, start seeds indoors 2–3 weeks before last frost. Set out when frost danger is past. Train to a fence or trellis; luffa vines grow to 15 feet (4.5 m) or more.

**Pests and diseases**  Little troubled by pests and disease, but provide good air circulation. In cooler areas,

pinch off flowers after several large fruits have set, to ensure maturity before the first frost.

**Harvesting and storage**  Pick fruits when 4–6 inches (10–15 cm) long and cook them as you would summer squash. For sponges, leave fruits on until they turn yellow, then hang up and dry in an airy place. Soak to loosen the skin from the fibrous interior, remove skin, and let dry again. Shake out the seeds.

**Special tips**  Named cultivars are not generally available. *L. acutangula* produces 1¼-foot (37.5 cm), dark green, smooth-skinned fruit; *L. cylindrica* produces 1¾-foot (52.5 cm), light green, ridged fruit.

*Lycopersicon esculentum* SOLANACEAE

**HARDINESS**
Zones 3 and warmer.

**DAYS TO MATURITY**
52–90 frost-free days from transplanting. Small-fruited cultivars mature fastest.

**COMMENTS**
Low-acid tomatoes, such as 'Orange Boy' (left), are milder and sweeter than some other cultivars.

# TOMATO

PURCHASED TOMATOES CAN'T COMPARE WITH AN OLD-FASHIONED TOMATO GROWN IN YOUR OWN GARDEN. TRY TO FIND SOME OF THE "HEIRLOOM" CULTIVARS FOR FLAVOR YOU WON'T BELIEVE.

**Position** Plant in full sun in fertile, deep, well-drained soil; pH 6.0–7.0.

**Cultivation** In long-season areas, tomatoes can be direct-seeded, but they are usually started indoors 5–6 weeks before the last spring frost. Set out 2–3 feet (60–90 cm) apart if plants are to be allowed to sprawl, or as close as 1¼ feet (37.5 cm) if they are to be staked or caged. Use black plastic mulch to prewarm the soil in short-season areas. Plant tomatoes by burying the

stem horizontally, right up to the topmost leaves. New roots will emerge from the buried stem, making a sturdier plant. If the tomato is staked, tie the vine to the stake with soft cloth strips, not wire or string, to avoid damaging the plant. Some gardeners prune tomatoes by pinching out leafy shoots that emerge from leaf axils, but this type of pruning is not necessary. Water tomatoes regularly but do not fertilize until the plant is well established and in full blossom. Then give weak compost tea or fish emulsion. Too much nitrogen will result in lots of foliage but few fruits. Mulch will help retain soil moisture but will also cool the soil,

# *Tomato* continued

Cherry tomatoes produce generous quantities of fruit in a variety of colors.
They are perfect for salads and lunch boxes.

so do not mulch tomatoes until the soil is well warmed.

**Pests and diseases** Protect young plants from cutworms with cardboard or metal collars. Handpick off tomato hornworms or control them with BT, a microbial insecticide. Folklore states that planting basil with tomatoes helps repel hornworms. To avoid soilborne diseases, do not plant where tomatoes or their relatives, such as eggplants (aubergines) and potatoes, have been grown in the preceding 2 years. If that is not possible, grow disease-resistant cultivars if you suspect your soil harbors diseases such as Fusarium

or Verticillium wilt. Blossom-end rot indicates that the plant is not taking up enough calcium from the soil. If soil calcium levels are adequate, the problem is probably a lack of soil moisture. Keep the soil moist but not soggy. Dark brown, circular spots on tomato leaves suggest fungal disease or blight, which can be a serious problem in prolonged humid weather. Provide good air circulation and do not disturb plants when they are wet.

**Harvesting and storage** Pick the fruit when it is evenly colored but still firm. Bottle, freeze or dry excess tomatoes. Cover tomato plants to protect them through a light, early

Paste tomatoes have fewer seeds and less juice than slicing tomatoes, which makes them the right choice for soups and sauces.

frost, but harvest all fruit when more severe frost threatens. Completely green tomatoes will not ripen; pickle them or make into chutney. Blemish-free fruit that has begun to whiten or change color will continue to ripen. Wrap each tomato in tissue or newspaper and keep in a spot that stays above 55°F (13°C); check often and discard any fruit that develops bad spots.

**Special tips** Tomato cultivars are usually described as "indeterminate" or "determinate." Indeterminates continue to grow and set fruit all season, and usually require a sturdy cage or stake. Determinates stop growing and flowering when they reach a certain height. They are often earlier to mature and may not require caging, but they produce fruit for shorter periods than indeterminates. The letters often given after a cultivar's name indicate resistance to the following diseases or pests: V—Verticillium wilt, F—Fusarium wilt, N—nematodes, T—tobacco mosaic virus. Where space is limited, plant tall-growing tomatoes at the back of the flower garden or tie them to a wire fence.

### Related plants
**Beefsteak tomato *L. esculentum***
Large, fleshy fruit, up to 2 pounds (1 kg) and more, with meaty flesh and often a thick central core. Most

# Tomato continued

The tiny fruits of currant tomatoes are produced in abundance. They look most attractive left in sprays in salads, and as garnishes.

are indeterminate. Cultivars include 'Burpee's Supersteak Hybrid', 'Beefmaster' and many "heirloom" cultivars such as 'Giant Belgium' and 'Pink Ponderosa'.

**Cherry tomato** *L. esculentum* **var. cerasiforme** Prolific bearers of fruit that is usually about 1 inch (2.5 cm) in diameter, often borne in grape-like clusters. Cultivars include 'Sweet 100' (red, indeterminate), 'Gold Nugget' (yellow-orange, determinate) and 'Green Grape' (green-yellow, determinate).

**Low-acid tomato** *L. esculentum* Reduced acidity usually means milder flavor, with sweet undertones. Yellow-skinned cultivars are often, but not always, low in acid. Try 'Pink Girl' (pink skin, indeterminate), 'Lemon Boy' (yellow skin, indeterminate), 'Jetstar' (red skin, determinate) and 'Orange Boy' (orange skin, indeterminate).

**Paste tomato** *L. esculentum* Meatier than other tomatoes, with fewer seeds and less juice. Most cultivars are determinate, and many have concentrated fruit-set, with up to 90 percent of the fruit ripening at once. Cultivars include 'Roma' (small, pear-shaped), 'Milano' (early maturity, plum-shaped) and 'Royal Chico' (large, flat-sided, plum-shaped).

**Patio tomato** *L. esculentum* Determinate cultivars bred for growing in containers, but also

The large, meaty beefsteak tomato is the classic, old-fashioned garden tomato. Because the fruits are so heavy, most cultivars need sturdy stakes or cages for support.

good for small gardens. Cultivars include 'Patio' and 'Better Bush'.

**Pear tomato *L. esculentum* var. *pyriforme*** The fruits look like tiny pears. Red and yellow variants are available. The vigorous, indeterminate vines will need staking or caging.

**Slicing tomato *L. esculentum*** Grown primarily for fresh use. Scores of cultivars are available in a wide range of colors, growth habits, maturity dates and disease resistance. Among the most popular are 'Early Girl' (small red fruit, early-ripening), 'Big Boy' (large, red fruit), 'Celebrity' (large, red fruit, very disease-resistant) and 'Jubilee' (large, yellow-orange fruit).

**Currant tomato *L. pimpinellifolium*** Has tiny, currant-sized fruit. Both red and yellow variants are available. The vigorous, indeterminate vines will need cages or stakes for support.

# *Nasturtium officinale*

HARDINESS
Zones 3 and
warmer; grow as a
winter vegetable in
warmer areas or
indoors in pots
almost anywhere.

DAYS TO MATURITY
120–150 days. In
short-season areas,
a newly established
watercress bed
may not produce
a harvest in the
first year.

COMMENTS
Named cultivars
are not generally
available.

# WATERCRESS

AT ITS BEST IN AUTUMN AND EARLY SPRING,
WATERCRESS IS A TASTY AND HEALTHFUL
ADDITION TO SALADS AND SANDWICHES.

**Position** Plant in full sun or partial
shade in wet, well-limed soil that is
rich in humus, preferably at the
edge of a stream or stream-fed
pond; pH 6.0–7.0.

**Cultivation** Start indoors 4–8 weeks
before the last spring frost, or
sprinkle seeds as thinly as possible
where they are to grow, about a
month before the last frost, pressing
them into the soil. Fill gaps in the
planting by breaking off pieces of
stem and pressing them into the
soil, where they will root easily.
Gardeners without access to
constantly moist soil can grow
watercress in pots, indoors or out.
Set pots in pans of water and
change the water daily to avoid the
soil becoming sour and to prevent
attracting breeding mosquitoes.

**Pests and diseases** Little troubled by
pests and diseases.

**Harvesting and storage** Harvest the
leaves as needed, midautumn
through early spring, and including
winter where the climate permits.

**Special tips** The flavor of the leaves
deteriorates during the period the
plants are flowering.

*Pastinaca sativa*

HARDINESS
All Zones.

DAYS TO MATURITY
126–140 days.

COMMENTS
Steam or bake
parsnips as you
would potatoes.
Popular cultivars
include 'Hollow
Crown' and
'Harris Model'.

# PARSNIP

PARSNIPS LOOK RATHER LIKE CREAMY WHITE
CARROTS BUT HAVE A DISTINCTIVE FLAVOR.

**Position** Plant in full sun in friable,
open, well-drained soil; pH 6.0–7.0.

**Cultivation** Sow after spring frosts
have finished. Sow seeds directly
where they are going to grow in a
furrow 2½ inches (6 cm) deep and
keep moist until germinated.
Parsnip seeds take 21–28 days to
germinate. Thin seedlings to
2–3 inches (5–7.5 cm) apart and
control weeds by hand-weeding
and cultivation. Do not overfeed
with nitrogen fertilizers.

**Pests and diseases** Rarely troubled
by pests. Shallow, heavy soil or
fresh manure in the soil may result
in misshapen roots. Remove stones
and break up clods before planting.

**Harvesting and storage** Start pulling
early to spread the harvest. Those
left keep well in the soil. In winter
cover crowns with a thick layer of
straw mulch and mark the bed. Dig
through mulch layer all winter for a
continuous, fresh harvest. Roots
store for up to 2 weeks on a shelf
and a little longer in the refrigerator.

**Special tips** If parsnips are grown
on a well-prepared and fertilized
bed, extra fertilizer is rarely needed,
but liquid feeds, such as compost
tea, applied in midseason, will
promote faster growth.

*Persicaria odorata* POLYGONACEAE

HARDINESS
Zones 9–10.

DAYS TO MATURITY
Leaves can be
picked as soon
as the plant is
established.

COMMENTS
This plant grows
1–2 feet
(30–60 cm) tall.
Its other common
names include
laksa leaf, laksa
plant and
knotweed.

# VIETNAMESE MINT

THE SPICY LEAVES OF THIS ATTRACTIVE PLANT
HAVE RED MARKINGS TOWARD THE STEM,
BUT THESE OFTEN DISAPPEAR IN WINTER OR
WHEN THE PLANT IS GROWN IN SHADE.

**Position** Plant in a well-drained,
moist position in partial shade to
full sun; pH 6.0–7.0.

**Cultivation** Set out plants about
1⅓ feet (40 cm) apart. Given ideal
conditions, Vietnamese mint can be
invasive as the stems root wherever
they touch the ground. However,
these spreading stems are easily
pulled out. Growing it in a pot or
hanging basket overcomes this
potential problem in warm, humid
areas. In colder areas it is best
grown as an annual as it does not
tolerate frost.

**Pests and diseases** Little troubled by
pests and diseases.

**Harvesting and storage** Cut the
stems as needed. The older leaves
are hotter, spicier and more
flavorsome than younger ones and
the strongly flavored stems can be
removed before serving.

**Special tips** Cuttings are easily
grown. Stems will quickly sprout
roots if they are placed in water,
or you can simply snip off the
new plants where the stems have
touched the soil and rooted.

*Petroselinum crispum* var. *tuberosum*

HARDINESS
Zones 4 and warmer.

DAYS TO MATURITY
78–90 days.
Will withstand severe frost (frost actually sweetens the flavor).

COMMENTS
This plant is also commonly known as turnip-rooted parsley. 'Early Sugar' is a short-rooted cultivar.

# PARSLEY, HAMBURG

GROWN FOR ITS THICK, WHITE TAPROOT RATHER THAN ITS LEAVES, HAMBURG PARSLEY IS ATTRACTIVE IN THE GARDEN AND TASTY AS WELL.

**Position** Plant in full sun in loose, deep, well-drained soil, free of stones; pH 6.0–7.0.

**Cultivation** Sow 4–6 weeks before the last spring frost and keep moist until germinated, which can take several weeks. Thin to stand 6–8 inches (15–20 cm) apart. If started indoors, set plants out while still small to avoid curled or forked roots. Cultivate or mulch to keep free of weeds. Water regularly in dry spells to produce large, more tender roots. Raised beds help.

**Pests and diseases** Shallow or heavy soil can result in misshapen roots. Break up clods, remove stones and don't step on seedbed. Handpick off any celery- or parsleyworms (green caterpillars with black and yellow stripes).

**Harvesting and storage** Dig up roots when large enough for you. The roots keep well in the ground (mulch to keep soil workable), or dig up before a hard freeze and store in a cool place in damp sand or sawdust.

**Special tips** Dig up overwintered plants before they begin to grow in spring. Roots shrink and toughen as the plants draw nutrients from them to set seed.

## *Phaseolus, Cicer, Lablab, Vigna* spp.

FABACEAE

# BEANS, DRIED

MANY OF THE BEAN TYPES THAT DRY AND
STORE WELL ARE PANTRY STAPLES IN THE
WORLD'S VARIED CUISINES. WHILE YOU MAY
NOT HAVE SPACE TO GROW EVERY BEAN YOU
WILL USE EACH YEAR, EVEN A SMALL CROP
GOES A LONG WAY AND IS FUN TO TRY.

**Position** Plant in full sun, in a site
with good air circulation. Well-
drained garden soil is acceptable;
pH 6.0–7.0.

**Cultivation** Sow seed after the last
frost and when soil has warmed,
1 inch (2.5 cm) deep and 3 inches
(7.5 cm) apart in single or double
rows. Cultivate shallowly until the
plants are large enough to shade
out weeds. Mulch between rows
to help prevent pods from rotting

if they touch the ground. Moisture
is critical when the plants are in
flower; when pods begin to mature,
withhold water to hasten drying.

**Pests and diseases** Provide good air
circulation to help prevent blights,
mosaic disease and anthracnose; to
avoid spreading rust, do not disturb
plants when foliage is wet. Till or
spade under all plant debris in
autumn to destroy any disease
organisms, and do not plant beans
or other legumes in the same place
more than once every 3 years.
Damp weather late in the season,
when the pods are maturing, can
encourage beans to sprout in the
pod. Pull plants when most of the

The black-eyed bean *Vigna unguiculata* subsp. *unguiculata* loves warmer climates. It is easy to grow and makes a wonderful, protein-rich addition to vegetable soups.

foliage has died and hang by the roots in a well-ventilated place to complete drying.

**Harvesting and storage** Harvest when pods are completely dry and the beans can barely be dented when bitten. Shell pods individually or thresh by placing in an old pillowcase and walking on it until pods are thoroughly crushed. Remove the resulting chaff by pouring the beans back and forth between two pans in a breezy area or in front of a fan. Store in airtight jars or bags in a dry, cool place.

**Special tips** To avoid potential problems with your crop being eaten by weevils, freeze the well-dried beans for several hours before storing. And remember that they will need to be soaked before cooking. One very good reason to grow beans is that they belong to the plant family that produces soil nitrogen by using the nitrogen in the atmosphere in cooperation with various soil bacteria. Grow a crop of beans in rotation with root and leafy green vegetables to ensure that your garden soil remains as healthy and productive as possible.

**Related plants**
**Black bean** *P. vulgaris* Sometimes called turtle bean or turtle soup bean, the black bean is especially popular in Caribbean and Latin

Pinto beans *Phaseolus vulgaris* are often used in Mexican cooking.
You can either use them fresh, or dry the seeds.

American cuisines. The beans are small and shiny jet black.

**Kidney bean** *P. vulgaris* Historically the term "kidney bean" was used for all common beans, green and shelled as well as dry. But today it is usually used to refer to large, dry beans with the characteristic kidney shape—not just the dark, red-brown ones familiar from the supermarket shelf, but white, brown, yellow, black and mottled beans as well. Smaller kidney beans are often referred to as navy beans. Among firm favorite kidney bean cultivars are 'Jacob's Cattle', a red-speckled white bean popular in short-season areas, and 'Soldier', an "heirloom" bean that derives its name from a soldier-like marking on its edge.

**Pinto bean** *P. vulgaris* The pinto bean is a medium-sized, oval bean, usually mottled on a buff background. Its resistance to heat and drought makes it a favorite in arid areas. It is the standard bean in Mexican cooking.

**Garbanzo bean** *Cicer arietinum* Also called chickpea, the large, round, buff-colored garbanzo is native to southern Europe and India, where it is eaten boiled or roasted. It is the main ingredient in the popular hummus spread, in which its nutty flavor is combined with that of sesame seeds. It requires a relatively long growing season, 120 days or more.

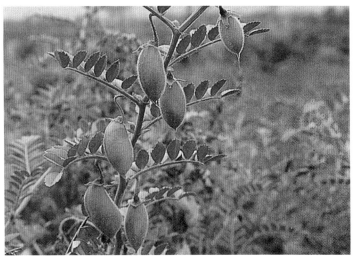

Soak garbanzo beans *Cicer arietinum* for two hours before cooking.
They are delicious boiled or roasted.

**Hyancinth bean** *Lablab purpureus*
This is a fast-growing, vining plant
that is grown in its native tropics for
both its pods and its seeds. It is a
perennial in warm climates, but can
also be grown in cooler areas as an
annual. The wisteria-like blossoms
are ornamental and the seeds can
be dried and eaten like beans.

**Adzuki bean** *Vigna angularis* Small,
dark red beans of Japanese origin.
They are highly valued for their
protein content. 'Express' is an
early-maturing cultivar, requiring
about 118 frost-free days.

**Mung bean** *V. radiata* The seeds
are often sprouted for use as bean
sprouts, but the dried beans are
also edible after soaking and
cooking. The pods can also be
eaten when immature.

**Black-eyed bean** *V. unguiculata*
**subsp.** *unguiculata* Also called
black-eyed pea, this warm-region
favorite is related to the asparagus
bean (see page 213), but is grown
for its seed rather than its pod. The
round, off-white beans are marked
with black. It does best in Zones 7
and warmer.

*Phaseolus, Vicia, Vigna* spp.                    FABACEAE

HARDINESS
Zones 3 and
warmer; cold
climates may
require a quick-
maturing cultivar.

DAYS TO MATURITY
A minimum of
42–55 frost-free
days, depending
on species/cultivar.

COMMENTS
The scarlet runner
(left) has clusters of
brilliant red edible
flowers, edible
pods and large
seeds, used as
fresh shelled beans.

# BEANS, FRESH

EVERY GARDEN CAN ACCOMMODATE SOME
FRESH BEANS, BE IT A FEW SMALL BUSH
PLANTS OR A FULL CROP ON A TRELLIS.

**Position** Plant in full sun. Likes soil
that is rich in humus but not
excessively fertile; pH 6.0–7.5.

**Cultivation** Sow seed after frost
danger is past. Sow bush snap
beans about 1 inch (2.5 cm) deep
and 3 inches (7.5 cm) apart in
single or double rows. Keep well
weeded or mulched. Regular
watering will increase yield;
thorough watering is critical when
beans are in flower. Bush snap
beans bear heavily but only for
a few weeks. To assure a steady
supply, make small plantings
3–4 weeks apart, ending 2 months
before the first autumn frost date.

**Pests and diseases** Mexican bean
beetles can be serious pests from
midseason onward; early plantings
are usually less troubled. Deter with
row covers. Avoid the bean patch
when the plants are wet to avoid
spreading bean rust. Sown too early
in cold, wet soil, bean seeds may
rot before germinating. Small
plantings for early harvest may be
worth the risk, but larger plantings
for freezing or bottling should be
delayed until the weather is settled.

**Harvesting and storage** Pick at any
size, but before seeds have begun
to swell noticeably inside the pod.

Plant butterbeans *Phaseolus lunatus* successively for a regular supply.
Water frequently when flowers appear for a heavy yield.

Tiny, fresh beans are a tender treat, but larger pods have a more characteristic "beany" flavor. Bottle, freeze or pickle snap beans, or leave pods on the plant to mature fully and then dry beans and use as you would other dried beans.

**Special tips** Increase yield by using an inoculant of nitrogen-fixing bacteria to help the plant make better use of nitrogen from the air. Add the inoculant to the seed or the soil at planting time.

### Related plants

**Scarlet runner bean *P. coccineus***
Climbing bean grown as a perennial in subtropical areas and as an annual in areas as cool as Zone 4.

Cold-tolerant cultivars include 'Prize Winner'.

**Lima bean *P. lunatus*** Climbing or pole limas require plenty of warm weather and a sturdy trellis, but are considered superior to the bush types in flavor. Require at least an 85-day growing season for the first beans to mature; a full harvest takes at least 100 days' favorable weather.

**Bush lima bean *P. lunatus***
Sometimes called butter or sugar bean, the bush lima is a heat-loving bean. It does best in Zones 7 and warmer. The seed, rather than the pod, is eaten, either as a fresh vegetable or as a dried bean. The beans are ready to pick when the pods are plump.

Romano beans *Phaseolus vulgaris* are flat-podded, tender beans, sometimes called Italian beans.

**Butterbean *P. lunatus*** Butterbeans are grown and used like limas but are flat, thin and much smaller. Also called Carolina bean.

**Horticultural bean *P. vulgaris*** Also called the shell bean, shelly bean, or cranberry bean, these plants are grown specifically for their seeds, which are eaten at the immature stage. Harvest horticultural beans when pods have started to turn rubbery but before the seeds inside have begun to harden. 'Tongue of Fire' is a striking bean, streaked with red on an off-white background; some seed suppliers may carry cultivars of French shelling beans, also known as "flageolets."

**Pole bean *P. vulgaris*** Also called runner beans, these beans require support for their long vines. They are often grown on a "teepee" framework, but can also be planted in a row and trellised. They bear over a longer period than bush beans and are a good choice where space is too limited for successive plantings to be made. They take longer to mature and some older cultivars will have strings that must be removed before eating. Cultivars include 'Kentucky Wonder', 'Case Knife' and 'Blue Lake'.

**Purple-podded bean *P. vulgaris*** Striking, quick-maturing purple bean that turns dark green when

Pick fava beans *Vicia faba* when pods are plump, but before the outer skin becomes tough. Where winter abruptly turns to summer, blossoms may fall without setting pods.

cooked. Cultivars include 'Royal Burgundy' and 'Royalty Purple Pod'.

**Romano bean** *P. vulgaris*  Tender, well flavored, early to mature. Cultivars include 'Romano II', 'Jumbo' and 'Greencrop'.

**Wax bean** *P. vulgaris*  Also called yellow snap bean. Slender, pale to golden yellow pods that are picked, prepared, and eaten exactly as green snap beans. Cultivars include 'Yellow Pencil Pod' and 'Goldkist'.

**Fava bean** *Vicia faba*  Also called broad bean, the fava is sometimes grown as a shell bean in place of limas in short-season areas. It is far more frost-tolerant than other beans and can be planted with the spring peas, 4–6 weeks before last frost of spring. It is best in areas with long, cool springs. 'Ipro' has some tolerance to hot weather; 'Windsor Long Pod' is widely available.

**Asparagus bean** *Vigna unguiculata* **subsp.** *sesquipedalis*  Also known as Chinese long bean, dow guak, snake bean or yardlong bean, this relative of the southern cowpea produces long, thin, crunchy pods best eaten at 10–12 inches (20–30 cm). It requires a trellis, likes warm weather, and needs a longer growing season than regular beans—at least 75 days of frost-free weather. Named cultivars are hard to find, but some variants are identified by the color of their seed.

# *Phyllostachys* spp.

HARDINESS
Zones 6–9;
hardiness varies
among species.
The "clumping"
*Bambusa
beecheyana* will
grow in Zone 10.

DAYS TO MATURITY
Depending on
species vigor, some
shoots can be
harvested in the
second spring.

COMMENTS
Cut stalks for
garden stakes
when 3 years
old or more.

## BAMBOO SHOOT

WHERE GARDEN SPACE ALLOWS, BAMBOO
PROVIDES EDIBLE YOUNG SHOOTS IN SPRING
AS WELL AS USEFUL GARDEN STAKES LATER.

**Position** Plant in full sun in fertile,
moist, well-drained soil; pH 6.0–7.0.

**Cultivation** Propagate by division
in late winter or very early spring.
Buy potted divisions by mail or in
garden centers in areas where
bamboo is hardy. Plant in early
spring and water until established.

**Pests and diseases** Little troubled
by pests. Most bamboos that
produce edible shoots are "running"
bamboos that spread by underground rhizomes. Build a strong
underground barrier or mow

frequently to keep the colony from
getting out of hand.

**Harvesting and storage** Cut tender
young shoots at ground level in
early to midspring. Stir-fry or use
fresh in salads.

**Special tips** Edible species vary
widely in their mature height and
hardiness. The smallest, *P. aurea*,
also called fishpole or golden
bamboo, grows to about 20 feet
(6 m) tall. *P. bambusoides*, or timber
bamboo, grows to 73 feet (22 m)
tall and 6 inches (15 cm) in
diameter. The hardiest bamboos
include *P. aureosulcata*, *P. dulcis*,
*P. nuda* and *P. viridiglaucescens*,
all up to 30–35 feet (9–10.5 m) tall.

*Pisum sativum*  FABACEAE

HARDINESS
Zones 2 and
warmer; grow as a
spring and autumn
crop in most
Zones, and as a
winter vegetable in
frost-free climates.

DAYS TO MATURITY
55–80 days. Young
plants will tolerate
moderate frost, but
frost will halt the
development of
autumn crops.

COMMENTS
The pods of crisp
snap peas (left)
are edible.

# PEA

TALL-GROWING PEAS WILL NEED THE
SUPPORT OF SOME TYPE OF TRELLIS FOR
THEIR CLIMBING STEMS.

**Position** Plant in full sun on a site
with good air circulation. Prefers
loose, well-drained soil; pH 6.0–7.0.

**Cultivation** Peas do poorly in hot
weather, so plant spring crops early
to beat the heat unless your springs
are long and cool. In Zones 7 and
warmer, seed planted in late
autumn often overwinters and
germinates in early spring. In colder
Zones, plant 4–8 weeks before the
last spring frost. Sow autumn crops
10–12 weeks before first autumn
frost. Plant bush types 1 inch
(2.5 cm) deep and about 1 inch
(2.5 cm) apart in double rows
spaced 6 inches (15 cm) apart.
Planted in this way, the plants will
help support each other and the
yield will be greater in very little
extra space. Plant tall types roughly
1 inch (2.5 cm) apart in single rows
and provide a trellis for them to
climb on. Do not thin. Cultivate
carefully to avoid uprooting plants,
or mulch to discourage weeds.
Peas do not need supplementary
fertilizer, especially if the soil has
been sufficiently well dug and
composted or manured during the
previous season. If your soil tends
to be acidic, apply a light dressing
of lime to correct the pH level.
Practice crop rotation with root

# *Pea* continued

Keep your pea plants well watered during flowering and pod set and they will continue to produce for a considerable time, especially if the pods are picked regularly.

vegetables and leafy greens to avoid soilborne diseases.

**Pests and diseases** Rarely troubled by insects. Good air circulation and resistant cultivars help to prevent powdery mildew. If root rot is a problem in your area, do not plant where peas have been grown in the preceding 2 years. Autumn plantings in humid areas, even of resistant cultivars, are often plagued by powdery mildew. Spray the foliage thoroughly with a baking soda solution (1 teaspoon per quart [liter] of water).

**Harvesting and storage** Pick shelling-type peas when pods are full and plump and peas are tender.

Pick snap peas when pods are rounded but still smooth, before the peas begin to bulge the sides of the pod. Pick snowpeas when pods are perfectly flat, showing only the tiniest hint of the pea inside. Peas are best eaten immediately or frozen or canned promptly, as their sugars begin to turn to starch quickly. Dry and store overmature crops as you would dried beans, for use in soups.

**Special tips** Make sure you provide adequate moisture when pea plants are in bloom. Even low-growing cultivars benefit from some vine support. Stick twiggy brush cuttings into the pea row to serve as what

If the space available for peas is limited, plant a variety such as 'Tall Telephone', which can be grown on a teepee-type support, or on a trellis.

old-time gardeners called "pea brush." Make plantings in late summer to extend the harvest, and remember to compost spent plants, as long as they are not diseased in any way. Time to maturity differs with the various cultivars, with the earlier ones generally producing a lower yield than those that grow taller and mature later.

### Related plants

**Shelling pea *P. sativum* var. *sativum*** Also called English pea or garden pea. Other cultivars include 'Laxton's Progress' (bush type), 'Tall Telephone' (trellis type) and 'Wando' (bush type, heat-resistant).

**Snap pea *P. sativum* var. *sativum*** Pods are not fibrous like shelling peas and may be eaten cooked or raw in salads. They are best if the strings are removed before cooking. Cultivars include 'Sugar Snap' (trellis type), 'Sugar Ann' (bush type) and 'Sugar Daddy' (bush type, stringless).

**Snowpea *P. sativum* var. *macrocarpon*** Also called edible-podded or sugar pea. Favored in oriental cuisines. Cultivars include 'Oregon Sugar Pod' (trellis type), 'Mammoth Melting Sugar' (trellis type) and 'Little Sweetie' (bush type).

*Portulaca oleracea* var. *sativa*

HARDINESS
Zones 4 and
warmer.

DAYS TO MATURITY
60–70 days,
although thinnings
can be eaten
sooner.

COMMENTS
Other common
names include
kitchen garden
purslane, pourpier,
pussley and
verdolaga.

# PURSLANE

POPULAR IN EUROPE AS A SALAD GREEN,
CULTIVATED PURSLANE IS TALLER AND MORE
SUCCULENT THAN ITS COUSIN, THE WEED.

**Position** Plant in full sun. Not fussy
about soil and will even grow in
sand; pH 6.0–7.0. Drought-resistant.

**Cultivation** Seed thinly in rows or
broadcast in small beds after frost
danger is past in spring. Do not
cover seeds but firm gently into the
soil with the back of a hoe. Keep
the soil moist until the seeds
germinate. Thin to 4–6 inches
(10–15 cm) apart (the thinnings
can be used in salads). Sow small
successive crops up to 2 months
before autumn frosts are expected.
Water frequently.

**Pests and diseases** Little bothered by
pests or diseases.

**Harvesting and storage** Harvest fresh
leaves and stems with scissors as
needed, leaving 1 inch (2.5 cm) or
more above ground to sprout new
leaves. May be harvested four or
five times. Best used fresh as it does
not store well.

**Special tips** Common purslane is
also edible. Collect seeds of the
best wild plants to grow in the
garden, saving seed each year from
plants with the best flavor and
growth habit. Named cultivars are
not generally available, but seed
suppliers may offer variants based
on leaf size or green or gold color.

*Psophocarpus tetragonolobus*

**HARDINESS**
Zones 7 and warmer; perennial in tropical climates.

**DAYS TO MATURITY**
120–150 frost-free days for edible pods; 180–210 days for tubers.

**COMMENTS**
Other common names are Goa bean, Manila bean, princess pea and winged bean.

# ASPARAGUS PEA

ITS UNIQUE FLAVOR AND HIGH PROTEIN CONTENT MAKE THE ASPARAGUS PEA POPULAR IN ASIAN STIR-FRIES AND OTHER DISHES. IT ALSO PRODUCES EDIBLE TUBERS.

**Position** Plant in full sun near a trellis or fence in loose and well-drained soil; pH 7.3–8.0.

**Cultivation** Plant after frost danger is past, 1 inch (2.5 cm) deep and 2–4 inches (5–10 cm) apart. The vines grow to a height of 6–8 feet (1.8–2.4 m), so support with a sturdy trellis or fence. Cultivate shallowly or mulch to control weeds. The purplish red flowers form in loose clusters. The pods are four-sided, rather than round, with distinct flanges or "wings" at each corner.

**Pests and diseases** Do not grow where legumes, such as peas and beans, have grown the preceding year. Keep vines growing strongly with regular watering to deter aphids. Requires a long, warm growing season. Where the weather is not to its liking, it may die without flowering.

**Harvesting and storage** Harvest the pods at 6–8 inches (15–20 cm) long and eat steamed or stir-fried. Pick frequently, as pods can quickly become oversized. Dig up marble-sized tubers after frost has killed the plants; use in stir-fries or stews.

**Special tips** Named cultivars are not generally available.

*Raphanus sativus*

# RADISH

FAST-GROWING RADISHES ADD A CRISP, COLORFUL TOUCH TO SPRING SALADS. HARVEST WHILE YOUNG AND TENDER.

**Position** Plant in loose, moisture-retentive soil; pH 5.5–6.8.

**Cultivation** Sow spring radishes 3–5 weeks before last spring frost, ½ inch (12 mm) deep in double or triple rows. Make the rows short and sow small crops every 2 weeks until a month after frost danger is past. Sow autumn crops starting 8 weeks before frost and continuing until frost. Thin spring radishes to 1–2 inches (2.5–5 cm) apart, or seed sparingly and thin by pulling radishes as they reach eating size. Sow winter radishes 8–10 weeks before autumn frost and thin to 4–6 inches (10–15 cm) apart. Keep moist to avoid strong flavor and toughness. Mulch between rows to keep soil moist in hot weather.

**Pests and diseases** Rotate radishes and other root crops to reduce damage from root maggots. Spring crops are more vulnerable than autumn crops. Spring radishes, especially slender French breakfast types, become woody and bitter when overmature. Plant small but frequent crops to keep tender radishes on the table. The roots of radishes planted in heavy soils are apt to be misshapen and have a number of branching side roots.

# *Radish* continued

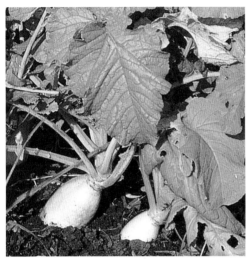

HARDINESS
All Zones; grow as
a winter vegetable
in mild areas.

DAYS TO MATURITY
21–35 days for
spring radishes;
50–60 days for
winter radishes.
Will withstand
moderate frost.

COMMENTS
Cultivars of the
daikon (left)
include 'Summer
Cross' and
'Miyashige'.

Japanese radish *Raphanus sativus* is a white, carrot-shaped radish, up to 2 feet (60 cm) long. Also known as daikon, it is often grated as a condiment.

**Harvesting and storage** Pull spring and autumn crops when large enough for use. Pull winter radishes as needed when they reach eating size; harvest all roots before a hard frost. Store in damp sand or sawdust in a cool place, or pickle.

**Special tips** Interplant spring radishes with slower-growing crops such as broccoli and cabbage. Harvest the radishes before the companion crops needs the space. Radishes are frequently mixed with beet or carrot seeds: the radishes germinate first and so mark the rows of the slower-growing crops. Because they grow quickly, they are a good crop for children to plant.

**Related plants**

**Black Spanish radish *R. sativus*** Up to 4 inches (10 cm) in diameter, with black skin and white flesh. Pungent, keeps well.

**Chinese radish *R. sativus*** Also called lo bok or lo po. Long and white like the Japanese radish, but sweet, not pungent. Oriental seed suppliers offer named cultivars or variants based on skin color.

**Winter radish *R. sativus*** A catch-all term for radish cultivars that are suitable for at least short-term storage as a root vegetable. In addition to those above, the German beer radish, which is large, white, and turnip-shaped, is very popular in Europe.

# *Rheum* x *cultorum*

**HARDINESS**
Zones 8 and cooler.

**DAYS TO MATURITY**
Harvest sparingly in the second year after planting and more heavily thereafter.

**COMMENTS**
Cultivars include 'MacDonald' and 'Valentine'. 'Victoria' is robust and green-stemmed rather than red.

# RHUBARB

RHUBARB'S STOUT LEAF STALKS, COOKED BY THEMSELVES OR WITH OTHER SEASONAL FRUITS, MAKE DELICIOUS DESSERTS.

**Position** Plant in full sun in rich, deep, well-drained soil; pH 5.0–6.8.

**Cultivation** Can grow from seed, but it is quicker to use divisions of this hardy perennial. Plant in early spring, 1–2 months before last spring frost. Dig a hole big enough to accommodate roots and cover the crown with no more than 2 inches (5 cm) of soil. Mix a shovelful of compost or well-rotted manure into the soil to get the plant off to a good start. Cultivate or mulch. Heavy feeder; top-dress every spring with compost or rotted manure. Drought-tolerant, but provide adequate moisture to ensure abundant, tender stalks.

**Pests and diseases** Little troubled by pests. Plant in well-drained soil to avoid root rot.

**Harvesting and storage** To harvest large, outer leaf stalks, grasp them near the base and pull with a slight twisting motion. Remove the leaves, which are toxic. Harvest sparingly in autumn as well as in spring, but spring stalks are more tender. Chop and freeze uncooked stems.

**Special tips** Cut off flower stems that rob the plant of energy, resulting in stringy leaf stalks.

*Rumex scutatus*

HARDINESS
All Zones.

DAYS TO MATURITY
60 days for first-year crop, although thinnings may be harvested sooner.

COMMENTS
Will withstand moderate frost. The leaves can be frozen for use in soup and sauces. Sheep's sorrel is also known as red sorrel.

# SORREL, FRENCH

A TENDER GREEN SALAD PLANT WITH A DELICIOUS LEMONY FLAVOR. FRENCH SORREL WITHSTANDS DRY WEATHER BETTER THAN SOME OTHER SORRELS.

**Position** Plant in full sun or partial shade in rich, moist soil; pH 6.0–7.0.

**Cultivation** Start the seeds indoors or sow directly in the garden 2–4 weeks before last spring frost. Thin to stand 6–8 inches (15–20 cm) apart, using the thinnings in salads. Cultivate or mulch to discourage weeds and keep watered for best production. Top-dress the bed with compost or well-rotted manure each autumn or spring. Sorrel is a perennial plant, but will decline after 3–4 years. Start a new bed from seed or divide existing plants.

**Pests and diseases** Use row covers to protect plants from leaf-eating insects. Keep flower stems cut back to extend the spring harvest.

**Harvesting and storage** Pick fresh leaves as needed. Produces abundantly in spring and autumn; less productive in hot weather.

**Related plants**
**Garden sorrel *R. acetosa*** Also called sour dock. Pictured above, it has longer leaves and milder flavor than French sorrel.
**Sheep's sorrel *R. acetosella*** This is the most common "weed" sorrel. It is edible, but invasive in the garden.

*Sechium edule*  CUCURBITACEAE

HARDINESS
Zones 7 and
warmer.

DAYS TO MATURITY
80–90 days for
fruits; shoots and
roots are harvested
in the second year.

COMMENTS
Other common
names for chayote
are cho-cho,
choko, chuchu,
christophene,
mirliton and
vegetable pear.

# CHAYOTE

CHAYOTE IS A SPACE-HUNGRY, AVID CLIMBER
SUITED TO WARM CLIMATES. SHOOTS, ROOTS
AND FRUITS ARE ALL EDIBLE.

**Position** Cooler areas may produce
fruits only; roots are not harvested
until the second year. Full sun,
adjacent to a wall or fence for
climbing. Deep, fertile, moist, but
well-drained soil; pH 5.5–6.5.

**Cultivation** After last spring frost,
plant the entire fruit (about 4 inches
[10 cm] long, containing one seed),
with 1 inch (2.5 cm) of narrow end
exposed. One plant will satisfy most
gardeners' needs. Plant near a fence
or trellis, or provide 12 feet (3.6 m)
of growing space. Keep well
watered. Perennial in mild areas;

may overwinter in cooler climates
with protection. Cut back after frost
and mulch roots; pull back mulch
after frost danger is past next spring.

**Pests and diseases** Provide good air
circulation to avoid fungal disease
and mildew.

**Harvesting and storage** Pick
immature fruits at 4–6 inches
(10–15 cm) long and use like
summer squash. Harvest mature
fruits before frost; store and use
like winter squash (see page 175).
Cut second-year shoots in spring;
marinate or steam as you would
asparagus. Dig up roots in autumn
of the second year; store and
use like potatoes.

*Solanum melongena*                                    SOLANACEAE

HARDINESS
Zones 5 and
warmer.

DAYS TO MATURITY
50–75 frost-free
days.

COMMENTS
Eggplant can be
grown in large pots
in disease-free soil.
Provide adequate
soil moisture and
calcium to prevent
blossom-end rot,
which shows up as
a soft, brown spot
at the blossom end
of the fruit.

# EGGPLANT (AUBERGINE)

EGGPLANT THRIVES IN HOT WEATHER. IT
NEEDS AMPLE AMOUNTS OF WATER AND
FERTILIZER TO PRODUCE ITS FRUITS.

**Position** Plant in full sun in light,
rich, well-drained, warm soil;
pH 5.5–6.8.

**Cultivation** It does not pay to start
the plants too early in the season or
set them out too early. Start 8 weeks
before night temperatures can be
counted on to stay above 50°F
(10°C). Night covers may be
needed in colder climates. Space
the plants 1½–2 feet (45–60 cm)
apart. Eggplant needs plenty of
water and food to produce well.
Apply fish emulsion or compost tea
at least once a month.

**Pests and diseases** Use row covers
to deter flea beetles. Pick off
Colorado potato beetles by hand;
a light dusting of ground limestone
helps to repel this pest. To avoid
soilborne diseases such as Fusarium
and Verticillium wilt, rotate eggplant
and other members of the
nightshade (Solanaceae) family,
such as tomatoes and potatoes.

**Harvesting and storage** Clip the fruit
with some stem attached; harvest
often to encourage further fruiting.
Standard eggplant cultivars, such as
'Black Beauty', will bear 4–10 full-
sized fruits, or more if picked small.
Oriental cultivars, such as 'Sanshi',
bear more but smaller fruits. It is

The white eggplant is as delicious as it is decorative. Harvest the glossy fruits at any size and keep picking regularly to keep the plants bearing.

better to harvest when a little small than to let eggplant become bitter and overmature. When frost threatens, harvest all fruits, leaving 2 inches (5 cm) of stem attached, and store in a cool, moist, well-ventilated place. They will keep for a month or longer.

**Special tips** Where the growing season permits, try making two small plantings a month apart.

### Related plants

**Baby eggplant S. *melongena***
A gourmet item, usually slender or egg-shaped, up to 4 inches (10 cm) long. Quick-maturing, good for short-season areas. Cultivars include 'Pirouette' and 'Little Fingers'.

**Italian eggplant S. *melongena*** There are many fine cultivars with tender, nonbitter white flesh and dazzling skin color. 'Rosa Bianca' is rosy lavender and white; 'Violetta di Firenze' has dark lavender, somewhat ridged fruit.

**Oriental eggplant S. *melongena***
Also called Japanese eggplant. Long, thin, purple-black fruits, but also light green and white-lavender. Cultivars include 'Orient Express' and 'Kurume'.

**White eggplant S. *melongena*** This variety has an attractive white skin, but may be less prolific than its purple siblings. 'Casper' has full-sized fruit; 'Osterei' and 'White Egg' bear smaller fruits.

*Solanum tuberosum*

**HARDINESS**
Zones 3 and
warmer.

**DAYS TO MATURITY**
55–80 days.

**COMMENTS**
Young plants
will withstand
a light frost.
Fingerling potatoes
(left) are long and
slender, with a
waxy texture that
makes them ideal
for use in salads.

# POTATO

POTATOES THRIVE IN RICH, LOOSE, WELL-
DRAINED, SLIGHTLY ACID SOIL. ALL POTATOES
CAN BE STORED FOR LATER USE.

**Position** Plant in full sun in loose,
well-drained, slightly acid soil with
plenty of potash; ideal pH 5.2–5.7,
but will also do well at pH 5.8–6.5.

**Cultivation** Most potatoes do not
come true from seed and are
planted from pieces of tuber called
"seed potatoes." Each piece should
be about the size of an egg and
contain one or more "eyes," or
dormant buds. Cut seed potatoes to
size and let the pieces dry for 1 day
to avoid having them rot in the
ground. Plant 2–4 weeks before last
spring frost, about 1 foot (30 cm)

apart in a trench 3–4 inches
(7.5–10 cm) deep. Rake the soil
level over the seed potatoes. Tubers
will form above the seed potato,
not below it, so plants must be
"hilled" to get good yields. With a
hoe or rake, draw soil up around
the plant when it is 6–8 inches
(15–20 cm) tall, burying all but the
topmost leaves. Repeat at least
once more as the plant grows.
Hilling also supports the plants
and protects new potatoes from
exposure to light. On level or
slightly sloping beds, the furrow
between rows can be used for
irrigating. You can also grow
potatoes under straw or leaf mulch,
adding layers as the plant grows.

White potatoes are good for all-purpose use. For easy harvesting, incorporate loose compost, leaves and straw into the hills and the potatoes will pull up readily.

In well-prepared and fertilized soil, no extra fertilizer is needed, but water regularly to promote smooth-skinned, well-developed potatoes.

**Pests and diseases** Rotate plantings of potato and its nightshade relatives, such as tomato and eggplant. Potatoes like soil that has recently been under sod, but prepare the area the autumn before planting and turn it over once during the winter, if possible, to destroy grubs. Do not use fresh manure on potato beds as it encourages scab. Covering plants with row covers or dusting them with ground limestone helps to deter flea beetles and Colorado potato beetles. A special strain of BT, a microbial insecticide, is available to control potato beetle larvae where the insect is a serious problem. If exposed to light, potato tubers develop green patches that contain the toxic alkaloid solanine. Hill or mulch deeply to prevent sunlight from reaching the tubers; store harvested potatoes in a dark place (never eat greened potatoes).

**Harvesting and storage** Blooming is usually the signal that the plant has begun to form tubers. Check by gently probing the soil around the base of the plant, taking no more than a few tubers per plant for early use. "New potatoes" are those that

When blossoms appear on the plants, you can harvest some small new potatoes. When the leaves die down, the mature potatoes are ready to harvest.

have been freshly harvested and eaten within a day, before the skin toughens and the sugars begin to be converted to starches. When foliage dies back, the potatoes are mature. Dig up as needed, completing the harvest before a hard freeze, because potatoes that have been frozen will rot in storage. Dry, without washing, and store in well-ventilated boxes or mesh bags in a cool to cold place, ideally about 40°F (4°C).

**Special tips** To speed up your harvest, try presprouting your seed potatoes. Set whole tubers in a cool, bright spot. Once they have developed short, bright sprouts (in

about 4–6 weeks), plant the whole potatoes out into the garden as you would normally.

### Related plants
**Fingerling potatoes *S. tuberosum***
Also called German potatoes, this variety (pictured on page 227) has long, slender tubers, often with a waxy texture that makes them ideal for potato salad. They are more prolific than standard potatoes. Dig up soon after they mature, because potatoes left in the ground tend to become knobby. Cultivars include 'German Fingerling', 'Yellow Fingerling' and 'Larota'.
**Red potatoes *S. tuberosum*** A red-skinned potato, usually with moist,

# *Potato* continued

Red potatoes are good for boiling or baking in their skins. Set aside any tubers that are nicked or damaged during harvesting and use them first.

white flesh, but some cultivars have cream-colored or yellow flesh. Small ones are often sold commercially as "new potatoes." Cultivars include 'Red Pontiac', 'Red Norland', 'Red Bliss' and 'Red Gold' (yellow flesh).

**Russet potatoes *S. tuberosum*** Usually oblong potatoes with netted skin, this variety has a mealy texture ideal for baking. Cultivars include 'Russet Burbank'.

**White potatoes *S. tuberosum*** With white- or buff-colored skin and white flesh, this variety is an all-purpose potato. 'Irish Cobbler' is a very thin-skinned and early cultivar. 'Kennebec' is well adapted to many areas. 'Green Mountain' is an old and reliable cultivar.

**Yellow potatoes *S. tuberosum*** Yellow-fleshed potatoes are gaining popularity for their delicate flavor, beauty and their appealing waxy texture. Some popular cultivars include 'Bintje', 'Yukon Gold' and 'Yellow Finn'.

*Spinacia oleracea*

HARDINESS
All Zones.

DAYS TO MATURITY
40–53 days,
although thinnings
can be harvested
sooner. Spinach
will withstand
moderate frost.

COMMENTS
Good, reliable
cultivars are
'Longstanding
Bloomsdale',
'Melody' and
'Tyee'.

# SPINACH

FRESH OR COOKED, SPINACH IS DELICIOUS AND NUTRITIOUS. IT NEEDS COOL WEATHER AND PLENTY OF WATER TO PRODUCE ABUNDANT, CRISP LEAVES.

**Position** Plant in full sun or partial shade in moist, fertile, well-limed soil; pH 6.0–7.0.

**Cultivation** Sow seed ½ inch (12 mm) deep, 4–6 weeks before the last spring frost. In very short-season areas, or where hot weather sets in abruptly, start spinach indoors. Set out or thin seedlings to 4–6 inches (10–15 cm) apart. Keep free of weeds and water regularly. Sow autumn crops 4–6 weeks before the first frost, or later for overwintering. Seed autumn crops heavily, because spinach germinates poorly in warm soil.

**Pests and diseases** Use row covers to protect from leaf miners and chewing insects.

**Harvesting and storage** Pick larger outside leaves or harvest the whole plant at its base. Spinach freezes well for use as a cooked vegetable.

**Special tips** Hot weather and lengthening days can cause spinach plants to bolt to seed. Choose heat-resistant cultivars and sow spring crops early to avoid this problem.

**HARDINESS**
Zones 4 and
warmer.

**DAYS TO MATURITY**
55–70 days.

**COMMENTS**
Named cultivars
are not generally
available.

# SPINACH, NEW ZEALAND

NEW ZEALAND SPINACH IS A BRANCHING,
MATLIKE PLANT THAT THRIVES IN WEATHER
THAT IS TOO HOT FOR TRUE SPINACH.

**Position** Plant in full sun in rich,
well-drained soil; pH 6.5–7.5.

**Cultivation** Soak seed overnight to
hasten germination and sow directly
in the garden 1–2 weeks before the
last spring frost. In warm climates,
prechill seed in the refrigerator for
1–2 days. In short-season areas,
start indoors 4–6 weeks before
the last frost. Set plants 1–1½ feet
(30–45 cm) apart when the danger
of frost is past.

**Pests and diseases** New Zealand
spinach is rarely troubled by pests.

Seed can be slow to germinate.
Mark the row well to avoid
weeding out young plants.

**Harvesting and storage** Pick about
4–6 inches (10–15 cm) of the
branch tips, together with the
leaves, which are small and brittle.
Whole plants may be cut above the
ground when they are small; the
stem will resprout. Cook as you
would true spinach.

**Special tips** New Zealand spinach is
good for hot, dry climates where
true spinach does poorly. It will
tolerate saline soils.

# *Tragopogon porrifolius*

HARDINESS
Zones 4 and
warmer; grow as
a winter vegetable
in mild climates.

DAYS TO MATURITY
120–150 days.

COMMENTS
Other common
names include
oyster plant and
vegetable oyster,
a reference to the
unusual flavor of
this easily grown
vegetable.

# SALSIFY

A HARDY ROOT VEGETABLE, SALSIFY LOOKS
LIKE A SLENDER PARSNIP WITH NARROW,
GRASSY LEAVES, BUT HAS A DELICATE,
OYSTER-LIKE FLAVOR.

**Position** Plant in full sun in deep,
light and rich soil; pH 6.0–8.0.

**Cultivation** Sow seed ½ inch
(12 mm) deep 2–4 weeks before
the last spring frost, or in autumn
in mild climates. Thin to stand
3–4 inches (7.5–10 cm) apart. Water
regularly and mulch to maintain
the soil moisture and produce
smoother, more tender roots.

**Pests and diseases** Salsify is little
troubled by pests or diseases. Spotty
or slow germination may indicate
that the seed is old. Purchase fresh
salsify seed each year.

**Harvesting and storage** Dig roots
as needed when large enough, but
mulch the bed before a hard freeze.
Store the harvested roots in damp
sand or sawdust in a cool place.

**Special tips** Young plants can
tolerate light frost; mature ones,
severe frost.

**Related plants**
**Black salsify *Scorzonera hispanica***
Cream root with black skin. Leaves
can be eaten in salads.
**Spanish salsify *Scolymus hispanicus***
Also called golden thistle, this
variety is quite mild in flavor.

# *Valerianella locusta*

HARDINESS
Zones 2 and
warmer. Over-
winters in Zones 5
and warmer; in
mild areas, grow as
a winter vegetable.

DAYS TO MATURITY
45–60 days from
spring seeding;
thinnings can be
harvested earlier.

COMMENTS
Other common
names are fetticus,
lamb's lettuce and
mâche. Reliable
cultivars are 'Elan',
'Piedmont' and 'Vit'.

## CORN SALAD

SMALL, TENDER, GREEN CORN SALAD CAN
BE PLANTED IN AUTUMN TO GRACE SPRING'S
EARLIEST SALADS. IT'S EXPENSIVE TO BUY,
BUT EASY TO GROW.

**Position**  Full sun or partial shade.
Not fussy about soil, but prefers it
rich with humus; pH 6.0–7.0. Will
withstand light frosts.

**Cultivation**  Sow seed in early
spring, 2–4 weeks before last frost;
just cover with fine soil and firm
with the back of a hoe. Plant thickly
in rows or more thinly in wide
beds; keep moist. Thin to stand
2 inches (5 cm) apart; use thinnings
in salads. Avoid plantings that will
mature in hot weather. Plant in
autumn near first frost date; mulch

lightly after a hard freeze. Remove
mulch in early spring.

**Pests and diseases**  Little troubled by
pests or diseases. In colder areas,
mulch more heavily over winter to
avoid plants being "heaved" up
above ground as the soil freezes.

**Harvesting and storage**  Harvest
entire rosettes by pinching off at
ground level. Some cultivars remain
sweet even when in flower, but
taste to check.

**Special tips**  In wide-bed plantings,
thin and weed simultaneously by
raking shallowly in two directions.

*Zea mays*

HARDINESS
Zones 3 and
warmer.

DAYS TO MATURITY
54–94 frost-free
days. Early cultivars
(54–70 days)
include 'Seneca
Horizon' and
'Earlivee'. Longer-
season cultivars
include 'Tuxedo',
the super-sweet
'Honey 'n Pearl',
and 'Silver Queen'.

COMMENTS
Use short-season
cultivars in
colder areas.

# CORN

TENDER AND SUCCULENT, FRESH SWEET
CORN IS A CLASSIC SUMMER TREAT FROM
THE GARDEN. IT'S WELL WORTH GROWING.

**Position** Plant in full sun, avoiding
areas subject to high winds. Accepts
many soil textures; prefers deep,
well-manured soil with high organic
content; pH 6.0–6.8.

**Cultivation** Sow seed after last spring
frost, or 1–2 weeks earlier if soil has
first been warmed by covering with
black plastic for a week or more in
sunny weather. Seed germinates
poorly in cold, wet soil and may
rot. Plant 1 inch (2.5 cm) deep and
4 inches (10 cm) apart in blocks at
least four rows wide, rather than in
long, single rows, to ensure good
wind-pollination. Rows should be
1½–2 feet (45–60 cm) apart. Thin
seedlings to stand 8–12 inches
(20–30 cm) apart; mulch or cultivate
shallowly to avoid damaging roots
near the soil surface. Corn grows
rapidly and needs adequate feeding
and water. Apply fish emulsion or
compost tea after 1 month and
again when the tassels appear.
Water is most critical when corn is
in tassel. Plant successive crops
every 10–14 days through
midsummer, or until about 90 days
before first frost. Choose an early-
maturing cultivar for the last
planting. Modern corn cultivars
include some known as "super-
sweet," which have been genetically

# Corn continued

Colorful ears of ornamental corn are very easy to grow. Hang them upside-down to finish drying and use for dramatic decorative effects.

modified to slow the conversion of sugar to starch. But if these cultivars cross-pollinate with other sweet corn cultivars, tough kernels will result. It is recommended that corn plots be separated by 25 feet (7.5 m) or more, but this is not always practicable in home gardens. Instead, time the plantings to ensure that at least 10 days elapse between pollination periods for the cultivars. For example, you could plant a super-sweet cultivar that matures in 82 days at the same time as a regular cultivar that matures in 72 days. Or you could plant an 82-day super-sweet cultivar next to an 82-day regular cultivar, as long as you sow it 10 days earlier or later.

**Pests and diseases** Plant in warm soil to avoid wireworms, which destroy seed. Late plantings are less prone to corn borers; early plantings are less susceptible to corn earworms. Help control earworms by dropping mineral oil into the immature ears as soon as you see the pests' sticky frass on the silks. Rotate corn plantings and shred or bury crop debris to reduce overwintering pests. Patchy spots on kernels, or poorly filled ears, indicate poor pollination.

**Harvesting and storage** Harvest when silks have turned brown and dry and ears feel full, usually about 3 weeks after the silks appear.

Plant corn in blocks rather than rows to get more effective pollination. To hand-pollinate corn, strip the pollen from the tassels and sprinkle it onto the silks.

Check by pulling back a husk and pressing a thumbnail into a kernel. It should squirt back a milky liquid. Holding the stalk firmly, snap the ear downward, then up. Bottle or freeze corn that cannot be eaten immediately after picking, as it begins to turn starchy within hours.

**Special tips** If space is limited, interplant a fast-growing crop such as lettuce between rows of corn. The lettuce can be used before the corn casts too much shade.

### Related plants

**Miniature corn Z. *mays* var. *rugosa*** Pick baby ears a day or two after silks appear and use whole in stir-fries or for pickling. 'Baby' and 'Baby Asian' are grown specifically for miniature corn, but any sweet corn cultivar will do.

**Ornamental corn Z. *mays* var. *indurata*** Also called Indian corn. These cultivars of field corn have colorful kernels. Many cultivars, such as 'Hopi Blue' and 'Mandan Bride', are ground as cornmeal or flour.

**Popcorn Z. *mays* var. *praecox*** The dense kernels explode into crisp puffs when heated. Harvest as dry as possible, pull back the husks, and hang in an airy place to "cure." Test-pop a few kernels to determine when the corn is dry enough to be shucked and stored in bags or jars. Cultivars include 'Matinee', 'White Cloud' and 'Strawberry'.

*Sprouts*

# SPROUTS

A WIDE VARIETY OF SEEDS, INCLUDING
ALFALFA AND LENTILS, ARE EASY TO SPROUT
WITHOUT SOIL. THEY ARE TASTY EATEN RAW
IN SALADS AND SANDWICHES, OR SPRINKLED
OVER STIR-FRIES AT THE LAST MINUTE.

**Position** Sprouts are grown indoors
and no soil is required.

**Cultivation** Use only seeds that have
not been treated with fungicides or
other chemicals; natural food stores
often carry seeds packaged
especially for sprouting. Use fresh
seeds to ensure good germination.
Soak large seeds overnight in water,
or smaller ones for an hour or two.
Pick out any broken seeds and
rinse the rest several times in warm
water in a strainer or colander.

(Don't waste the rinse water. Some
potplants, for example African
violets, thrive on it, but test with
small diluted amounts until you are
sure.) You will find several styles of
sprouting systems at natural food
stores, but you can simply put the
seeds in a wide-mouthed jar, cover
it with cheesecloth and invert it
over a dish to catch any remaining
rinse water. Good air circulation is
very important. Keep the container
in a warm place, rinsing the seeds
twice daily with tepid water. In hot
weather, rinse more often.

**Harvesting and storage** Sprouts are
ready to eat in 3–5 days, or slightly
longer if you are sprouting some of

1. **The tube system** is, after a screw-top jar, perhaps the simplest of all. It has three screen lids and one solid lid for transportation. Made from clear plastic, it affords excellent drainage and air circulation.

2. **The SproutMaster** is a system of stackable trays that come in two tray sizes. Excellent drainage and air circulation and perhaps the best choice if you like to have a few types of sprouts on the go at the same time.

3. **The hemp bag system** has excellent drainage and air circulation. It is very good for beans, grains and the larger seeds, but it's fine for smaller seeds, too. It really comes into its own when you are traveling.

4. **The miniature garden** is perfect for baby greens. It's so small you can keep it on your desk at work to supply fresh sprouts for your lunch. Simply sprinkle small seeds on the moist felt pads for a mini-crop.

the hard-seeded vegetables. Store sprouted seeds in the refrigerator and use promptly; many sprouts become moldy quite quickly, especially in hot weather.

**Special tips** Old seeds may not germinate or do so only slowly. Visit www.sproutpeople.com for more information on the types of sprouting systems that are available.

Part Six

# Plant
# Directory
# ~
# Fruits

*Actinidia deliciosa*

HARDINESS
Zones 7–9. In the colder parts of this range, protect plants from late-spring frosts.

HEIGHT
4–6 feet
(1.2–1.8 m)

SPREAD
15 feet (4.5 m)

COMMENTS
You'll need to control enthusiastic kiwi growth so the vine won't tangle or shade itself out.

# KIWI FRUIT

KIWI VINES MAKE EXCELLENT COVERING FOR TRELLISES AND ARBORS. WHILE YOU ENJOY THE SHADE, REACH UP TO PICK THE FRUIT.

**Position** Plant in full sun to light shade in average to poor, well-drained soil.

**Cultivation** With the exception of a few self-fertile cultivars, such as 'Issai' and 'Blake', kiwi vines have either male or female flowers. For pollination, plant a male vine within about 40 feet (12 m) of females— closer if possible. One male will pollinate up to eight female vines. Keep the soil moist up to harvest time, but water less as winter approaches. Mulch well, but fertilize lightly, if at all.

**Pruning** Before planting, install a sturdy post-and-wire trellis (as you would for grapes). Insert a stake next to the vine at planting time, and cut out all but one stem. Prune off sideshoots from the remaining stem and train it up the stake.

**Propagation** Propagate using cuttings or by grafting.

**Pests and diseases** Surround young plants with a circle of wire mesh fencing to prevent cats from rolling or chewing on leaves and stems.

**Harvesting and storage** Pick kiwi fruit in autumn, when the seeds are black and most of the fruit is still firm. Peel before eating.

*Akebia quinata*

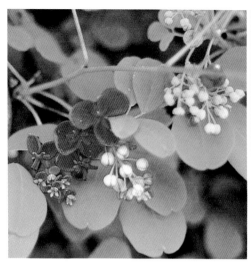

HARDINESS
Zones 4–8.

HEIGHT
10–20 feet (3–6 m)

SPREAD
15–20 feet
(4.5–6 m)

COMMENTS
The fruit has a mild flavor reminiscent of watermelon.

# AKEBIA

AKEBIA VINES PRODUCE BLUISH OR PURPLE FRUITS WITH NUMEROUS DARK SEEDS EMBEDDED IN THEIR EDIBLE, JELLY-LIKE FLESH.

**Position** Akebia grows best in full sun but tolerates light shade. The plants are not finicky about soil, as long as it is well drained. The flowers appear early, so choose a site not prone to late-spring frosts.

**Cultivation** Plant container-grown vines anytime the ground isn't frozen, or set out bareroot plants in spring or autumn, while they are dormant. Space plants 10 feet (3 m) apart to spread out on a trellis or an arbor. If fruit set is poor, try hand-pollination: Transfer pollen with a paintbrush from the male flowers

(the ones toward the end of each flower stalk) to the female flowers (near the base of each flower stalk).

**Pruning** Just before spring growth, thin out spindly or tangled stems.

**Propagation** Mix seed with moist peat moss and keep at temperatures just above freezing for 1–2 months; sow seed in a warm, bright place. Or root from softwood cuttings.

**Pests and diseases** Generally no significant problems.

**Harvesting and storage** When fruit is ripe, the skin splits lengthwise. Pick the fruit at this point for fresh eating, or just as it starts to split along its seam for storage.

# *Ananas comosus*

HARDINESS
Zone 10.

HEIGHT
3–6 feet
(90–180 cm)

SPREAD
3–6 feet
(90–180 cm)

COMMENTS
Inside the
pineapple's
inedible and tough
outer covering,
the edible flesh is
yellow or almost
white, with a tangy
and sweet flavor.

# PINEAPPLE

PINEAPPLE FLOWERS FUSE TO FORM A WARTY,
GREEN-AND-YELLOW SKIN OVER THE FRUIT.

**Position** Pineapples need full sun
and well-drained, acid soil;
pH 4.5–6.5. They are reasonably
tolerant of dry conditions.

**Cultivation** Plant anytime, setting
out plants 1 foot (30 cm) apart in
double rows 2 feet (60 cm) apart.
No pollination needed. In areas
cooler than Zone 10, grow plants in
containers, with a growing mix that
contains extra sand or perlite for
good drainage. Avoid overwatering.
When plant is about 2 years old,
induce flowering by covering the
crown for a few days with a paper
bag containing a slice of apple.

**Pruning** Prune 1–2 months after
harvest, cutting off sideshoots
arising near ground level as well as
those originating along or at the
base of the fruit stalk. If remaining
sideshoots along the stem are
crowded, thin them out.

**Propagation** Pull off and plant
sideshoots. Or twist the crown of
leaves off the top of the fruit, let
it dry for a few days, and plant it.

**Pests and diseases** Control
mealybugs with oil sprays.

**Harvesting and storage** Cut or snap
fruit from stem when color changes;
slight softening and aroma indicate
ripeness. Store above 50°F (10°C).

# *Annona cherimola*

**HARDINESS**
Zone 10, with a period of cool, but not cold, winter weather.

**HEIGHT**
15–30 feet (4.5–9 m)

**SPREAD**
10–25 feet (3–7.5 m)

**COMMENTS**
Cherimoya is a rich-textured, luxurious fruit that can be frozen and eaten with a spoon, like ice cream.

## CHERIMOYA (CUSTARD APPLE)

INSIDE THE PALE GREEN SKIN, CHERIMOYA FLESH IS WHITE AND CUSTARDY, WITH A COMBINATION OF BANANA, PINEAPPLE AND PAPAYA FLAVORS. EAT THE FLESH BUT NOT THE SEEDS OR SKIN.

**Position** Plant in a sheltered spot in full sun and well-drained, slightly acid soil.

**Cultivation** Plant container-grown stock anytime, or set out bareroot plants in spring or autumn, while they are dormant. Space plants 10–25 feet (3–7.5 m) apart. Hand-pollinate flowers with a fine brush for best yields of large fruits. Water less in winter to encourage the plants to go dormant.

**Pruning** Prune just before the new-season growth begins, while the plant is leafless. Keep fruiting branches close to main stems by removing a moderate amount of wood each year.

**Propagation** For the best-tasting fruits, graft cultivars to seedling rootstock just as buds are swelling.

**Pests and diseases** Generally no significant problems.

**Harvesting and storage** Clip firm fruits from the tree when their color changes to pale green or yellow; let them soften at room temperature. Store harvested fruits at 50°F (10°C) before ripening at room temperature.

# *Asimina triloba*

HARDINESS
Zones 4–8.

HEIGHT
10–25 feet
(3–7.5 m)

SPREAD
5–15 feet
(1.5–4.5 m)

COMMENTS
Papayas are
delicious raw
or cooked into
puddings and pies.
Use only slight
heat while cooking
so as to preserve
the delicate flavor.
Eat the flesh only.

# PAPAYA (PAWPAW)

RIPE PAPAYA FRUIT HAS GREENISH YELLOW
SKIN SPECKLED WITH BROWN. THE ORANGE,
CUSTARDY FLESH TASTES LIKE BANANA, WITH
HINTS OF PINEAPPLE, MANGO AND VANILLA.

**Position** Papayas prefer full sunlight
but aren't finicky about soil, as long
as it is well drained.

**Cultivation** Plant young trees in
spring, 15 feet (4.5 m) apart.
Papayas need cross-pollination,
so plant at least two seedlings, a
seedling and a named cultivar, or
two different cultivars. Papayas
sometimes need hand-pollination
for good fruit set.

**Pruning** Little or no pruning is
necessary for papayas.

**Propagation** Seed germinates easily
after you keep it cool and moist for
2–3 months. Growth is very slow
for the first 3 years and it takes
6 years or more for fruits to appear.
For quicker fruit of more reliable
quality, graft selected cultivars onto
seedling papayas just as the buds
are swelling in spring.

**Pests and diseases** Generally no
significant problems.

**Harvesting and storage** Ripe
papayas are slightly soft and have
black specks on their skin. Either let
the fruits ripen on the tree, or pick
slightly underripe for refrigerated
storage. When ready to use, ripen
the fruits at room temperature.

*Averrhoa carambola* OXALIDACEAE

HARDINESS
Zone 10.

HEIGHT
20–30 feet (6–9 m)

SPREAD
15–25 feet
(4.5–7.5 m)

COMMENTS
Carambolas come
in either sweet or
sour types. For
jelly, use slightly
underripe sweet
types or fully ripe
sour types. Ripe
carambolas can be
cooked in tarts and
puddings or added
to curries.

# CARAMBOLA (STAR FRUIT)

CARAMBOLA TREES PRODUCE FLESHY FRUITS
THAT ARE STAR-SHAPED IN CROSS SECTION
AND ENCLOSED WITHIN A WAXY, YELLOW
SKIN. BOTH THE SKIN AND THE CRISP FLESH
ARE EDIBLE.

**Position** Plant in full sun and well-
drained, slightly acid soil with low
salt content. Avoid sites that are
subject to hot, dry winds.

**Cultivation** Work compost into the
soil before planting, and also use
it as a mulch to prevent nutrient
deficiencies. Set out container-
grown plants anytime. Space trees
15–25 feet (4.5–7.5 m) apart. Better
yields can usually be obtained with
cross-pollination.

**Pruning** Carambola needs little
pruning beyond the removal of
vigorous, upright shoots.

**Propagation** Seed germinates readily
when fresh. However, grafted plants
bear more quickly, and their fruit
quality is more predictable.

**Pests and diseases** Plants have no
significant pest or disease problems.

**Harvesting and storage** Pick the
fruits when they are pale green with
some yellow. Ripe fruits often fall to
the ground. Fruits will keep for a
few weeks at 50°F (10°C). Pickle
underripe fruits or cook them as
you would a vegetable.

*Berberis* spp.

HARDINESS
Zones 3–9.

HEIGHT
3–12 feet
(90–360 cm)

SPREAD
3–12 feet
(90–360 cm)

COMMENTS
Common barberry
*Berberis vulgaris*
and other species,
including raisin
barberry
*B. asiatica* and
Nepal barberry
*B. aristata*, are
used for their fruits.

# BARBERRY

BARBERRIES PRODUCE RED, YELLOW OR BLACK BERRIES; BOTH THE FLESH AND SKIN OF THE BERRIES ARE EDIBLE. THE FLAVOR IS USUALLY TART, BUT IN SOME SPECIES THE FRUITS HAVE ENOUGH SUGAR TO BE DRIED INTO "RAISINS."

**Position** Barberries prefer full sun and moist, well-drained soil. (Evergreen species are generally less hardy than deciduous species.)

**Cultivation** Set out container-grown plants anytime the soil isn't frozen, or plant bareroot shrubs in spring or autumn, while they are still dormant. Space plants 3–12 feet (90–360 cm) apart, depending on how big the particular species gets.

**Pruning** Cut a few of the oldest stems to the ground in winter. Also shorten spindly stems and thin out suckers if the stems are crowded.

**Propagation** Mix seed with moist peat moss and refrigerate it for 2–3 months before sowing in a warm, bright place. Or dig up and transplant suckers from the base of a bush.

**Pests and diseases** Generally no significant problems.

**Harvesting and storage** Harvest the berries after they are fully colored. Make the fruit into conserves, jams or pickles for storage, or dry them and store in airtight jars.

# *Carissa macrocarpa*

**HARDINESS**
Zone 10.

**HEIGHT**
2–18 feet
(60–540 cm), but
cultivars vary in
their eventual
height and spread.

**COMMENTS**
Natal plum fruit is
usually cooked into
jellies, sauces
and pies.

# NATAL PLUM

THE ROUNDISH FRUIT OF NATAL PLUM IS
THE SIZE OF A PING-PONG BALL, WITH A
CRIMSON SKIN AND STRAWBERRY-RED FLESH.
THE WHOLE FRUIT IS EDIBLE; SOME PEOPLE
PREFER TO REMOVE THE SMALL SEEDS.

**Position** Plant in full sun or partial
shade in well-drained soil. Natal
plum withstands salt spray and is
moderately drought-tolerant.

**Cultivation** Set out container-grown
plants anytime, spacing them
roughly 10 feet (3 m) apart,
depending on the eventual size of
the particular cultivar. Natal plum
generally needs cross-pollination,
so plant at least two seedlings or
cultivars. Hand-pollination often
helps when fruiting is poor. In areas
where Natal plum is not hardy,
grow it indoors in a container.

**Pruning** Prune only as needed to
shape the plant and to remove dead
or crossing branches. You can even
shear this plant as a hedge.

**Propagation** Take cuttings of
semi-woody shoots, or layer a
branch from an established plant.

**Pests and diseases** Generally no
significant problems.

**Harvesting and storage** For fresh
eating, pick fruit when fully ripe
(fully colored); pick fruits slightly
underripe for cooking. Plants
produce fruit almost year-round,
so pick it as you need it.

*Carya illinoensis*                                    JUGLANDACEAE

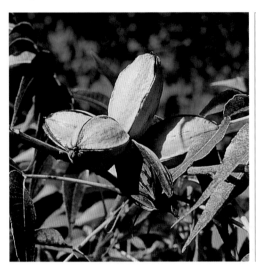

HARDINESS
Zones 6–9.

HEIGHT
50–150 feet
(15–45 m)

SPREAD
35–50 feet
(10.5–15 m)

COMMENTS
If the growing
season in your
area is closer to
the 150-day range,
choose extra-hardy
and early-maturing
cultivars such as
'Major' or 'Giles'.

# PECAN

LARGE, RICH-FLAVORED NUTS EMERGE EASILY
FROM THEIR SHELLS—A BIG TIME-SAVER.

**Position** Plant in full sun in average
to rich, well-drained soil.

**Cultivation** Male (pollen-providing)
and female (nut-producing) flowers
on pecan trees usually don't open
at the same time. For this reason,
you usually need to plant another
tree that can provide pollen when
the main crop tree is ready. Space
trees 35–50 feet (10.5–15 m) apart.
Mulch with compost and irrigate
during dry periods.

**Pruning** Pecans naturally take on a
central-leader shape, so established
pecans seldom need much pruning.

Remove any branches that are
competing with the main trunk and
trim out dead or damaged branches
as you spot them. Call an arborist to
remove large limbs.

**Propagation** Propagate by grafting.

**Pests and diseases** Diseases such as
scab can be a problem in humid
areas. Pecan weevils lay their eggs
in almost-mature nuts. Rake up and
destroy damaged nuts.

**Harvesting and storage** Grafted trees
will begin bearing nuts in 4–7 years.
Tap limbs with a padded stick or
pick up fallen nuts. Remove the
husks and dry the nuts for several
weeks. Store in a cool place.

# *Casimiroa edulis*

HARDINESS
Zone 10.

HEIGHT
15–50 feet
(4.5–15 m)

SPREAD
15–50 feet
(4.5–15 m)

COMMENTS
Only the flesh is
edible, not the
seeds or skin.
(The seeds are
poisonous.)

# SAPOTE, WHITE

THE ROUND OR OVAL FRUIT OF WHITE
SAPOTE IS COVERED WITH A THIN, PALE
GREEN OR GOLDEN YELLOW SKIN. THE
BUTTERY FLESH IS WHITE OR YELLOW
AND IT HAS A SWEET AND SLIGHTLY
RESINOUS FLAVOR.

**Position** White sapote needs full
sun and well-drained soil.

**Cultivation** Set out container-grown
plants anytime, spacing them
15–50 feet (4.5–15 m) apart. Many,
but not all, cultivars are self-fruitful.
Do not plant where the fallen fruit
will be a nuisance. The trees
require very little care.

**Pruning** Shorten stems on young
trees to promote branching. Prune

mature trees to keep them from
growing too large.

**Propagation** Propagate cultivars by
grafting onto seedling rootstock.

**Pests and diseases** Generally no
significant problems.

**Harvesting and storage** Watch for
the color change, which is subtle on
green-skinned cultivars. This signals
that it is time to clip fruits from the
tree. Leave a piece of stem attached
and allow the harvested fruit to
ripen at room temperature.

## *Ceratonia siliqua*

**HARDINESS**
Zones 9–10.

**HEIGHT**
25–50 feet
(7.5–15 m)

**SPREAD**
15–35 feet
(4.5–10.5 m)

**COMMENTS**
The pods have a rather chocolate-like flavor. Munch on raw pods, or remove the seeds and roast and grind the pods, for use as a substitute for chocolate.

# CAROB

CAROB TREES YIELD FLAT, BROWN, EDIBLE PODS THAT ARE FILLED WITH A ROW OF SEEDS AND SOFT, SWEET, BROWN FLESH.

**Position** Carob prefers climates with a hot, dry summer; plant in full sun and alkaline, well-drained soil.

**Cultivation** Transplant young plants or set out container-grown stock carefully. Plant potted plants anytime, or set out bareroot plants in spring or autumn, while they are dormant. Space plants 15–35 feet (4.5–10.5 m) apart. Male trees are usually needed to pollinate female trees; either plant a male for every 25–30 females, or graft a single male branch onto a female tree.

**Pruning** No regular pruning needed.

**Propagation** Fresh seed germinates readily, but dry seed germinates slowly and at a low rate even when helped along by being nicked with a file. Propagate cultivars by budding or grafting scions onto seedling rootstock.

**Pests and diseases** Keep deer and rabbits from trees with traps and fences. Where scale insects are a problem, spray with horticultural oil.

**Harvesting and storage** Pods turn dark brown when ripe. Pick before wet weather or even heavy dew. Shake or knock ripe pods from the branches and dry them in the sun.

# x *Citrofortunella microcarpa*

**HARDINESS**
Zones 9–10 for outdoor culture.

**HEIGHT**
6–24 feet
(1.8–7.2 m)

**SPREAD**
3–12 feet
(90–360 cm)

**COMMENTS**
The sweet, edible rind easily peels away from the segmented flesh, which is juicy, but too tart to eat plain. Use fruits to flavor drinks or to make marmalade.

# CALAMONDIN

CALAMONDINS GROW AS BUSHES OR SMALL TREES, PRODUCING BOUNTIFUL HARVESTS OF SMALL, ROUND, REDDISH ORANGE FRUITS.

**Position** Give calamondins full sun and slightly acid, well-drained soil.

**Cultivation** Set out container-grown plants anytime, spaced 3–12 feet (90–360 cm) apart, depending on whether you want a hedge or individual plants. Calamondins are self-fruitful, so you need only one plant. They are easy to grow in containers. Water your tree regularly to keep the soil evenly moist, especially during bloom.

**Pruning** Calamondins don't need regular pruning, unless you want to keep the plant small. Plants can be sheared as hedges.

**Propagation** Propagate calamondins by sowing fresh seed, taking stem cuttings, or grafting. Trifoliate orange *Poncirus trifoliata* is a good disease-resistant, dwarfing rootstock to use for grafting.

**Pests and diseases** Problems are usually minimal if soil drainage is good, but keep an eye out for scale, mealybugs, mites and whiteflies.

**Harvesting and storage** Harvest when fruits are fully colored, or let them hang on the tree until you are ready to use them. Store in a refrigerator crisper.

# *Citrus* spp.

# CITRUS

ONE FACTOR COMMON TO ALL CITRUS
FRUITS IS THEIR RICH VITAMIN C CONTENT.
LEMONS AND LIMES HAVE THE POWER TO
PERK UP THE FLAVOR OF MOST DISHES;
ORANGES AND GRAPEFRUIT ARE REFRESHING
AS SNACKS AND IN SALADS.

**Position** Frost will damage the fruit
of any citrus plants and sometimes
the rest of the tree. Plant in full sun
to light shade in average to rich,
well-drained soil. If your area gets
surprise frosts, plant these trees
near a sunny wall that will radiate
heat on cold nights.

**Cultivation** Citrus trees are nearly
all self-fertile, so you need to plant
only one to get a good harvest.
Space large citrus trees at least
25 feet (7.5 m) apart and dwarf
trees 10 feet (3 m) apart. Paint the
trunk with white latex paint (diluted
with an equal amount of water) to
prevent sunburn. Keep the soil
moist to prevent early fruit drop.
Mulch with compost, adding a fresh
layer several times during the year
as the old layer breaks down.
Fertilize lightly but often to
encourage good tree vigor.

**Pruning** Remove damaged or
diseased branches and upright-
growing shoots that emerge from
the roots. Trim back long branches
to shape the plant. Wear gloves
when pruning thorny types to
protect your hands.

HARDINESS
Zones 8–10.

HEIGHT
10–30 feet (3–9 m)

SPREAD
10–30 feet (3–9 m)

COMMENTS
If you need a smaller tree, choose one that has been grafted onto a dwarfing rootstock, or look for dwarf cultivars such as 'Meyer' and 'Snow' lemons or 'Valencia' oranges.

Citrus make attractive garden features, but if space is limited, consider planting just one tree grafted with two or three types of citrus fruits.

**Propagation** Propagate by bud grafting onto disease-resistant stock.

**Pests and diseases** Start with virus-free, disease-resistant plants and provide good growing conditions to minimize problems. Keep an eye out for scale (small, hard-shelled insects on leaves and stems), whiteflies (small, white flies on leaf undersides), thrips (tiny insects that cause scarring on leaves and fruits), and mites (tiny insects that cause yellow-stippled leaves). Use beneficial insects, traps and insecticidal soap to prevent infestations and control diseases.

**Harvesting and storage** Most citrus trees produce fruit 3–4 years after planting. Finding out when the fruit is ripe can be tricky, since you can't rely on the skin color as an indicator. For example, some oranges remain green when they are ripe unless the temperature falls to below 45°F (7°C). Other cultivars color up early, well before the fruit is ready. The only way to really know if the fruit is ripe is to taste it. Even when they're ripe, many citrus fruits can linger on the tree for weeks without loss of quality. The exception is mandarin oranges; pick these fruits promptly before the flavor deteriorates. Store citrus fruit in the refrigerator for up to two weeks.

# *Cornus mas*

HARDINESS
Zones 4–8.

HEIGHT
15–25 feet
(4.5–7.5 m)

SPREAD
10–20 feet (3–6 m)

COMMENTS
You can enjoy the
fruits out of hand,
although they are
normally used to
make a drink,
preserves, or a
thickened, sweet
syrup called *rob
de cornis.*

## CHERRY, CORNELIAN

THE RED FRUITS OF CORNELIAN CHERRY LOOK
LIKE TRUE CHERRIES. THE FLAVOR IS TART—
RATHER LIKE A SOUR CHERRY. YOU CAN EAT
THE WHOLE FRUIT, BUT NOT THE SEED.

**Position** Give plants full sun and
average, well-drained soil.

**Cultivation** Set out container-grown
plants anytime, as long as the
ground is not frozen, or plant
bareroot stock in spring or autumn,
while it is still dormant. Space
plants 10–20 feet (3–6 m) apart. The
flowers are partially self-fertile, but
cross-pollination increases yields.

**Pruning** No regular pruning needed.

**Propagation** Cornelian cherry is
easy to graft onto seedling

rootstock. To grow seedlings, either
nick the seed with a file or keep it
warm and moist for 4 months. Then
pot the seed and move to a cool,
moist spot for 1–4 months before
putting the pots in a warm, bright
place so the seeds will sprout.

**Pests and diseases** Generally no
significant problems.

**Harvesting and storage** Harvest the
fruits anytime after they are fully
colored. (Most turn red; a few kinds
ripen yellow or white.) The longer
they hang on the tree, the more
mellow they become in flavor.
Harvested fruits also mellow if
kept at room temperature.

# *Corylus* spp.

HARDINESS
American and
beaked hazels
are hardy in
Zones 2–8. Turkish
filberts are hardy
in Zones 4–9.
European hazels
are hardy in
Zones 4–8.

HEIGHT
6–70 feet
(1.8–21 m)

SPREAD
Up to 20 feet (6 m)

COMMENTS
Destroy damaged
nuts to eliminate
filbertworms.

# HAZELNUT

HAZELNUTS, OR FILBERTS, ARE SMALL, PLUMP
NUTS PRODUCED ON TREES AND SHRUBS.

**Position** Hazelnuts do best in full
sun (or light afternoon shade in hot
climates) in well-drained, loamy soil.

**Cultivation** Mulch to reduce weeds.
Water mature trees during dry times
or grow drought-tolerant cultivars.

**Pruning** European, beaked and
American hazels naturally grow into
dense bushes that make good
hedges; thin out the older wood
each winter to encourage new
growth. Turkish hazels grow into
tall trees that need little pruning.

**Propagation** Grow from seed, or by
layering or grafting.

**Pests and diseases** If eastern filbert
blight is a problem, plant less-
susceptible American hazels, or
moderately resistant European
cultivars such as 'Hall's Giant' and
'Barcelona'. Net shrub forms to keep
animal pests away from the nuts.

**Harvesting and storage** Hazels begin
bearing nuts in 2–3 years. They
ripen in autumn and are ready to
pick when nuts come free from the
husks easily. Pluck them or tap the
limbs with a padded stick to make
the nuts drop onto a cloth. The
European cultivar 'Barcelona' drops
its nuts without tapping. Let the
nuts dry until crunchy. Store in a
cool place for up to a year.

# Melon

VINE-RIPENED MELONS ARE A GREAT FLAVOR
TREAT, WELL WORTH THE LITTLE EXTRA CARE
THEY DEMAND FOR A SUCCESSFUL CROP.

**Position** Full sun in a site with good
air circulation. Plant in well-drained,
well-manured soil, not too acid;
pH 6.0–7.0.

**Cultivation** Set out plants 2–3 weeks
after germination into soil that has
first been warmed with black plastic
mulch. Use row covers to increase
warmth and protect from cucumber
beetles; remove covers when the
plants bloom. Cultivate shallowly to
reduce competition from weeds
until plants begin to vine. Water
weekly with compost tea or fish
emulsion to maintain growth.

**Pruning** Trim to confine only.

**Propagation** In long-season areas,
sow seed directly into the ground
when the soil is thoroughly warm.
Plant three or four seeds to a hill
and site hills 4–5 feet (1.2–1.5 m)
apart. In colder areas, start indoors
in individual pots, two seeds to a
pot, around the time of last frost.

**Pests and diseases** Plant radishes or
basil in the hill with melons to help
deter cucumber beetles. Or protect
plants with row covers; remove
covers when plants start to flower
to aid pollination. Spray foliage
thoroughly with a baking soda
solution (1 teaspoon per quart [liter]
of water) to control mildew. Rotate

# *Melon* continued

HARDINESS
Zones 4 and
warmer. In colder
areas, grow short-
season cultivars.

SPREAD
If space is limited,
melon vines can
be supported on a
frame or trellis.

COMMENTS
Melons do not
tolerate frost. Most
cantaloupes and
muskmelons mature
in about 68 days,
watermelons and
honeydews take
up to 95 days.

Muskmelon *Cucumis melo*, also called Persian melon or nutmeg melon. Melons do not ripen after picking, so for the best flavor leave on the vine until fully ripe.

plantings of melons and relatives, such as squash and cucumber, to reduce pest populations. Wilt spread by cucumber beetles causes plants to collapse before fruit ripens. Do not allow plants to become stressed from lack of water or nutrients. In warm areas, successive plantings increase the odds of a good harvest.

**Harvesting and storage** Pick muskmelons when cracks appear where fruit is attached to the stem. They should "slip" from the stem easily with a slight tug. Let them sit for 1–2 days at room temperature to ripen perfectly. Watermelons are ripe when the tendril closest to the fruit is brown and shriveled. When

ripe, hard-rind melons, such as honeydews, casabas and true cantaloupes, will show a subtle change of rind color. Most melons have a short storage life; some late-season melons will keep up to 2 months in a cool, dry place.

**Related plants**

**Apple melon *C. melo*, Chito Group**
Also called mango melon, vegetable orange, garden lemon or vine peach. Small yellow or orange fruit, used in preserves and pickles. No named cultivars.

**Cantaloupe *C. melo*, Cantalupensis Group** Also called rockmelon. Most commercial cantaloupes are muskmelons. Widely grown in

# *Melon* continued

Watermelon *Citrullus lanatus*. The cultivars 'Charleston Gray' and 'Jubilee' are both resistant to Fusarium wilt, which is spread by the striped cucumber beetle.

Europe, true cantaloupes don't have a netted rind. Try 'Charentais'.

**Casaba melon *C. melo*, Inodorus Group** Large, football- or banana-shaped fruit with gold skin and white flesh. Late-maturing, good keeper. Cultivars include 'Juan Canary' and 'Santa Claus'.

**Crenshaw melon *C. melo*, Inodorus Group** Pear-shaped with pale tan skin, delicately flavored, light pink or salmon flesh. Cultivars include 'Burpee Early Hybrid Crenshaw'.

**Honeydew melon *C. melo*, Inodorus Group** Smooth rind, usually pale green or ivory, with green flesh. Generally late-maturing; early cultivars include 'Earlidew' and 'Venus Hybrid'.

**Muskmelon *C. melo*, Reticulatus Group** Also called Persian melon, nutmeg melon, and, incorrectly, cantaloupe. Rind is netted and usually ridged, flesh is orange or green, sweet and fragrant. Cultivars include 'Harper Hybrid' (small, early melon), 'Ambrosia' and 'Iroquois'.

**Watermelon *Citrullus lanatus*** More drought-tolerant than other melons and less vulnerable to insect pests. Rind can be dark to light green, solid, striped or mottled. Usually red-fleshed, but some orange-, yellow- and white-fleshed cultivars. Cultivars include 'Sugar Baby' (a small melon), 'Charleston Gray' (large, long season), and 'Yellow Doll' (yellow-fleshed).

# Cydonia oblonga

HARDINESS
Zones 5–9.

HEIGHT
15–20 feet
(4.5–6 m)

SPREAD
15–20 feet
(4.5–6 m)

COMMENTS
The skin and spicy, white or yellowish flesh are edible cooked, but the flesh is too astringent to be eaten raw. Quince adds pizzazz to an apple pie.

# QUINCE

QUINCE TREES PRODUCE YELLOW FRUIT COVERED WITH DOWNY HAIRS.

**Position** Plant in full sun in well-drained and moderately fertile soil.

**Cultivation** Plant container-grown stock anytime, as long as the ground is not frozen; or set out bareroot plants in spring or autumn, while they are dormant. Space plants 15–20 feet (4.5–6 m) apart. Quinces are self-fertile, so you need only one plant.

**Pruning** Train as a small tree or large shrub. Each winter, prune off enough wood to keep the plant open to sunlight and air, removing any diseased or misplaced branches.

**Propagation** Graft cultivars onto quince rootstock, propagated by layering or from seed.

**Pests and diseases** In summer, watch for blackened leaves and curled-over stems—signs of fireblight, which is a big problem in many areas.

**Harvesting and storage** Pick fruits when they are scented and fully colored. Handle ripe fruit gently. It can be stored for 2–3 months at temperatures near freezing with high humidity, such as in a refrigerator. Alternatively, make it into a fine, clear, pink jelly or a dense paste for use with cheese and crackers.

# *Diospyros* spp.

EBENACEAE

HARDINESS
Zones 7–10 for
most oriental
persimmons; Zones
4–9 for American
persimmons.

HEIGHT
25–60 feet
(7.5–18 m)

SPREAD
20–35 feet
(6–10.5 m)

COMMENTS
Fresh persimmons
will keep for about
2 months in the
refrigerator. Eat
fresh, or freeze
or dry them.

# PERSIMMON

PERSIMMON FLESH HAS A HONEY-LIKE
SWEETNESS, SMOOTH AS SILK IN ORIENTAL
PERSIMMON *DIOSPYROS KAKI*, BUT DRIER
AND RICHER IN THE CASE OF THE AMERICAN
PERSIMMON *D. VIRGINIANA*.

**Position** Give persimmons full sun
and well-drained soil.

**Cultivation** Plant in spring,
preserving as much of the taproot
as possible. Space plants 20–35 feet
(6–10.5 m) apart. The pollination
needs vary with the cultivar. Thin
oriental persimmon fruits by hand
if they seem too crowded.

**Pruning** Shorten long, willowy
growth on young trees to stimulate
branching. Prune mature trees only
enough to stimulate new growth for
regular fruiting and to keep bearing
wood near the main branches.

**Propagation** Graft selected cultivars
onto *D. virginiana*, *D. kaki* or
*D. lotus* rootstocks in spring, just
as the buds are swelling.

**Pests and diseases** Where
persimmon girdler is a problem,
pick up and burn fallen twigs
regularly in autumn.

**Harvesting and storage** Clip ripe
persimmons from trees. Harvest
non-astringent oriental types when
fully colored and firm. Astringent
oriental and American types are not
edible until very soft.

# *Eriobotrya japonica*

**HARDINESS**
Zones 8–10.

**HEIGHT**
20–30 feet (6–9 m)

**SPREAD**
25–35 feet
(7.5–10.5 m)

**COMMENTS**
Eat loquats fresh,
cook them into a
sauce or cut them
in half and dry
them. Fresh fruits
will keep in the
refrigerator for
1–2 weeks.

# LOQUAT

LOQUAT TREES PRODUCE YELLOW, PLUM-
SIZED, ROUND, OVAL OR PEAR-SHAPED FRUIT
WITH SCENTED WHITE PULP THAT IS SWEET
WITH A BIT OF A TANG. REMOVE THE SKIN
AND SEEDS BEFORE EATING LOQUATS.

**Position** Plant in full sun or partial
shade in well-drained soil. Loquats
are somewhat drought-resistant.

**Cultivation** Set out container-grown
plants anytime, spacing them
20–30 feet (6–9 m) apart. Most
cultivars are self-fruitful. Thin fruits
in winter by clipping off some of
the clusters or individual fruitlets.
Mulch to protect the shallow roots.
Fertilize regularly. To grow loquats
in containers, choose a dwarf
cultivar and repot annually.

**Pruning** Thinning the fruits by
removing clusters takes care of
much of the pruning. Shorten
additional stems to let in light.

**Propagation** Graft cultivars onto
seedling loquat rootstock. Both
quince and pyracantha have been
used as dwarfing rootstocks.

**Pests and diseases** Watch for
blackened leaves and curled-over
shoots—signs of fireblight, a big
problem in many areas. Enclose
fruits in paper bags to protect them
from sunburn if plants are growing
in full sun.

**Harvesting and storage** Clip off fruits
when fully colored and slightly soft.

*Feijoa sellowiana*                                            MYRTACEAE

HARDINESS
Zones 9–10;
possibly Zone 8.

HEIGHT
15–20 feet
(4.5–6 m)

SPREAD
15–20 feet
(4.5–6 m)

COMMENTS
The fleshy flower
petals, white with
a tinge of purple,
are also sweet
and edible.

# FEIJOA

THE GREEN FRUIT OF FEIJOA FORMS ON A
LARGE, BUSHY PLANT. THE EDIBLE, GREENISH
FLESH, EMBEDDED WITH SMALL, EDIBLE
SEEDS, HAS A FLAVOR COMBINING THE BEST
OF PINEAPPLE, STRAWBERRY AND MINT.

**Position** Feijoa needs some winter
chilling to flower and fruit. Plant in
well-drained soil and full sun,
except in desert areas, where some
midday shade is needed.

**Cultivation** Set out container-grown
plants anytime. Space them at least
3 feet (90 cm) apart. Most feijoas
need cross-pollination, but a
number of cultivars are self-fertile.
In cool climates, you can grow
feijoas in pots; move them indoors
to a cool, bright location in winter.

**Pruning** Train as a shrub, small tree
or sheared hedge. Train grafted
plants as single-trunked trees,
removing all shoots that come off
the base of the stem. Feijoas don't
require much pruning, but can be
tidied up after harvest.

**Propagation** Propagate cultivars by
taking cuttings or by grafting them
onto seedling rootstock.

**Pests and diseases** Generally no
significant problems.

**Harvesting and storage** Ripe fruits
drop to the ground; gather them
every few days. Nearly ripe fruits
will ripen indoors. Fruits keep well
refrigerated with high humidity.

*Ficus carica*                                    MORACEAE

HARDINESS
Grow figs outdoors
in Zones 8–10 or in
protected areas up
to Zone 6.

HEIGHT
10–25 feet (3–8 m)

SPREAD
10–25 feet (3–8 m)

COMMENTS
Figs such as
'Conadria', 'Genoa'
and 'Panachee'
need long, hot
summers; cultivars
such as 'Venture'
and 'Osborne
Prolific' do best
with cool summers.

# FIG

FIGS ARE PRODUCTIVE AND GENERALLY EASY
TO GROW. THEY ARE SELDOM TROUBLED BY
PESTS, EXCEPT FOR BIRDS. NET THE TREE TO
DISCOURAGE THESE GREEDY FIG-LOVERS.

**Position** Plant in full sun in average,
well-drained soil. In cool climates,
plant figs in large containers and
move them inside for winter.

**Cultivation** Select self-pollinating
cultivars. Space large cultivars up
to 25 feet (8 m) apart; smaller trees
can be as close as 5 feet (1.5 m)
apart. Mulch generously with
compost as needed.

**Pruning** Thin out excess growth as
needed to control plant size and
allow for good light penetration into
the center of the plant. You can
also train figs as espaliers to grow
on sun-warmed walls.

**Propagation** Propagate by cutting
rooted suckers off the roots or
taking hardwood cuttings.

**Pests and diseases** Place netting over
trees to discourage birds, or grow
green-fruited cultivars, which are
less appealing to birds.

**Harvesting and storage** Fig trees
produce their first crop a year after
planting. Ripe figs are soft, with a
slightly flexible "neck;" sometimes
the skin splits. You can keep figs
for a few days in the refrigerator, or
cut them in halves and dry them.

# *Fortunella* spp.

**HARDINESS**
Zones 9–10.

**HEIGHT**
8–15 feet
(2.4–4.5 m)

**SPREAD**
6–12 feet
(1.8–3.6 m)

**COMMENTS**
Fruits are tasty
fresh, candied or
cooked into a
marmalade or
a sauce. They
keep well in
the refrigerator.

# KUMQUAT

THE FRUIT OF THE KUMQUAT LOOKS LIKE A
MINIATURE ORANGE—ABOUT THE SIZE OF A
CHERRY AND EITHER ROUND OR ELONGATED.
THE SKIN IS EDIBLE AND SWEET, AND THE
JUICY FLESH RANGES FROM TART TO SWEET.

**Position** Plant in full sun in well-
drained, slightly acid soil. Kumquat
tolerates winter weather as cold as
18°F (–7.7°C), but without sufficient
heat in summer, the fruits will be
few and of poor quality.

**Cultivation** Plant container-grown
stock anytime, or set out bareroot
plants in spring or autumn, while
they are dormant. Space plants
6–12 feet (1.8–3.6 m) apart.
Kumquats make beautiful potted
plants that fruit reliably. Put in

a cool, sunny room in winter and
repot every year.

**Pruning** Kumquats need no pruning
other than to shape the plants and
thin out crowded branches.

**Propagation** Kumquats are usually
grafted onto the rootstock of
trifoliate orange *Poncirus trifoliata*,
which also dwarfs the tree, or onto
sour orange *Citrus aurantium* or
grapefruit rootstocks.

**Pests and diseases** Problems are
usually minimal if soil drainage is
good, but look out for scale,
mealybugs, mites and whiteflies.

**Harvesting and storage** Harvest fruits
when fully colored.

## *Fragaria* spp.

HARDINESS
Zones 3–10.

HEIGHT
10 inches (25 cm)

SPREAD
1–2 feet
(30–60 cm)

COMMENTS
Strawberries are
self-fruitful. For the
longest possible
harvest, grow
plants of more
than one type
(June-bearers,
ever-bearers and
day-neutrals).

# STRAWBERRY

YOU'LL AVOID MOST PROBLEMS BY STARTING
WITH CERTIFIED DISEASE-FREE PLANTS OF
DISEASE-RESISTANT CULTIVARS.

**Position** Choose cultivars that are
appropriate for your climate. For
warmer areas, try 'Apollo', 'Arking',
'Chandler' and 'Sequoia'. In cooler
climes, try 'Crimson King' or 'Fort
Laramie'. Of the day-neutral types,
'Tristar', 'Tribute', 'Fern' and 'Selva'
can grow well in a fairly wide range
of climates; 'Brighton' and 'Heckler'
are best in cooler, temperate areas.
Plant in an area of full sun (or light
afternoon shade for day-neutral
strawberries) free from late-spring
frosts. The soil should be fertile and
well drained. If possible, avoid

garden areas previously used to
grow bell peppers (capsicum),
tomatoes, potatoes, eggplant
(aubergine), melons, okra, mints,
raspberries or blackberries, mums
or roses—crops that may leave
behind problems that can attack
strawberries. Add extra organic
matter before planting to make
the soil rich and moist.

**Cultivation** For an easy-care
strawberry bed, mound your garden
soil in a bed about 6 inches (15 cm)
tall and 2 feet (60 cm) wide, install
drip irrigation, and cover it all with
plastic mulch before planting. Cut
X-shaped slits in the plastic, and
plant through the slits into the soil.

## *Strawberry* continued

Strawberries do well in containers, such as special strawberry pots or hanging baskets. A bonus with such ways of growing is that the fruits are easier to protect from birds.

This hill system is especially good for ever-bearing or day-neutral strawberries. If planting in a flat bed, space plants 1–2 feet (30–60 cm) apart and keep the soil moist until berries are almost ripe. In early winter, cover plants with 2 inches (5 cm) of straw to prevent cold damage. Pull back the mulch as soon as plants begin to grow again in spring. If frost threatens new growth, cover the plants overnight with a floating row cover.

**Pruning** Weed, pinch out unwanted runners and mow along edge of bed as needed to keep walkways clear.

**Propagation** Propagate by transplanting disease-free rooted runners.

**Pests and diseases** Pick ripe fruit regularly to keep gray mold (botrytis blight) at bay. Remove and destroy damaged flowers and fruits as you spot them. Several problems can cause wilted plants. To determine the cause, dig up a few plants. If there are few or no side roots and the roots are reddish inside when cut lengthwise, red stele is the problem. If the roots are black and rotting, the culprit is root rot. Destroy all wilted plants.

**Harvesting and storage** Pick berries, leaving some stem on for better storage, when fully colored, tender and sweet. Eat fruit fresh, or make into jam or freeze immediately.

# *Fragaria vesca* 'Semperflorens'

ROSACEAE

HARDINESS
Zones 3–10.

HEIGHT
6 inches (15 cm)

SPREAD
6–12 inches
(15–30 cm)

COMMENTS
Plants will fruit
generously, even in
small pots. Eat the
fruits fresh as they
do not store well.

# STRAWBERRY, ALPINE

ALPINE STRAWBERRIES PRODUCE POINTED
FRUITS ON LOW, CLUMP-FORMING PLANTS.
THE RIPE FRUITS ARE USUALLY RED,
ALTHOUGH SOME WHITE CULTIVARS EXIST.
THE WHOLE FRUIT IS EDIBLE.

**Position** Plant in full sun or partial
shade, with well-drained soil that is
rich in humus.

**Cultivation** Set out container-grown
plants anytime the ground isn't
frozen, or plant bareroot stock in
spring or autumn, while the plants
are dormant. Set plants 6–12 inches
(15–30 cm) apart, planting so that
the ground level is just below the
lowest leaves on the crown. Alpine
strawberries are self-fruitful, so you
will get fruit from just one plant.

**Pruning** None is necessary.

**Propagation** To divide old plants,
dig them up and cut off young
crown pieces (with attached roots)
from the outside of the clump.
Throw away the old center part and
replant the divisions immediately.
To grow alpine strawberries from
seed, scatter the fine seed on the
surface of potting soil in a
container. Transplant seedlings
when large enough to handle.

**Pests and diseases** Keep birds at bay
with netting, or grow white-fruited
cultivars, which birds leave alone.

**Harvesting and storage** Harvest the
fruits when soft and scented.

# *Gaylussacia* spp.

**HARDINESS**
Plants vary in
adaptability,
according to origin,
but generally
Zones 5–8.

**HEIGHT**
1–6 feet
(30–180 cm)

**SPREAD**
3 feet (90 cm)
or more (some
spread via
underground
stems).

**COMMENTS**
The whole fruit is
edible, including
the seeds.

# HUCKLEBERRY

HUCKLEBERRY FRUIT LOOKS AND TASTES
SIMILAR TO A BLUEBERRY. YOU'LL KNOW
WHAT YOU'RE EATING, HOWEVER, BY THE
CRUNCH OF HUCKLEBERRY'S SMALL SEEDS.

**Position** *G. frondosa* and
*G. dumosa* enjoy wet sites;
*G. baccata* prefers drier sites. All
huckleberries like full sun and very
acid soil; pH 4.5–5.5.

**Cultivation** Plant container-grown
shrubs anytime the ground isn't
frozen, or set out bareroot plants in
spring or autumn, while dormant.
Space plants 3 feet (90 cm) apart.
Before planting, make sure the soil
is very acid and rich in humus. Dig
acid peat moss into the soil to meet
both of these needs.

**Pruning** No regular pruning needed.

**Propagation** Fresh seed germinates
fairly well, but for best results, keep
the seed warm and moist for a
month, then cool and moist for
1–2 months. Cuttings taken from
late summer through autumn root
well in a mix of peat and either
sand or perlite.

**Pests and diseases** Generally no
significant problems.

**Harvesting and storage** Pick fruits
when fully colored. One way to
harvest is to spread a clean cloth
on the ground and shake the plant;
ripe fruits fall on the cloth. Store in
the refrigerator with high humidity.

# *Juglans cinerea*

HARDINESS
Zones 3–7.

HEIGHT
40–60 feet
(12–18 m)

SPREAD
30–50 feet
(9–15 m)

COMMENTS
Other members of
this nut-producing
family include
English walnuts
*Juglans regia* (also
called Persian
walnuts) and black
walnuts *J. nigra*.

# BUTTERNUT

BUTTERNUTS ARE LARGE TREES THAT
PRODUCE EDIBLE NUTS ENCASED IN A HUSK
AND SHELL. THE HARD SHELL IS SOMEWHAT
ELONGATED AND ENDS IN A POINT. THE MEAT
WITHIN IS RICH AND BUTTERY.

**Position** Full sun and deep, moist,
rich soil is best, but plants will
tolerate dry, rocky soil, especially
on limestone.

**Cultivation** Transplant in spring,
taking care to preserve as much of
the taproot as possible if the plant
is not growing in a container. Space
plants 30–50 feet (9–15 m) apart.

**Pruning** Train young trees to form a
sturdy framework of well-spaced,
wide-angled branches. On mature

trees, just cut out diseased or dead
wood and odd untidy branches.

**Propagation** Mix seed with damp
peat moss and refrigerate for
3–4 months before sowing in a
warm, bright place. Graft cultivars
onto black walnut rootstock.

**Pests and diseases** Small, black
pustules and dying limbs indicate
butternut dieback disease. Cut
diseased branches back to healthy
wood, and fertilize and water trees.

**Harvesting and storage** Harvest nuts
after they fall. Allow husks to dry,
so they crumble off when you are
ready to crack the nut. Store kernels
in the refrigerator at high humidity.

# APPLE

To get high yields from your apples, you'll need to grow at least two cultivars that flower at the same time so they can cross-pollinate.

**Position**  Plant apple trees in full sun and well-drained soil.

**Cultivation**  There are more than 1,000 different apple cultivars available. For extra-high yields, you can choose spur-type trees, which are so heavily loaded with short fruit-bearing spur branches that they stay about 25 percent smaller than the same cultivar without spurs. You can also choose grafted trees with different combinations of rootstocks, interstems (short pieces of trunk) and tops to make just

about any kind of apple tree you can imagine. Plant full-sized apple trees 25–30 feet (7.5–9 m) apart, semidwarfs 12–15 feet (3.6–4.5 m) apart and dwarfs 6–8 feet (1.8–2.4 m) apart. Provide plenty of moisture and nutrients to keep young trees growing quickly. Mulch with compost in spring, and make sure the soil is moist around mature trees when they're in bloom.

**Pruning**  Apple trees grow best when trained into a pyramidal, central leader form, with one trunk and several sets of branches off it. Start pruning young trees just after spring planting (or in the spring following autumn planting).

A mulch of marigold roots has been found to suppress populations
of parasitic nematodes in the soil around apple trees.

Continue thinning and pruning each year until the trees mature.

**Propagation** Propagate by grafting.

**Pests and diseases** Some problems that might occur are apple maggots, codling moths, plum curculios, rust, scab, mildew and fireblight. You can prevent many problems by planting disease-resistant cultivars. Among these, 'Prima', 'Dayton' and 'William's Pride' are early ripening; 'Jonafree', 'Freedom' and 'Liberty' ripen in midseason; and 'Enterprise' ripens late. When rust, mildew or scab do strike, carefully rake up all dropped leaves in autumn. If the diseases were a major problem last year, spray sulfur as often as once a week from the time growth begins until midsummer. Fireblight is a difficult-to-control disease that has become an epidemic across the United States and elsewhere. Use blight-resistant cultivars or you'll have problems.

**Harvesting and storage** Depending on the rootstock, apples will start producing fruit in 2–5 years. Pick apples when they develop full color and flavor but are still crunchy and crisp. You can leave late-maturing apples on the tree as long as the temperature remains above 28°F (–2°C). Use bruised fruit at once. Store unblemished apples at 32°F (0°C) and 90 percent humidity.

*Malus* spp.

**HARDINESS**
Zones 3–9.

**HEIGHT**
8–25 feet
(2.4–7.5 m)

**SPREAD**
8–25 feet
(2.4–7.5 m)

**COMMENTS**
Fruits of most crab
apples are used for
cooking, but a few
cultivars are also
excellent for eating.

# CRAB APPLE

SOME CRAB APPLES TASTE DELICIOUS OUT
OF HAND, WHILE OTHERS TASTE GOOD ONLY
WHEN COOKED WITH SWEETENER INTO
JELLIES. YOU CAN EAT THE WHOLE FRUIT,
EXCEPT FOR THE SEEDS.

**Position** Plant in full sun and
well-drained soil.

**Cultivation** Plant container-grown
stock anytime the ground isn't
frozen, or set out bareroot plants in
spring or autumn, while dormant.
Space plants 8–25 feet (2.4–7.5 m)
apart. The plants need cross-
pollination, but the pollinator can
be an apple or a crab apple.

**Pruning** Train young plants to a
sturdy framework of wide-angled,

well-spaced main limbs. Mature
plants need little pruning beyond
removing water sprouts and
thinning congested growth.

**Propagation** Graft or bud cultivars
onto seedling apple or crab
apple rootstock. Seed, for seedling
rootstocks, germinates readily if
kept cool and moist for 2–3 months.

**Pests and diseases** Crab apples can
have the same pest and disease
problems as apples but are usually
less troubled by them.

**Harvesting and storage** Pick fruits
when fully colored and they pull off
the plant easily. Store, refrigerated,
in a plastic bag with air holes in it.

*Mangifera indica* ANACARDIACEAE

HARDINESS
Zone 10.

HEIGHT
50–90 feet
(15–27 m)

SPREAD
30–125 feet
(9–37.5 m)

COMMENTS
Remove the seed
and skin before
eating the pulp.
The fruits are good
fresh or when used
for chutney, sauces
and ice cream.

# MANGO

THE RIPE FRUIT OF MANGO TREES IS LARGE
AND ELONGATED WITH SKIN IN SHADES OF
RED, YELLOW AND GREEN. INSIDE, THE JUICY,
ORANGE PULP HAS A SWEET, RICH FLAVOR.

**Position** Mangoes need full sun and
well-drained soil that is not too rich.

**Cultivation** Set out container-grown
plants anytime, spacing them
30–60 feet (9–18 m) apart. Plants
are self-fruitful, so you need only
one to get a harvest. Thin fruits
and fertilize during years of good
production; otherwise, the tree
tends to bear only every other year.

**Pruning** Remove dead and crowded
wood to keep the tree within
bounds. In late summer, shorten

some of the stems and remove any
vigorous, upright ones.

**Propagation** Some cultivars come
true from seed, which should be
sown fresh, with the top of the seed
at soil level. A more reliable way to
propagate any cultivar is to graft or
bud it onto a mango seedling while
the tree is actively growing.

**Pests and diseases** In areas where
anthracnose disease is a problem,
rake up and dispose of infected
leaves and fruit.

**Harvesting and storage** Pick fruits
when they soften slightly and
change color. To store, pick them
firm and ripen at room temperature.

# *Mespilus germanica*

**HARDINESS**
Zones 4–8.

**HEIGHT**
9–20 feet
(2.7–6 m)

**SPREAD**
9–20 feet
(2.7–6 m)

**COMMENTS**
The ripening
process takes more
than 2 weeks in
cool temperatures.
Eat the flesh but
not the seeds or
the skin.

# MEDLAR

MEDLAR FRUIT LOOKS LIKE A SMALL,
RUSSETED APPLE, TINGED WITH DULL YELLOW
OR RED. THE FLESH IS SOFT AND BROWN
AND TASTES LIKE THICK APPLESAUCE.

**Position** Give medlars full sun and
moderately rich, well-drained soil.

**Cultivation** Plant container-grown
stock anytime the ground isn't
frozen, or set out bareroot plants in
spring or autumn, while they are
dormant. Space plants 12–25 feet
(3.6–7.5 m) apart. Plant with the
graft union below ground level so
the scion also takes root. Medlars
are self-fertile, and virtually every
blossom sets fruit. On young trees,
pinch off some blossoms to channel
more energy into shoot growth.

**Pruning** This small tree needs very
little pruning; simply trim as needed
to shape and to remove odd dead
or diseased branches.

**Propagation** Graft medlar onto
pear, hawthorn, quince or medlar
seedling rootstock.

**Pests and diseases** No pest or
disease problems worth noting.

**Harvesting and storage** Harvest the
fruits as the leaves begin to drop in
autumn. Although the fruits may
feel rock-hard, handle them
carefully to avoid bruising. Place
them on a shelf in a cool room to
"blet," or soften. Fruits will be soft
and ready to eat in about 2 weeks.

# *Morus* spp.

HARDINESS
Zones 5–10.

HEIGHT
15–30 feet
(4.5–9 m)

SPREAD
10–20 feet
(3–6 m)

COMMENTS
Do not plant
mulberries where
falling fruits will
cause problems
with staining.
For cooking, pick
the fruit when it
is still firm and
slightly underripe.

# MULBERRY

MULBERRY TREES PRODUCE BLACK, RED OR
WHITE BLACKBERRY-SHAPED FRUITS. FLAVOR
RANGES FROM SWEET WITH A SHARP TANG
TO PURELY SWEET. EAT THE WHOLE FRUIT.

**Position** Plant in full sun and
average, well-drained soil.

**Cultivation** Plant container-grown
stock anytime the ground isn't
frozen, or set out bareroot plants in
spring or autumn, while dormant.
Space plants 10–30 feet (3–9 m)
apart. Cultivars selected for fruit
production generally do not need
cross-pollination.

**Pruning** No regular pruning needed.

**Propagation** Russian mulberry
*M. alba* 'Tartarica' makes a good
rootstock for most other mulberries.
Softwood or hardwood cuttings of
most species usually root readily.
With hardwood cuttings, either
split the lower end or take a small
"heel" of 2-year-old wood along
with the 1-year-old wood used for
the cutting.

**Pests and diseases** Control scale
insects with dormant oil, and
handle dieback by cutting off
infected portions.

**Harvesting and storage** To harvest in
quantity, spread a clean sheet under
the tree and shake the branches.
Ripe fruits do not keep well fresh
but can be frozen or dried.

# Musa spp.

HARDINESS
Zone 10.

HEIGHT
8–30 feet
(2.4–9 m)

SPREAD
8–20 feet
(2.4–6 m)

COMMENTS
The edible flesh
of all bananas is
creamy-yellow,
with a smooth
texture and a
sweet, rich flavor.

# BANANA

BANANAS ARE PRODUCED ON LARGE, SOFT, PERENNIAL PLANTS THAT GROW TO THE PROPORTIONS OF A SMALL TREE.

**Position** Give bananas full sun and well-drained, slightly acid soil.

**Cultivation** Plant anytime of year, spacing plants 10–20 feet (3–6 m) apart. Bananas do not need cross-pollination, so you can get fruit from just one plant. The "stem" is really a pseudostem, a tightly wound sheath of leaves, which dies to the ground after fruiting but is replaced by others growing up from the rhizome (a thick underground stem). Cut off male flowers, which form at the far end of the fruit stalk. These plants are heavy feeders, so fertilize regularly, and provide abundant water in warm weather.

**Pruning** Remove all but three pseudostems—one fruiting, one ready to follow and one just peeking up from below. Cut down the fruiting pseudostem at harvest.

**Propagation** Divide rhizomes or dig up suckers with some attached roots.

**Pests and diseases** Generally no significant problems.

**Harvesting and storage** Cut off the entire stalk when some fruits begin to change color. Ripen fruits at room temperature to yellow. Bananas are best eaten fresh, but can also be dried for storage.

## *Olea europaea* subsp. *europaea*

**HARDINESS**
Zones 9–10.

**HEIGHT**
30 feet (9 m)

**SPREAD**
Up to 30 feet
(9 m)

**COMMENTS**
Do not plant olives
along walkways,
driveways or
patios, where fallen
fruit will be a
nuisance.

# OLIVE

OLIVE TREES PRODUCE GRAPE-SIZED FRUIT
WITH EDIBLE FLESH AND SKIN (DON'T EAT THE
SEEDS). THE FRUITS HAVE A RICH, OILY
TASTE, ESPECIALLY WHEN THEY ARE RIPE.

**Position** Give olives full sun and
well-drained soil. They bear best
where summers are long and hot,
with low humidity.

**Cultivation** Plant container-grown
stock anytime, or set out bareroot
plants in spring or autumn, while
dormant. Space plants 20–80 feet
(6–24 m) apart, with the greater
distances reserved for drier climates
where the trees will not be
irrigated. Cross-pollination usually
increases yield. Where fruits are
close together on a stem, thin by
just cutting back the stem, or
removing excess fruits individually.

**Pruning** Young trees need little
pruning. Prune mature trees to keep
them from growing too large.

**Propagation** Propagate olives by
hardwood or softwood cuttings.

**Pests and diseases** Where olive knot
disease is a threat, prune in summer
to prevent problems. Cut away galls
produced by this disease.

**Harvesting and storage** Harvest fruit
when it is green (unripe) or black
(ripe). Don't expose olives intended
for eating to cool temperatures.
Olives are usually brined for storage
after bitterness has been removed.

# *Opuntia* spp.

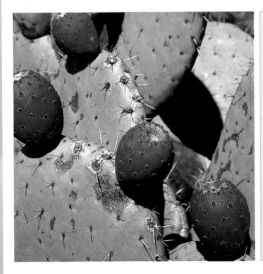

**HARDINESS**
Zones 5–10,
depending on
the species.

**HEIGHT**
1–15 feet
(30–450 cm)

**SPREAD**
3–15 feet
(90–450 cm)

**COMMENTS**
Both the fruit and
the fleshy green
pads are edible.
Eat the fruits raw.
Slice the pads and
cook as you would
string beans.

# PRICKLY PEAR

PRICKLY PEAR FRUITS ARE ABOUT THE SIZE OF
AN EGG WITH RED (OR SOMETIMES YELLOW
OR GREEN) SKIN. THE EDIBLE PULP IS USUALLY
RED, WITH A MILD FLAVOR AND MANY
SMALL, EDIBLE SEEDS.

**Position** Prickly pear needs full sun
and very well-drained soil.

**Cultivation** Plant anytime, unless
the ground is frozen, spacing plants
3–15 feet (90–450 cm) apart
(depending on their mature size).

**Pruning** No pruning is necessary.

**Propagation** Sow seed and keep it
in the dark until sprouts appear.
You can also use the fleshy pads to
start new plants. Cut a pad from the
mother plant and let it dry for a few

days before setting it upright with
the bottom part in well-drained soil.
Water sparingly until roots form
and growth begins.

**Pests and diseases** Generally no
significant problems.

**Harvesting and storage** Wear thick
leather gloves to harvest the flat,
green pads, then remove the spines
(and the tiny hairlike needles at the
base of the spines) by rubbing them
off with a rough cloth or peeling
them off with a vegetable peeler.
Also wear gloves when harvesting
the fruits, which are ripe when fully
colored. Rub off the needles and
peel away the skin before eating.

## *Passiflora incarnata*

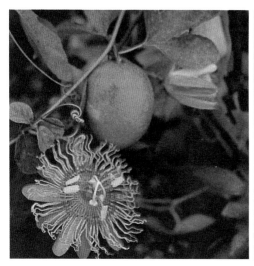

**HARDINESS**
Zone 4–10.

**HEIGHT**
20 feet (6 m)

**SPREAD**
Up to 20 feet
(6 m) or more,
if unrestricted.

**COMMENTS**
Eat the fleshy seed
covering with or
without the seeds.

# MAYPOP

MAYPOP FRUITS ARE YELLOW TO YELLOW-
GREEN WITH MANY SEEDS, EACH ENCASED IN
GELATINOUS PULP WITH A TROPICAL FLAVOR.

**Position** Plant in full sun in
well-drained soil.

**Cultivation** Plant container-grown
vines anytime the ground isn't
frozen, or set out dormant bareroot
plants in spring or autumn. Space
plants 6–18 feet (1.8–5.4 m) apart,
depending on whether you plan to
train vines upward or outward. This
vine likes to have a fence, arbor or
deciduous shrub to climb on. The
roots spread fast and far, so contain
them with a barrier strip or mowed
lawn. Maypops are cross-pollinators;
hand-pollination may help fruit set.

**Pruning** Cut the whole plant to the
ground each year at the end of the
growing season.

**Propagation** Suckers root readily if
dug from the mother plant when a
few inches high. To grow maypops
from seed, first soak the seed in
water for 24 hours. After sowing,
provide a warm, dark environment
until sprouts appear.

**Pests and diseases** No significant
pest or disease problems.

**Harvesting and storage** Fruit drops
to the ground when ripe; gather it
as soon as possible. Store in high
humidity, such as in a plastic bag,
in cool, not cold, temperatures.

# Passiflora spp.

# PASSIONFRUIT

A GRAFTED VINE WILL BEAR FRUIT, AS IT HAS BOTH MALE AND FEMALE CHARACTERISTICS.

**Position** Grow in full sun or, in very hot areas, partial shade. The vines need well-drained soil, rich in humus and low in salts.

**Cultivation** Set out container-grown plants anytime, spacing them about 9 feet (3 m) apart. Some need cross-pollination, so it's smart to plant at least two seedlings or cultivars to be on the safe side. The vines need some support, such as a fence or trellis, on which to climb. Where they are not cold-hardy, grow passionfruit vines in a well-drained soil mix in containers. The plants can wait out winter without full sun in a cool room; in spring, trim and provide full sunlight.

**Pruning** Regular pruning is not a necessity, but it will help to keep the vine untangled. For the neatest growth, train one or two permanent "arms" along the top of the support. Each winter, cut all sideshoots to within a few inches of these arms.

**Propagation** Sow fresh seed, take cuttings (or buy a grafted plant).

**Pests and diseases** Generally no significant problems.

**Harvesting and storage** Pick up ripe fruits from the ground. Fruit can be stored for a few weeks in a plastic bag at about 50°F (10°C).

*Persea americana*

HARDINESS
Zones 9–10.

HEIGHT
20–60 feet
(6–18 m)

SPREAD
25–35 feet
(7.5–10.5 m)

COMMENTS
Because of its
rough skin and
green, sometimes
almost black, color,
the avocado was
once called the
"alligator pear."

# AVOCADO

THE AVOCADO'S PALE GREEN, EDIBLE FLESH
IS BUTTERY SMOOTH, WITH A RICH FLAVOR.

**Position** Plant in full sun. Avocado grows best in well-drained soil with a pH between 5.5 and 6.5.

**Cultivation** Plant in spring, with the base of the trunk slightly higher out of the ground than it was in the nursery. Space plants 25–35 feet (7.5–10.5 m) apart. Avocados can self-pollinate (so you can get fruit from just one plant), but cross-pollination may improve yields.

**Pruning** Prune as necessary after harvest to limit the size of the tree.

**Propagation** Graft onto seedlings or rootstocks grown from cuttings.

**Pests and diseases** Avocado root rot can occur where drainage is poor. Avoid this problem by planting certified disease-free plants in a good site. There is no cure for infected trees. In humid areas, watch for leaf diseases. Minimize damage by keeping trees fertilized and watered as needed, pruning to promote air circulation among branches, and cleaning up infected leaves that fall to the ground.

**Harvesting and storage** When fruit is mature but still hard, clip it off with a piece of stem attached. Dark-skinned cultivars turn dark when mature; green cultivars yellow slightly. Allow fruit to soften slightly.

*Physalis pruinosa*

# CAPE GOOSEBERRY, DWARF

THE PALE YELLOW BERRIES OF DWARF CAPE
GOOSEBERRY RIPEN WITHIN A HUSK ON A
SMALL, SPREADING BUSH.

**Position** Cape gooseberry is a
perennial in the tropics, but you
can grow it as an annual wherever
you can grow tomatoes. It needs
full sun and well-drained soil that
is not overly rich in nitrogen.

**Cultivation** Start seed indoors about
8 weeks before the average date
of your last killing spring frost.
Transplant outdoors 1 week after
that last frost date. Space plants
3 feet (90 cm) apart.

**Pruning** No pruning is necessary,
but in year-round warm climates,
cut plants back hard after the first
harvest to reduce pest problems.

**Propagation** Grow from seed sown
indoors in early spring. Even where
Cape gooseberries are perennial,
yields are better if you start new
plants every 2–3 years.

**Pests and diseases** Plants usually
have no significant problems in
temperate climates.

**Harvesting and storage** Harvest fruits
when the husks are dry and papery.
Pick them individually, or shake the
plant and gather those that drop.
Fruit can be stored for months if
kept dry and intact in their husks.
The husk is not edible.

# *Pinus* spp.

**HARDINESS**
Zones 3–8,
depending on
the species.

**HEIGHT**
25–150 feet
(7.5–45 m)

**SPREAD**
10–75 feet
(3–22.5 m).
Eventual size varies
with species.

**COMMENTS**
The dry-textured,
delicate-flavored,
cream-colored
nuts are usually
about ½ inch
(12 mm) long.

# PINE NUT

MANY PINE SPECIES YIELD ELONGATED,
EDIBLE NUTS, HELD WITHIN THE CONES.

**Position** Plant in full sun in well-drained soil. Grows best in rich soil, but will tolerate infertile conditions.

**Cultivation** Plant container-grown stock anytime the ground isn't frozen, or set out small bareroot plants between spring and autumn where winters are mild, or in spring where winters are severe. Space plants 10–75 feet (3–22.5 m) apart, depending on the eventual size of the plant, which varies with species.

**Pruning** Pines need little pruning. If desired, pinch out the shoot tips in spring for bushier growth.

**Propagation** Enhance germination by keeping sown seed warm for 2–3 months, then cool for a few months. Graft pines using a side graft indoors in winter or, where winters are mild, outdoors in late summer or early autumn.

**Pests and diseases** Generally no significant problems.

**Harvesting and storage** Gather cones of species that drop ripe seed just before the cones open. With other pines, open the fallen cones either by heating them in the oven or smashing them with a hammer. Store nuts in cool, dry conditions.

HARDINESS
Zones 8–10.

HEIGHT
20–25 feet
(6–7.5 m)

SPREAD
25–30 feet
(7.5–9 m)

COMMENTS
One male tree
can pollinate
8–12 female trees.
At maturity, the
nut shell is pale
(perhaps blushed
with pink) and the
nut loosens within.

# PISTACHIO

PISTACHIO PLANTS GROW AS SHRUBS OR
TREES AND PRODUCE EDIBLE NUTS.

**Position** Pistachios prefer full sun
and average, well-drained soil,
although they tolerate alkaline and
saline conditions. They need some
winter cold (about 1,000 total hours
below 45°F [7.2°C]), as well as
summers that are long, hot and dry.

**Cultivation** Set out container-grown
plants anytime, spacing them at
least 25 feet (7.5 m) apart. You'll
need both male (nonfruiting) and
female (fruiting) trees to get nuts.

**Pruning** Prune young plants to
make them bushy, shortening stems
by about 8 inches (20 cm) when

they are 3 feet (90 cm) long. Prune
mature plants lightly, shortening
some of the branches in winter.

**Propagation** Propagate by grafting
onto selected rootstock, depending
on climate and soil conditions.
*Pistacia terebinthus* is cold-resistant;
*P. integerrima* is resistant to
Verticillium fungi; and *P. terebinthus*
and *P. atlantica* resist nematodes.

**Pests and diseases** Avoid root
diseases by selecting a suitable site
and rootstock.

**Harvesting and storage** Shake the
branches to dislodge ripe nuts. Rub
off the hulls and dry the nuts at
150°F (65.5°C) for 8–10 hours.

# *Prunus armeniaca*

**HARDINESS**
Zones 5–9.

**HEIGHT**
8–24 feet
(2.4–7.2 m)

**SPREAD**
16–24 feet
(4.8–7.2 m)

**COMMENTS**
In frost-prone areas, select later-blooming cultivars, such as 'Harglow', or the more frost-tolerant 'Alfred' and 'Manchurian Bush Apricot'.

# APRICOT

FULLY RIPE APRICOTS ARE SO SOFT THAT THEY DON'T SHIP WELL, SO THE BEST WAY TO ENJOY THEM AT THEIR PEAK IS TO GROW YOUR OWN.

**Position** Plant in full sun in average to poor, well-drained soil. Early-opening flowers should be sheltered from frost.

**Cultivation** Many apricots are self-fertile and will produce some fruit if planted alone. But with most, yields will increase if you plant a second cultivar for cross-pollination. Plant dwarf trees 12–15 feet (3.6–4.5 m) apart and full-sized trees 25 feet (7.5 m) apart. Mulch with compost to keep the soil moist in spring and fertilize as needed.

**Pruning** Some cultivars will fruit only every other year unless the fruits are thinned out to leave them 2 inches (5 cm) apart. Apricot trees should be pruned using the open-center system where the leader branch is removed and the tree is pruned to an open vase shape.

**Propagation** Propagate by bud graft.

**Pests and diseases** Susceptible to Eutypa dieback, a disease that attacks through pruning cuts. Treat scale, mite and aphid infestations with oil sprays.

**Harvesting and storage** Pluck the fruits when they're soft and sweet. Can be made into jam or frozen.

**HARDINESS**
Zones 4–9.

**HEIGHT**
15–30 feet
(4.5–9 m)

**SPREAD**
15–30 feet
(4.5–9 m)

**COMMENTS**
Sweet cherries
often need a
compatible
partner for cross-
pollination. Sour
cherries *Prunus
cerasus* are self-
fertile, so you can
get a harvest from
just one tree.

# CHERRY, SWEET

CHERRIES ARE IN SEASON FOR ONLY ABOUT
6 WEEKS SO CAN BE VERY EXPENSIVE. IT'S A
LUXURY TO HAVE A TREE IN THE GARDEN.

**Position** Plant in full sun in average
to poor, well-drained soil. Cherries
prefer arid climates.

**Cultivation** Space standard sweet
cherry trees 20–30 feet (6–9 m)
apart, sour cherries 20 feet (6 m)
apart, and dwarf cherries 10 feet
(3 m) apart. Mulch with compost
in early spring. In cooler climates,
plant from valleys to protect cherry
flowers from frost.

**Pruning** Train naturally spreading
cherry trees to an open-center form;
for more upright growing trees,

prune to a central leader form. Ask
the nursery for specific information.

**Propagation** Propagate by grafting.

**Pests and diseases** The main
predator with cherries is birds. Be
prepared to net the trees once the
fruit starts to ripen to keep the birds
away. Choose cultivars that are
resistant to the diseases most
prevalent in your area.

**Harvesting and storage** Cherries
begin to bear fruit 3–7 years after
planting. If the weather is dry, let
cherries ripen on the trees for best
flavor. They should be fairly soft
and very sweet.

## *Prunus* x *domestica*

ROSACEAE

HARDINESS
Zones 4–10.

HEIGHT
8–20 feet
(2.4–6 m)

SPREAD
8–20 feet
(2.4–6 m)

COMMENTS
'Santa Rosa' is a
Japanese plum
*Prunus salicina*
with large, high-
quality fruit. It
yields best when
planted with other
Japanese plums.

# PLUM, EUROPEAN

PLUMS COME IN A WIDE RANGE OF COLORS,
FLAVORS AND SIZES, SOME FRUITING EARLIER
THAN OTHERS. SPEND SOME TIME CHOOSING
THE ONE BEST SUITED TO YOUR NEEDS.

**Position** Plant plum trees in full sun
in average to rich soil.

**Cultivation** Many European plums
and damson plums will self-
pollinate, so one tree is enough.
But if you plant two compatible
cultivars, they may set more fruit.
Space full-sized plum trees
20–25 feet (6–7.5 m) apart and
dwarf trees 8–12 feet (2.4–3.6 m)
apart. Mulch with compost in spring
and keep the soil moist through the
growing season. Apply a complete
fertilizer when the petals drop.

**Pruning** Train upright-growing
cultivars to a central leader. Open-
center training works better for
more spreading plums, including
most Japanese types. Thin the fruit
on trees that are overburdened.

**Propagation** Propagate by bud graft.

**Pests and diseases** Plums are prone
to black knot, a fungus that causes
dark swellings on tree limbs. If
black knot was a problem in the
previous year, spray with lime-sulfur
when the buds swell, then reapply
a week later.

**Harvesting and storage** Plum trees
start to bear 3–4 years after planting.
Pick the fruit when soft and sweet.

# *Prunus dulcis*

HARDINESS
Zones 6–9.

HEIGHT
15–30 feet
(4.5–9 m)

SPREAD
15–30 feet
(4.5–9 m)

COMMENTS
To spread out your harvest, choose early- and later-maturing almonds. One of the earliest-producing cultivars is 'Nonpareil'; 'Monterey' and 'Fritz' bear a month or so later.

# ALMOND

MOST ALMONDS NEED CROSS-POLLINATION TO SET THEIR CROP, SO CHECK THE CATALOG DESCRIPTIONS TO MAKE SURE YOU PLANT THE BEST COMPANIONS.

**Position** Grow in full sun in average to fertile, well-drained soil.

**Cultivation** Most almonds require another tree to pollinate them. Plant trees 25 feet (7.5 m) apart and mulch with compost each spring. Water plants regularly when the weather is hot.

**Pruning** Train almonds to an open-center form, but as you prune each year, do more heading and less thinning than you would for trees such as peaches. The aim is to develop a thick branch network, which will promote better fruiting.

**Propagation** Propagate by grafting.

**Pests and diseases** Unfortunately, disease resistance is minimal in almonds so they're best grown in a dry climate. Keep mulch away from the trunk to discourage rodent activity. Pick up all fallen nuts and destroy bad ones to reduce problems with navel orangeworms—the white caterpillars with brown heads that feed on the nut meat.

**Harvesting and storage** Most almond trees begin to produce nuts after 3–4 years. Use a padded stick to knock the nuts off the tree.

# *Prunus* hybrids

**HARDINESS**
Zones 6–9.

**HEIGHT**
8–20 feet
(2.4–6 m)

**SPREAD**
8–20 feet
(2.4–6 m)

**COMMENTS**
Dwarf cultivars
can be grown
successfully
in containers.

# PLUMCOT

IN BOTH APPEARANCE AND FLAVOR, PLUMCOTS RESEMBLE THEIR PARENTS, PLUMS AND APRICOTS. THE FLESH AND SKIN OF THE FRUIT ARE EDIBLE, BUT NOT THE SEED.

**Position** Plant in full sun and well-drained soil. Avoid sites subject to late frost early in the season.

**Cultivation** In colder regions, plant only in spring; elsewhere, plant in either spring or autumn. Plumcots need cross-pollination, although the pollinator can vary, depending on the cultivar. (Ask the nursery or check catalog descriptions to get the right pollinator for your plant.)

**Pruning** Prune out a moderate amount of wood each year, just before the blossoms open, to keep the plant open to light and air at the center.

**Propagation** Graft cultivars onto either seedling or cutting-grown apricot or plum rootstock.

**Pests and diseases** Brown rot may damage the fruit. Remove and destroy any shriveled fruit left hanging on the tree at the end of the season.

**Harvesting and storage** Pick the fruits when they are fully colored and slightly soft. They can be stored for up to a couple of weeks at high humidity and temperatures just above freezing.

FRUITS 291

*Prunus persica* ROSACEAE

HARDINESS
Zones 5–9.

HEIGHT
8–15 feet
(2.4–4.5 m)

SPREAD
10–20 feet (3–6 m)

COMMENTS
Genetic dwarfs
with especially
good fruit flavor
include 'Nectar
Babe', 'Bonanza'
and 'Southern
Flame'. Trees that
are grafted onto
dwarfing roots
grow to 8–10 feet
(2.4–3 m) tall.

# PEACH AND NECTARINE

BOTH PEACHES AND NECTARINES ARE
ATTRACTIVE WHEN GROWN AS FAN-SHAPED
ESPALIERS. GROWING THEM ON A WALL
ALSO PROVIDES THEM WITH EXTRA WARMTH.

**Position** Plant in full sun in average
to poor, well-drained soil.

**Cultivation** Most peaches and
nectarines are self-pollinating, so
you can get a full crop from just
one tree. Fertilize with compost
in early spring and again with a
balanced organic fertilizer when the
fruit first forms. Spray the leaves
with liquid kelp every 3–4 weeks
during the growing season.

**Pruning** Train peach trees to an
open-center form. Thin young trees

lightly in summer to remove excess
branches. With mature trees, cut
half the older branches back by
about half of their total length
during the dormant season so they
resprout productive new wood.

**Propagation** Propagate by bud graft.

**Pests and diseases** If you live in an
area that is prone to peach tree
diseases, start with disease-resistant
cultivars. Otherwise, you may have
to spray to control diseases.

**Harvesting and storage** Peach and
nectarine trees begin producing fruit
2–4 years after planting. Harvest
when fruit is soft and sweet. Can
be made into jam or frozen.

# *Prunus tomentosa*

HARDINESS
Zones 3–6.

HEIGHT
9–15 feet
(2.7–4.5 m)

SPREAD
9–15 feet
(2.7–4.5 m)

COMMENTS
Although it has a delicate beauty, Nanking cherry is a tough shrub. Its blossoms resist frost, and the plants tolerate drought, extremely cold winters and hot summers.

# CHERRY, NANKING

NANKING CHERRIES GROW AS LARGE BUSHES WITH SMALL RED OR YELLOW FRUIT. DEPENDING ON THE PLANT, THE FRUIT MAY TASTE LIKE SWEET CHERRIES OR SOUR CHERRIES. EXCEPT FOR THE SEED, THE WHOLE FRUIT IS EDIBLE.

**Position** Nanking cherries need full sun but tolerate a wide range of soil types as long as they are provided with good drainage.

**Cultivation** Set new plants out in spring, spacing them 6–16 feet (1.8–4.8 m) apart. Nanking cherries generally need cross-pollination, so grow at least two plants. This shrub thrives with little or no care.

**Pruning** No pruning is needed, but you can keep the plants smaller or even train them as hedges with regular, late-winter pruning.

**Propagation** Keep the seed moist and cold for 3 months before sowing it in a warm, bright place. Seedlings typically begin to bear fruit by their third season.

**Pests and diseases** Twigs or stems occasionally die back; cut them back to healthy wood.

**Harvesting and storage** Harvest the fruit as soon as it fully turns color. Harvested fruits store poorly, so just pick and eat them fresh.

# *Psidium* spp.

HARDINESS
Zone 10.

HEIGHT
10–25 feet
(3–7.5 m)

SPREAD
7–15 feet
(2.1–4.5 m)

COMMENTS
Tropical guava
*Psidium guajava*
has larger fruits
than strawberry,
or Cattley, guava
*P. littorale*. The
flesh of both is
edible. Both make
excellent jelly,
jam or juice.

# GUAVA

WHEN RIPE, THE TROPICAL GUAVA GIVES OFF A MUSKY AROMA BUT THE FLAVOR IS SOMEWHAT INSIPID; THE STRAWBERRY GUAVA HAS A SPICY FLAVOR.

**Position** Plant in full sun. Well-drained, slightly acid soil rich in organic matter is ideal.

**Cultivation** Set out container-grown plants anytime, spacing them 9–15 feet (2.7–4.5 m) apart. Plants are partly self-fruitful, so growing two or more seedlings or cultivars may increase yields. Fertilize often to keep your plants vigorous.

**Pruning** Prune heavily to stimulate new growth and keep fruits close to the center of the plant.

**Propagation** Dig suckers from around the base of an established bush, or take stem cuttings. The seed germinates fairly easily.

**Pests and diseases** Generally not a problem in home plantings.

**Harvesting and storage** The aroma and color change tell you when the fruits are ripe. Tropical guava turns yellow when ripe. It is usually stored just below 50°F (10°C). Strawberry guava turns yellow or red when ripe and is best stored at temperatures just above freezing. Slightly underripe fruit will keep for a few weeks at cool temperatures with high humidity.

## *Punica granatum*

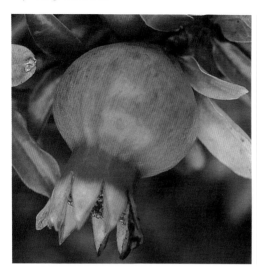

HARDINESS
Will grow in
Zone 8 but fruits
best in Zones 9–10.

HEIGHT
10–20 feet
(3–6 m)

SPREAD
6–8 feet
(1.8–2.4 m)

COMMENTS
Dwarf cultivars are
good in pots in
colder climates.
Besides eating
fresh pomegranate
seeds and flesh,
use the juice for
jelly, or in punch.

# POMEGRANATE

POMEGRANATE FRUIT IS USUALLY RED AND
THE SIZE OF A SOFTBALL. INSIDE, THE SEEDS
ARE SUPPORTED WITHIN MEMBRANES. EAT
BOTH SEEDS AND FLESHY SEED COVERING.

**Position** Pomegranates prefer a hot,
dry climate. Give the plants full
sun. They tolerate a wide range of
well-drained soil types.

**Cultivation** Set out container-grown
plants anytime, or plant bareroot
stock from spring to autumn. Space
plants 18 feet (5.4 m) apart. Cross-
pollination sometimes increases
yields, so grow at least two plants
if you have room.

**Pruning** Train the plant as a
multiple-stemmed bush or as a
single-stemmed tree. Prune mature
plants lightly each winter—just
enough to stimulate some new
growth and thin out excess fruit.
Also remove suckers, unless they are
needed to replace a damaged trunk.

**Propagation** Seed germinates
readily. Propagate cultivars by
hardwood cuttings.

**Pests and diseases** Generally no
significant problems.

**Harvesting and storage** Clip fruits
from the plant as soon as they are
fully colored. Fruits refrigerated at
high humidity keep well for several
months. For grenadine syrup, cook
juice with an equal weight of sugar.

# *Pyrus communis*

**HARDINESS**
Zones 4–9.

**HEIGHT**
8–20 feet (2.4–6 m)

**SPREAD**
8–20 feet (2.4–6 m)

**COMMENTS**
Plant cultivars that mature at different times. For example, 'Clapp's Favorite' and 'Moonglow' (ripen mid-August), 'Bartlett' (early September), 'Seckel' and 'Magness' (mid-September), 'Comice' and 'Kieffer' (October).

# PEAR

MOST PEARS REQUIRE CROSS-POLLINATION TO SET FRUIT, SO YOU'LL NEED TO PLANT AT LEAST ONE COMPATIBLE COMPANION TO GET A GOOD CROP.

**Position** Plant in full sun in average to poor, well-drained soil.

**Cultivation** Space full-sized trees 15–20 feet (4.5–6 m) apart and dwarfs 8–12 feet (2.4–3.6 m) apart. Water and mulch as necessary to keep the soil moist and prevent damage to foliage and fruit. Mulch with compost in spring.

**Pruning** Use the central leader system to shape upright-growing European pears. Heavy-bearing trees will need some fruit thinning.

In late spring, remove the smaller fruits, leaving one or two of the best fruit per cluster.

**Propagation** Propagate by grafting.

**Pests and diseases** Keep an eye out for pear psyllas, tiny insects that suck sap from tender shoot tips and fruit, spreading diseases as they go. During the growing season, use insecticidal soap or horticultural oil sprays to control psyllas. Select pear cultivars resistant to fireblight.

**Harvesting and storage** Pear trees generally begin to produce fruit 3–5 years after planting. Pick European pears when they are mature but not quite ripe.

# *Ribes* spp.

HARDINESS
Zones 3–7.

HEIGHT
3–7 feet
(90–210 cm)

SPREAD
3–7 feet
(90–210 cm)

COMMENTS
Buy gooseberry
cultivars that are
resistant to mildew.
Mildew-resistant
currant cultivars
are also available.

## CURRANT AND GOOSEBERRY

THE TART BERRIES OF CURRANTS ARE
EXCELLENT FOR JAMS OR JUICE. IF POSSIBLE,
PLANT TWO OR MORE CULTIVARS, AS CROSS-
POLLINATION WILL INCREASE YIELDS.

**Position** Plant in full sun to light
shade in average soil.

**Cultivation** Most currants and
gooseberries are self-pollinating;
however, if interplanted with two or
three other culivars, they'll produce
higher yields. Space the plants
6 feet (1.8 m) apart and mulch well.
Add compost and a potassium-rich
fertilizer in early spring. Water
regularly in dry weather.

**Pruning** At planting time, select one
branch as the main trunk and
remove the rest. Each winter,
remove all shoots that are more
than 3 years old (or more than
2 years old on blackcurrants);
then remove all but six of the
remaining shoots.

**Propagation** By hardwood cuttings.

**Pests and diseases** Powdery mildew
can devastate gooseberries, and
sulfur sprays are not always an
effective treatment.

**Harvesting and storage** For cooking
or making jelly, pick currants and
gooseberries when they are not
quite ripe. For fresh eating, let them
ripen on the bush until they taste
right to you.

*Rubus fruticosus*

HARDINESS
Zones 5–9.

HEIGHT
4–7 feet
(1.2–2.1 m)

SPREAD
3–6 feet
(90–180 cm)

COMMENTS
Look for thornless,
highly productive
cultivars, such as
'Navaho Erect' and
'Arapaho', which
stand erect with no
support necessary.

# BLACKBERRY

THE FLAVOR OF BLACKBERRIES IS AT ITS BEST
WHEN THE FRUITS TURN DARK AND LOSE
SOME OF THEIR GLOSSINESS. SOME
THORNLESS CULTIVARS NEED SUPPORT.

**Position** Plant in full sun in average
to rich soil.

**Cultivation** Buy blackberries as
bareroot plants, or as tissue-cultured
plantlets. They need plenty of
space and good air circulation.
Plant thorny cultivars 3–4 feet
(90–120 cm) apart and thornless
cultivars 4–6 feet (1.2–1.8 m) apart.
Make paths between the rows for
good sun exposure and adequate
air circulation. Keep the soil evenly
moist and mulch with compost in
early spring.

**Pruning** Cut fruit-bearing canes to
the ground right after harvest. In
early spring, thin to leave only
seven strong canes per plant.
Shorten side branches to about
1 foot (30 cm) long. For maximum
yields, train blackberries to a trellis.

**Propagation** By division or layering.

**Pests and diseases** Watch for
distorted growth, sterile canes or
orange-spotted leaves that drop
early. These are all symptoms of
incurable viral or orange rust
diseases. Remove infected plants.

**Harvesting and storage** Eat soft,
sweet blackberries as soon as
possible after picking, or freeze.

*Rubus idaeus*

# RASPBERRY

IF BIRDS ARE BEATING YOU TO YOUR BERRIES,
COVER THE PLANTS WITH NETTING. ROLL
BACK THE COVER AS NEEDED TO HARVEST.

**Position** Plant in full sun in average
to poor soil.

**Cultivation** If possible, buy bareroot
plants and plant them 2 feet (60 cm)
apart in a row. They'll fill in within
a year or two. Apply compost and a
little balanced organic fertilizer in
late winter, if needed, for good
growth. Water during dry spells and
mulch to discourage weeds and
keep the soil evenly moist.

**Pruning** Cut off all the old canes
at ground level when they have
finished fruiting. Leave the new
current-season canes to produce
berries next year.

**Propagation** Propagate by division
or layering, but only if you are sure
your plants are healthy.

**Pests and diseases** Buy only certified
disease-free plants. Several fungal
diseases may attack raspberries:
powdery mildew, anthracnose and
cane blight. If these diseases were a
problem in the previous year, spray
with lime-sulfur when the buds
begin to turn green. Remove and
destroy plants affected by disease.

**Harvesting and storage** Harvest
berries when they're sweet and
ripe. Eat fresh or freeze for later.

*Rubus* x *loganobaccus*                    ROSACEAE

**HARDINESS**
Zones 8–9.

**HEIGHT**
8–12 feet
(2.4–3.6 m)

**SPREAD**
8–12 feet
(2.4–3.6 m)

**COMMENTS**
Completely ripe
fruits have a
delectable flavor
and aroma. Use
quickly, as they
are very soft
and fragile.

# BOYSENBERRY

RIPE BOYSENBERRY FRUITS ARE LARGE,
MAROON AND ALMOST SEEDLESS.

**Position** Plant canes in full sun in
well-drained soil, rich in humus.

**Cultivation** Plant container-grown
stock anytime the ground isn't
frozen, or set out bareroot plants in
spring or autumn, while dormant.
Boysenberries are self-fruitful, so
you can get fruit from just one
plant. Space plants 3–6 feet
(90–180 cm) apart. Set up a post
next to each plant or erect a one-
or two-wire trellis on which to
support the canes. The canes are
biennial, bearing fruit in their
second season.

**Pruning** In winter, cut canes that
fruited the previous summer to the
ground—they are dead anyway.
Thin remaining canes, leaving
eight to 10 of the most vigorous
ones per plant. Shorten these to
7 feet (2.1 m), and cut back any
sideshoots to 1–1½ feet (30–45 cm).

**Propagation** Propagate by layering.

**Pests and diseases** Given good
growing conditions, boysenberries
usually have few major problems.

**Harvesting and storage** For full
flavor, harvest when the fruit
practically drops off into your hand.
Even at cool temperatures and high
humidity, fruit keeps only 2–3 days.

# *Sambucus* spp.

HARDINESS
Zones 2–9.

HEIGHT
6–10 feet
(1.8–3 m)

SPREAD
3–6 feet
(90–180 cm)

COMMENTS
Edible species
include blueberry
elder *Sambucus
caerulea*, American
elder *S. canadensis*
and European elder
*S. nigra*. But some
species (such as
*S. ebulus*) have
poisonous berries.

# ELDERBERRY

ELDERBERRIES PRODUCE CLUSTERS OF SMALL
BLUE-BLACK BERRIES. THE FLAVOR IS VERY
MILD, SO ELDERBERRIES TASTE BEST COOKED
WITH A SWEETENER AND ANOTHER, MORE
ACIDIC FRUIT. THE WHOLE FRUIT IS EDIBLE.

**Position** Plant in full sun or partial
shade and evenly moist soil.

**Cultivation** Plant container-grown
shrubs anytime, or set out bareroot
plants in spring or autumn, while
they are dormant. Space plants
6 feet (1.8 m) apart. Plant two
seedlings or two different cultivars
for best yields.

**Pruning** On established bushes, cut
stems that are more than 3 years
old to ground level each winter.

Also prune away suckers to control
the spread of the plants.

**Propagation** Dig up and transplant
suckers from around the base of the
plant. You also can take cuttings or
sow seed.

**Pests and diseases** If necessary,
cover the bushes with netting to
keep birds at bay.

**Harvesting and storage** Harvest the
berries when they are fully colored.
An easy way to pick fruit from the
clusters is to pop it off with the
tines of a dinner fork. Store the fruit
in a covered container in the
refrigerator. The fruit is most often
used in jams, pies and preserves.

# *Vaccinium corymbosum*

HARDINESS
Lowbush cultivars
grow well in Zones
3–7. Midhighs grow
up to Zone 4.
Highbush types
thrive in Zones
5–7. Rabbiteyes are
normally adapted
to Zones 6–9, but
cultivars, such as
'Briteblue', can also
grow in Zone 10.

HEIGHT
2–15 feet
(60–450 cm)

SPREAD
3–10 feet
(90–300 cm)

# BLUEBERRY

SOME BLUEBERRIES NEED CROSS-
POLLINATION, SO MAKE SURE YOU CHECK
CATALOG DESCRIPTIONS TO GET THE
APPROPRIATE PARTNERS.

**Position** Plant in full sun in average
to rich, well-drained soil.

**Cultivation** Depending on whether
you're growing lowbush, highbush,
midhigh or rabbiteye blueberries,
plant them 2–8 feet (60–240 cm)
apart. Apply a thick layer of mulch
to keep the soil evenly moist. Add
compost each spring.

**Pruning** Pinch off all the flowers on
a young blueberry bush the first
year after planting so the bush will
grow strong. The next year you'll
have to remove only dead or
damaged wood. Let plenty of sun
and air penetrate the entire plant.

**Propagation** Propagate by
hardwood or softwood cuttings, or
by division, depending on cultivar.

**Pests and diseases** If stems begin to
die back or show unusual cankers
or cracks, cut them back to healthy
tissue. Use sticky red balls (such as
apple maggot traps) to catch
blueberry maggots before they can
tunnel into the ripening berries.

**Harvesting and storage** Harvest after
the berries turn blue. Don't pick
underripe berries; they won't ripen.
Eat immediately or freeze.

# *Vaccinium macrocarpon*

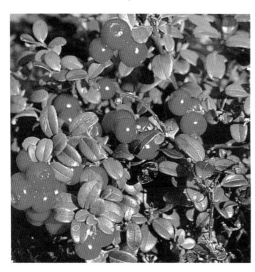

HARDINESS
Zones 2–6.

HEIGHT
Up to 1 foot
(30 cm)

SPREAD
Unlimited. (The
sprawling stems
root where they
touch the ground
and continue to
grow outward.)

COMMENTS
The tart berries are
completely edible.

# CRANBERRY

CRANBERRIES GROW AS LOW, CREEPING
BUSHES. THEIR WHITE FLOWERS ARE
FOLLOWED BY HARD, RED BERRIES, EACH
ABOUT THE SIZE OF A THUMBNAIL.

**Position** Cranberries thrive in sun
and moist, well-drained, humus-rich
and very acid soil; pH 4.0–5.5.
The plants do not tolerate dry soil,
but they can withstand flooding in
cold weather.

**Cultivation** Plant in spring or
autumn where winters are mild or
in spring where winters are severe.
Space plants 1–2 feet (30–60 cm)
apart. Mix plenty of acid peat into
the soil before planting. Mulch with
sawdust or sand, renewing the
mulch periodically.

**Pruning** Cut away some of the
sprawling stems and some of the
upright fruiting stems when they
become overcrowded.

**Propagation** Summer stem cuttings
root readily. Where winters are
mild, set rooted cuttings outdoors in
autumn; otherwise, set them out as
early as possible in spring.

**Pests and diseases** Generally no
significant problems.

**Harvesting and storage** Pick berries
in autumn, after they are fully
colored. Cranberries will keep for
2–4 months at high humidity and
temperatures just above freezing.
They can also be dried.

# *Vaccinium vitis-idaea*

**HARDINESS**
Zones 2–6.

**HEIGHT**
6–24 inches
(15–60 cm)

**SPREAD**
Unlimited. (Plants
send up shoots
from creeping
underground
stems.)

**COMMENTS**
The round, red
berries are a little
larger than peas
and have a flavor
similar to, but less
sharp than that of
true cranberries.

# LINGONBERRY

LINGONBERRY IS A LOW, CREEPING BUSH
THAT PRODUCES WHOLLY EDIBLE FRUIT.

**Position** Give lingonberries full sun
or partial shade and well-drained,
humus-rich, acid soil; pH 4.5–5.5.

**Cultivation** Set out container-grown
plants anytime the ground isn't
frozen, or plant bareroot stock in
spring or autumn, while dormant.
Space plants of the species *vitis-
idaea* 1½ feet (45 cm) apart and
those of the variety *minus* 10 inches
(25 cm) apart. Lingonberries
compete poorly with weeds, so
weed thoroughly before planting.
Also dig in plenty of acid peat
moss. Mulch with sand or sawdust
to further suppress weeds and to
keep the shallow roots cool and
moist. Plants are partially self-fertile,
but planting at least two seedlings
or cultivars may increase yields.

**Pruning** Once plants are a few
years old, mow a different third
or quarter of the planting in late
autumn each year (so each part gets
mowed every 3–4 years) to about
1 inch (2.5 cm) high.

**Propagation** Take cuttings in spring.

**Pests and diseases** Generally no
significant problems.

**Harvesting and storage** Delay harvest
until fruit is thoroughly red and
ripe. Store fruit at temperatures just
above freezing with high humidity.

# *Viburnum trilobum*

**HARDINESS**
Zones 4–9.

**HEIGHT**
8–12 feet
(2.4–3.6 m)

**SPREAD**
8–12 feet
(2.4–3.6 m)

**COMMENTS**
The seeds must be strained out when you make jam or jelly. There is an offensive odor while the fruit is cooking, but it is not present in the finished product.

## CRANBERRY, HIGHBUSH

THE SHINY, BRIGHT RED BERRIES OF HIGHBUSH CRANBERRY RIPEN IN DROOPING CLUSTERS. THE TART FRUITS CONTAIN A SINGLE, LARGE SEED. EAT THE WHOLE FRUIT, EXCEPT FOR THE SEED.

**Position** Plant in full sun or partial shade in moist, well-drained soil.

**Cultivation** Plant container-grown shrubs anytime the ground isn't frozen, or set out bareroot plants in spring or autumn, while they are dormant. Space plants 6–9 feet (1.8–2.7 m) apart. Plant several of them close together for a bright spot when they are in fruit, or along a border as an informal hedge, or grow just one as a specimen shrub.

**Pruning** Cut off old, nonproductive stems at ground level in winter.

**Propagation** Take hardwood or softwood cuttings. Seed does not germinate until it has been kept warm and moist for 4 months, then cool and moist for 3 months.

**Pests and diseases** Generally no significant problems.

**Harvesting and storage** Harvest anytime after the berries turn fully red. Fruits not harvested hang on the bush well into winter, shriveling with time. Store at cool temperatures and high humidity, such as in a covered container in the refrigerator.

# *Vitis* spp.

**HARDINESS**
Zones 4–10.

**HEIGHT**
4–6 feet
(1.2–1.8 m)

**SPREAD**
8–15 feet
(2.4–4.5 m)

**COMMENTS**
Grapes come in a variety of different types. The hardiest are American, or fox, grapes *Vitis labrusca*, robust growers with rich flavor for fresh eating, or making jelly or juice.

# GRAPE

To prevent growing clusters from ripening unevenly, thin in early summer, when fruits are small and hard.

**Position** Plant in full sun in average to rich soil.

**Cultivation** Start with 1-year-old plants that are virus-indexed and certified disease-free. Set up a support system before planting for the vines to cling to. After planting, let the grapevine grow untrained for a year to develop strong roots. Pinch off grape flowers during that year. Keep the soil moist and mulch well. Feed with compost in spring.

**Pruning** Train the vine over wire strung between posts. In late winter, cut the vine back to a stump with two buds. When the buds start growing, leave the stronger shoot and remove the other one.

**Propagation** Propagate by cuttings, grafting or, for some types, layering.

**Pests and diseases** Black rot causes reddish brown leaf spots and hard, shriveled fruit. Botrytis bunch rot causes a fluffy gray-brown coating on the fruit. Anthracnose infection produces sunken, dark-ringed spots on leaves and fruit. Remove and destroy all infected fruit and leaves.

**Harvesting and storage** Harvest the bunches of grapes by clipping them off the vine with clean secateurs.

# Ziziphus jujuba

**HARDINESS**
Zones 5–8.

**HEIGHT**
Up to 30 feet
(9 m)

**SPREAD**
Up to 20 feet
(6 m)

**COMMENTS**
The skin is pale
green, mottled with
brown. You can eat
the skin and flesh
but not the seed.
Dried fruits taste
rather like dates.

# JUJUBE

FRESH JUJUBE FRUITS HAVE A CRUNCHY
TEXTURE AND A FLAVOR SIMILAR TO APPLES.

**Position** Jujube needs full sun and
abundant summer heat but grows
in almost any soil, and will tolerate
even very wet or dry conditions.

**Cultivation** Plant container-grown
trees anytime the ground isn't
frozen, or set out bareroot plants in
spring or autumn, while dormant.
Space plants 20 feet (6 m) apart.
Pollination needs are not well
defined, but cross-pollination
generally increases fruit size and
yield. The trees tend to sucker,
especially when young.

**Pruning** No regular pruning needed.

**Propagation** Increase cultivars by
grafting or, if the mother tree is not
grafted, by digging up suckers. To
grow a seedling for a rootstock,
open the seed lengthwise to extract
the two kernels, then keep the
kernels cool and barely moist for
2 months to assist germination.

**Pests and diseases** Generally no
significant pest or disease problems.

**Harvesting and storage** Harvest fruits
for fresh eating just as they become
mottled with brown. Will store for
a month or more at 50°F (10°C).
Fruits left hanging on the tree turn
completely brown, then shrivel and
lose moisture. Dried fruits keep for
over a year at cool temperatures.

# Plant Hardiness Zone Maps

These maps of the United States, Canada and Europe are divided into ten zones. Each zone is based on a 10°F (5.6°C) difference in average annual minimum temperature. Some areas are considered too high in elevation for plant cultivation and so are not assigned to any zone. There are also island zones that are warmer or cooler than surrounding areas because of differences in elevation; they have been given a zone different from the surrounding areas. Many large urban areas, for example, are in a warmer zone than the surrounding land. Plants grow best within an optimum range of temperatures. The range may be wide for some species and narrow for others. Plants also differ in their ability to survive frost and in their sun or shade requirements.

*PACIFIC OCEAN*

## Average Annual Minimum Temperature °F (°C)

| | | | | | |
|---|---|---|---|---|---|
| **ZONE 1** | | Below -50°F (Below -45°C) | **ZONE 6** | | -10° to 0°F (-23° to -18°C) |
| **ZONE 2** | | -50° to -40°F (-45° to -40°C) | **ZONE 7** | | 0° to 10°F (-18° to -12°C) |
| **ZONE 3** | | -40° to -30°F (-40° to -34°C) | **ZONE 8** | | 10° to 20°F (-12° to -7°C) |
| **ZONE 4** | | -30° to -20°F (-34° to -29°C) | **ZONE 9** | | 20° to 30°F (-7° to -1°C) |
| **ZONE 5** | | -20° to -10°F (-29° to -23°C) | **ZONE 10** | | 30° to 40°F (-1° to 4°C) |

Canada

United States
of America

*ATLANTIC
OCEAN*

The zone ratings indicate conditions in which designated plants will grow well, and not merely survive. Many plants may survive in zones that are warmer or colder than their recommended zone range. Remember that other factors, including wind, soil type, soil moisture, humidity, snow and winter sunshine, may have a great effect on growth.

Keep in mind that some nursery plants have been grown in greenhouses, so they might not survive in your garden. It's a waste of time and money, and a cause of heartache, to buy plants that aren't suitable for your climate zone.

## AUSTRALIA AND NEW ZEALAND

These maps divide Australia and New Zealand into seven climate zones which, as near as possible, correspond to the USDA climate zones used in the United States, Britain and Europe and in this book. The zones are based on the minimum temperatures usually, or possibly, experienced within each zone. This book is designed mainly for cool-climate gardens, but the information in it can be adapted for those in hotter climates.

In this book, the ideal zones in which to grow particular plants are indicated and when you read that a plant is suitable for any of the zones 7 through to 10, you will know that it should grow successfully in those zones in Australia and New Zealand. There are other factors that affect plant growth, but temperature is one of the most important. Plants listed as being suitable for zone 10 may also grow in hotter zones, but to be sure, consult a gardening guide specific to your area.

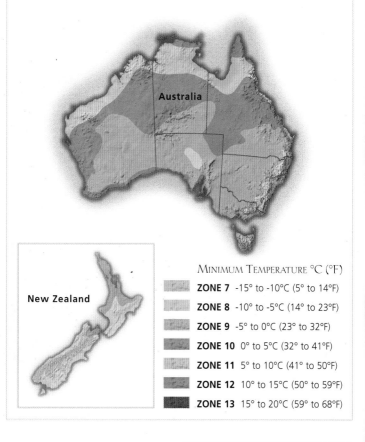

MINIMUM TEMPERATURE °C (°F)

**ZONE 7**  -15° to -10°C (5° to 14°F)

**ZONE 8**  -10° to -5°C (14° to 23°F)

**ZONE 9**  -5° to 0°C (23° to 32°F)

**ZONE 10**  0° to 5°C (32° to 41°F)

**ZONE 11**  5° to 10°C (41° to 50°F)

**ZONE 12**  10° to 15°C (50° to 59°F)

**ZONE 13**  15° to 20°C (59° to 68°F)

# INDEX

Page references in *italics* indicate
photos and illustrations.

# ACKNOWLEDGMENTS

KEY l=left, r=right, c=center, t=top, b=bottom

APL=Australian Picture Library; AZ=A–Z Botanical Collection; BCL=Bruce Coleman Ltd; CM=Cheryl Maddocks; CN= Clive Nichols; DF=Derek Fell; DW=David Wallace; GDR=G.R. "Dick" Roberts; GP.com=gardenphotos.com; GPL=Garden Picture Library; HA=Heather Angel; HSC=Harry Smith Collection; HSI=Holt Studios International; IH=Ivy Hansen; JP=Jerry Pavia; JY=James Young; LC=Leigh Clapp; LR=Lorna Rose; OSF=Oxford Scientific Films; PD=PhotoDisc; PH=Photos Horticultural; SM=Stirling Macoboy; SOM=S. & O. Mathews; TE=Thomas Eltzroth; TPL=photolibrary.com; WO=Weldon Owen; WR=Weldon Russell

1t OSF/Steffen Hauser; c WO/JY; b WR/John Callanan 2c WO 5c LC 6t WO/JY; c WO/JY; b APL/ Corbis/Lynda Richardson 7t JY; c OSF/Richard Kolar; b GPL/Howard Rice 10c APL/Corbis/Michael Boys 13b GPL/Eric Crichton 15b LR 16tl DF 17tr PH 20tr HSC 21bl TE 23c GPL/Howard Rice 24t GPL/John Millar 25b PH 26c APL/Corbis/Michael Boys 28–29b WR 30b GPL/Joanne Pavia 31t GPL/Michael Howes 33c, b DW 37t DF 38b WO 39tl WO; br GP.com/Judy White 41c HSC 42t PH; b HSI/Nigel Cattlin 43b PH 44t HSI/Nigel Cattlin 45tr PH 46b TE 47t WO 48t HSI/Nigel Cattlin 49b BCL/Jane Burton 50br WR 51br PH 52t APL/Corbis/Patrick Johns; c, b TE 53l WR 54c GPL/John Glover 56tl WO; br WR 57r WO/Kevin Candland 59t PD 61b PD 62bl John Callanan 63 DW 67 DW 70t Andrew Lawson; b TE 71b CN 74–75b PH 75tr GPL/Mel Watson 76tl GPL/John Glover; br GPL/Stephen Robson 77t TE 78b GP.com/Judy White 80c LC 82tl Denise Greig 83c CN 84t APL/Corbis/Eric Crichton 84–85b GPL/Juliette Wade 86–87b APL/Corbis/Eric Crichton 87t GPL/John Glover 88t, b TE 89t APL/Corbis/Bohemian Nomad Picture Makers 90tl TE 91b GPL/Howard Rice 92bl GPL/Mayer/Le Scanff 93tr TE 95t GPL/Michael Howes 96b GPL/ Mel Watson 97tr Corbis 99t GPL/Mel Watson 100cl DF; bl GPL/Robert Estall 102tl GPL/Marijke Heuff 103b 105t APL/Corbis/Michael Boys 106t PH 106–107b Denise Greig 107t AZ/Anthony Cooper 108t PH 109t Artville; b GPL/Ron Sutherland 110tr AZ/Bjorn Svensson 110–111b GPL/JP 111t PH 112t GPL/JP 114t JY 115t PH 116t JP 117t GPL/Sunniva Harte 118t TE 119t DW 120t GDR 121t DF 122t GDR 123t WO/JY 124t WR 125t DW 126t PH 127t Ardea London/Don Hadden 128t HA 129t HA 130t WR 131t CM 132t PH 133t DF 134t WO/JY 135t GDR 136t DW 137t BCL 138t GDR 139t DF 140t 141t TE 142t GDR 143t GPL/John Glover 144t GDR 145t DW 146t JY 147t DW 148t WO 149t GDR 150t GPL/Jacqui Hurst 151t GDR 152t WR 153t DW 154t GPL/Christi Carter 155t TE 156t TE 157t WO/Michael Freeman 158t TE 159t WO/JY 160t WR 161t WO/JY 162t WO/JY 163t AZ 164t DW 165t TE 166t WO/JY 167t BCL 168t JY 169t PH 170t GPL/John Glover 171t GDR 172t JY 173t DW 174t WO 175t DW 176t GPL/Lamontagne 177t APL/Corbis/Michael Boys 178t HA

179t CM 180t SM 181t PH 182t DW 183t GDR 184t DW 185t DW 186t DW
187t HSC 188t IH 189t DW 190t WO/JY 191t WO 192t PH 193t DW 194t
HSC 195t HSC 196t DW 197t TE 198t GPL/Lamontagne 199t Auscape/
C. Andrew Henley 200t PH 201t JY 202t DW 203t TE 204t LR 205t DW
206t DW 207t TE 208t SM 209t Tony Rodd 210t CM 211t DW 212t Rodale
Stock Images 213t GDR 214t DW 215t DW 216t GDR 217t TPL/Maximilian
Stock Ltd/AGSTOCK 218t DW 219t GP.com/Judy White 220t SM 221t DW
222t DW 223t DW 224t DW 225t DF 226t DW 227t TE 228t APL/
Hackenberg/Zefa 229t GPL/John Glover 230t WR/DW 231t HSC 232t DW
233t CM 234t DW 235t OSF/John McCammon 236t APL/Corbis/Robert
Maass 237t DW 238t TPL/Wen Jia Feng 240c GP.com/Judy White 242t PH
243t HSC 244t OSF/Harold Taylor 245t TE 246t TE 247t TE 248t HSC
249t TE 250t IH 251t TE 252t TE 253t SOM 254t WO 255t GPL/Mayer/Le
Scanff 256t TE 257t APL/Corbis/Maurice Nimmo 258t GPL/Tamara Richards
259t GPL/Christi Carter 260t WO/JY 261t HSC 262t TE 263t TE 264t TE
265t TE 266t TE 267t PH 268t GPL/John Glover 269t PH 270t SOM 271t
WO 272t GDR 273t GDR 274t GDR 275t OSF/R. F. Head 276t HSI/Nigel
Cattlin 277t TE 278t OSF/Bill Paton 279t TE 280t TE 281t BCL/Hans
Reinhard 282t GP.com/Judy White 283t TE 284t SOM 285t PH 286t TE
287t GDR 288t HSC 289t TE 290t GDR 291t TE 292t DF 293t GP.com/Judy
White 294t TE 295t GDR 296t DF 297t GPL/John Glover 298t PH 299t PH
300t TE 301t SOM 302t PH 303t BCL/Charlie Orr 304t GPL/John Glover
305t TE 306t GPL/Neil Holmes 307t TE

Illustrations by Tony Britt-Lewis, Edwina Riddell, Barbara Rodanska,
Jan Smith, Kathie Smith.

The publishers would like to thank Puddingburn Publishing Services,
for compiling the index, and Bronwyn Sweeney, for proofreading.